NOTABLE QUOTES

"How 'Varsity Blues' Swept-up an Innocent Father" "I've practiced criminal law for more than a half century, but I'm still capable of shock at how easy it is for an innocent person to be falsely charged and convicted. ... Mr. Wilson was innocent, yet prosecutors charged him and smeared his children."
—Harvey Silverglate, *Wall Street Journal*

"John Wilson did not receive a fair trial."
—Brief by eleven former United States Attorneys as Amicus Curiae, United States of America v. John Wilson

"Wilson was convicted not for what he did, but for what others did."
—Noel Francisco, former solicitor general of the United States

"You have to pile on inference on top of inference" to believe the parents knew they were participating in a nationwide fraud conspiracy."
—David Barron, chief US circuit court judge, First Circuit Court of Appeals

"[Johnny was] 'an A+ by USC standards for speed and work ethic' [and] 'could contribute to a high-level program like USC' by his junior or senior year." "Without a doubt, Johnny was legitimately in the group of Division I college-recruitable athletes."
—Jack Bowen, Menlo High School water polo coach

"[Superior Court Judge Michael K. Callan] denied Netflix's motion to dismiss Wilson's defamation case ... [and] ruled Wilson has plausibly alleged Netflix defamed him and his son."

—Michael McCann, *Sportico*

"Generous, philanthropic, doing for others less fortunate than himself, leading, a visionary selfless to his own plight… This is the John Wilson I had the honor and pleasure of getting to know while serving the autism community and continuing to know to this day."

—Mark Roithmayr, former chief executive officer of Autism Speaks

"The government admits that if Wilson genuinely believed Singer's side door was legitimate, he would not be guilty of any crime.… Yet his own emails showing that were excluded from his trial. The district court reflexively excluded it all."

—Appeals court filings, *United States v. John Wilson*

"It's not a bribe if the beneficiary of the payment—in this case, USC—is also the alleged victim.… The government has not identified a single case in all of American history that says that paying money to an institution in exchange for a benefit is a bribe."… "Wilson was convicted not for what he did, but for what others did."

—Noel Francisco, former solicitor general of the United States

"People may think you're lying and that you committed fraud, but I know that you didn't and that you're telling the truth."

—Ken Shull, former head of the FBI's worldwide polygraph division

"How can you argue that [the excluded] evidence was not relevant?"
—Kermit Lipez, senior US circuit court judge,
First Circuit Court of Appeals

"Criminal trials don't need to be perfect, but they do need to be fair."
—Hank Asbill, partner, Schertler, Onorato, Mead & Sears

VARSITY BLUES

THE SCANDAL WITHIN THE SCANDAL

BY JOHN WILSON WITH LESLIE WILSON

Copyright © 2025 by John Wilson

All rights reserved.

No portion of this book may be reproduced, stored in a retrieval system, or transmitted in any form by any means–electronic, mechanical, photocopy, recording, or other–except for brief quotations in printed reviews, without prior permission of the author.

Hardcover ISBN: 9798822910171
Paperback ISBN: 9798822910188
eBook ISBN: 9798822913202

Dedication

Though we wish we never had to write this, we dedicate this book to our three incredible children: Johnny, Courtney, and Mamie. Each of you is uniquely talented, and we are endlessly proud of you.

We love you with all our hearts.
Mom and Dad

Book Proceeds

Sharing our story is about restoring our family's honor and reputation, not making money. We commit to donating all proceeds from book sales to three nonprofit organizations that we feel strongly about: the South Peninsula Water Polo Association, Autism Speaks, and the NACDL Foundation for Criminal Justice.

For more info and videos about the facts, law, and media in this case, scan the QR code below.

CONTENTS

Introduction xi

Chapter 1: Handcuffed in Houston:
   From a Ten-Hour Flight to a Federal Prison 1

Chapter 2: A Boy and His World Record:
   False Narratives Ignored the Truth 9

Chapter 3: Escaping the Projects:
   Rising from Hell to Harvard 25

Chapter 4: Sharing the Wealth:
   But No Good Deed Goes Unpunished 43

Chapter 5: The Crooked Singer:
   The Bernie Madoff of College Consulting 61

Chapter 6: Guilt by Association:
   A Media Firestorm Scorches Everyone in Its Path 79

Chapter 7: Against All Odds:
   Deciding to Fight the Federal Government 93

Chapter 8: Becoming Collateral Damage:
   The "Hook" to Bring All the Trials to Boston 111

Chapter 9: Prosecutorial Overreach:
   The Long Arm of the Federal Bureau of Entrapment 125

Chapter 10: Critical Evidence Vanishes:
   How Proof of My Innocence "Disappeared" 139

Chapter 11: The Fine Art of Judge Shopping:
> *How Prosecutors Achieve Near-Absolute Power* 153

Chapter 12: The Proof Is in the Polygraph:
> *FBI and CIA Leaders Reveal the Truth* 165

Chapter 13: Smeared by a Streaming Giant:
> *A Netflix "Documentary" Causes Worldwide Defamation* 179

Chapter 14: No Turning Back:
> *Preparing for Trial* 191

Chapter 15: Our Judicial Nightmare:
> *Were We in the Wrong Courtroom?* 199

Chapter 16: Overruled and Overwhelmed:
> *Prosecutors Blocked 98.3 Percent of our Evidence* 215

Chapter 17: Appeals Court Reversal of Fortune:
> *All My Core Convictions Were Overturned* 231

Chapter 18: Prosecutorial Malice:
> *Vindictive Lawfare and Double Standards* 253

Chapter 19: The Truth Begins to Prevail:
> *The Media Slowly Turns in Our Favor* 263

Chapter 20: Striking Back at the Streamer:
> *Netflix Blurred Fact and Fiction to Maximize Profits* 277

Chapter 21: Taking on the Trojans:
> *USC Defrauded Us to Protect Their Dark Secrets* 293

Epilogue: Our Fight to Restore Our Family's Honor Continues 313

Acknowledgments 331

INTRODUCTION

How far would you go to defend your family's honor if you were falsely accused of a crime? What if your adversary was the federal government with a 99.6 percent conviction rate?[1] What if you also had to fight a global streaming giant and a prestigious university to clear your family's name? Would you spend your entire life savings? Could you endure seven years of emotional, psychological and financial hell fighting three Goliaths at once?

My name is John Wilson, and I had to answer these impossible questions when a nightmare that no one imagines ever happening to them became my reality. For over fifty years, I lived by the rules and worked long and hard hours day in and day out. I did everything I thought was right and built a life which I was proud of—until a wrongful arrest and prosecution devastated my life.

***

I was born into poverty, raised by an abusive single mother in the Bowles Park housing projects in Hartford, Connecticut. From the ages of twelve to sixteen, I picked tobacco to help my family scrape by. For years, my surrogate father was a homeless World War II veteran who lived in a nearby shanty camp; he taught me the importance of hard work, perseverance, and standing up for what's right.

---

1 *Pew Research Center analyses; reports by John Gramlich from June 11, 2020, and June 14, 2023. Pew Research Center analyses; reports by John Gramlich from June 11, 2020, and June 14, 2023.*

THE SCANDAL WITHIN THE SCANDAL

Education transformed my life and helped me break free from poverty. I worked hard in high school to become valedictorian and got a scholarship to college. I earned a BS in chemical engineering from Rensselaer Polytechnic Institute and graduated from Harvard Business School with an MBA at twenty-three—the youngest in my class. I built a successful career from the ground up, and by my thirties, I held senior roles at some of America's most respected corporations. In 1990, I married the love of my life, Leslie Quartermain, and together we raised three remarkable children with the same values that had guided us.

Then, in March 2019, our American dream turned into a nightmare when I stepped off a plane for a business trip in Houston and two FBI agents arrested me. I had never been charged with a crime or arrested before in my life. I was blindsided, accused of crimes I did not commit, and thrown into a federal prison.

I was swept up in Operation Varsity Blues—the largest college admissions scandal in US history. The case captivated the media and became a sensationalized symbol of wealthy people abusing their privilege. Hollywood celebrities like Felicity Huffman and Lori Laughlin and dozens of wealthy West Coast parents were accused of bribery, test cheating, and fraud to get their *unqualified* children into elite colleges.

Except for one thing: that was *their* story—it wasn't *our* story.

Our children did not cheat on their college tests nor were they fake athletes. We never bribed anyone. No allegations against me contradict the facts that our children were highly qualified for admission to each school they applied to based on their own hard-earned merits.

Our son, Johnny, a nationally ranked water polo player, trained year-round for a decade, was twice selected for the US Olympic Team water polo development program, and was recruited by another top-ten Division I college for water polo. He joined and participated fully on the USC water

Introduction

polo team. Our twin daughters earned perfect and near-perfect scores on their ACTs. (To put that into perspective, only 4,879 students out of 1.8 million test-takers got a perfect score in 2019.[2])

Yes, we hired Rick Singer, a college consulting expert with thousands of clients, back in 2010 on the recommendation of a trusted advisor at Goldman Sachs. And like many families, we donated to the University of Southern California (USC) through Singer's IRS certified organization. This was entirely legal. It's shocking that USC, the very institution that encouraged us to donate, who provided us with an official USC receipt and Thank You letter, and has kept our money to this day, would later accuse us of bribery.

Our situation was fundamentally different from *all* the other parents charged. However, the Boston-based prosecutors needed a Massachusetts defendant to anchor the case and justify bringing all the West Coast defendants (and the media spotlights that could catapult a prosecutor's career) to trial in Boston. As the only charged parent from Massachusetts, I became their jurisdictional hook, targeted not for evidence of wrongdoing but to help the Boston prosecutors boost *their* careers. We don't believe that this was a simple mistake; given the overwhelming amounts of evidence they had proving my innocence (which we will share throughout this book). We believe it was a calculated, strategic maneuver designed to maximize headlines for themselves.

The brutality of their approach was shocking. Our family was treated like mere pawns, deliberately sacrificed to serve their ambition. The sheer ruthlessness of it all was staggering—an abuse of authority wielded with precision, each move calculated not just to win but to destroy. The prosecutors falsely accused me and ignored the overwhelming amounts of exculpatory evidence they had in my case and instead treated our family as mere collateral damage in *their* turf battles for this high-profile case.

---

2 *Annual ACT statistics, www.act.org*

THE SCANDAL WITHIN THE SCANDAL

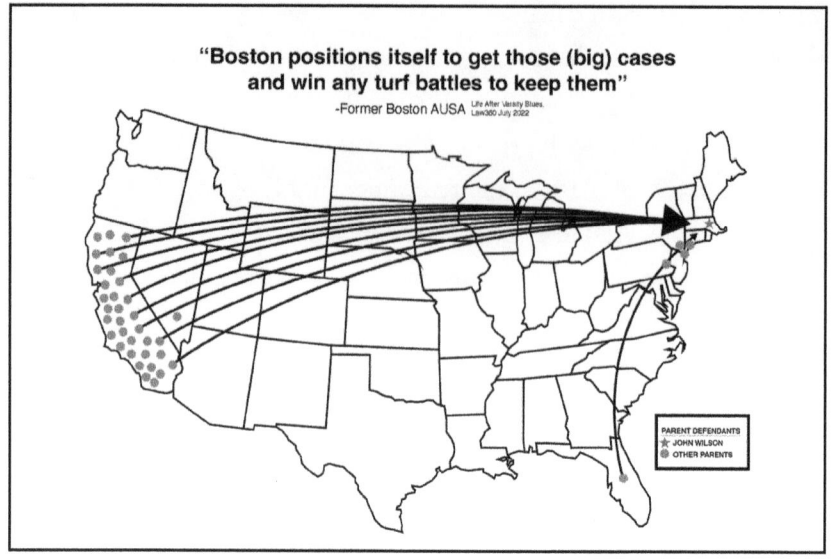

As former Assistant US Attorney David G. Lazarus told *Law360* in 2022 about the Varsity Blues case, "Boston positions itself to get those (big) cases and win any turf battles to keep them." Years later, when I called Mr. Lazarus about his quote, he confirmed its accuracy and shared that he was criticized by his former colleagues about his public statement. He told me his response to them was, "It's the truth!"

While the government worked to manipulate opaque allegations of any wrongdoing on my part into convictions in the court of law, Netflix worked to convict me in the court of public opinion with the actions of the other indicted parents. My legal team and I sent Netflix a 550-page notice letter with the publicly available record of our exculpatory facts *before* they aired their purported "documentary." Netflix blatantly ignored our notice letter and rushed to release the film to their 280 million subscribers months before my trial, severely tainting the jury pool.

Although the financial costs of defending our family's honor were enormous, the emotional costs have been far greater. As a husband, I cannot

Introduction

describe the heartache of watching Leslie cry herself to sleep nearly every night for six years as she worried about our children and their futures. There is nothing more painful as a father than feeling helpless while seeing our innocent children suffer from false attacks, not by schoolyard bullies but by federal prosecutors, a streaming media giant, and a university we had trusted.

We know the risks of speaking out, especially given the potential for further retaliation by federal prosecutors who can weaponize our system of criminal justice for their own agendas. However, for us, silence is not an option. What the prosecutors, Netflix, and USC did to our family should never happen to anyone.

The truth matters. Our family's honor is worth more than our entire life savings. By standing up for what's right, we can hold our heads high and hope to inspire others to find their voices. We will continue the fight to restore our reputations and help ensure that no other family endures the hardships we have faced.

You might think you know all there is to know about the Varsity Blues scandal, but the reality we will share is far more complicated and profoundly disturbing than you might imagine.

Varsity Blues: The Scandal Within the Scandal exposes the many dirty tactics three of America's most powerful institutions used as they knowingly trampled over truth, justice, and innocent lives to serve their own self-interests and hide their dark secrets.

This is the shocking truth behind the headlines. It's the untold story of how far a family will go to defend their honor and the brutal reality and costs of fighting for justice in America today.

Chapter 1

HANDCUFFED IN HOUSTON

From a Ten-Hour Flight to a Federal Prison

Before March 11, 2019, I had never been arrested or set foot inside a federal courtroom, not for a criminal case, a civil lawsuit, or even a tour. I had *never* been charged with a crime in my life. I lived my life by the rules, built my career through hard work and integrity, and never once thought that I would find myself accused of a crime.

So imagine my shock when, without warning, two FBI agents arrested me at Houston's George Bush Intercontinental Airport (IAH) after I arrived from a ten-hour flight from Europe to meet with a Texas-based client. Those meetings never happened as I was swept up as part of Operation Varsity Blues—the largest college admissions scandal in US history.

I heard the sharp clicks of the handcuffs and the agent's stern voice telling me, "You're under arrest." In that instant, as I felt the cold steel of the handcuffs wrapping around and biting into my wrists, my world changed forever. In a matter of seconds, the life I had spent fifty years building, based on hard work and integrity, began to disintegrate. I unknowingly said goodbye to nearly everything I held dear; the safety and security of my family was now in jeopardy.

In seconds, I went from a respected businessman, father and husband to a criminal in the eyes of the law—without ever committing a crime. What I didn't know then was that this moment marked the beginning of a seven-year nightmare.

THE SCANDAL WITHIN THE SCANDAL

The FBI agents told me that I was being arrested for "honest services fraud."[3] I asked what that meant and was even more shocked when they admitted *they* didn't know; of the charge, they said, "We've never heard of it before."

It seemed like a scene from *The Twilight Zone*. I remember thinking, How could the FBI agents arresting me not even know what they are charging me with? Their uncertainty left me dumbfounded. I wanted to scream, to demand answers. Instead my throat went dry.

My mind raced. I thought this had to be a mistake. "You must have the wrong person," I said, thinking it *had* to be a mix-up with one of the other fifteen thousand John Wilsons in the US. I had never committed fraud in my life.

The agents confirmed my address in Massachusetts and told me I was indeed the person they were looking for as they escorted me through the airport halls, handcuffed, to a waiting car. I was still in shock as they drove me to a local FBI processing facility. As the car moved through Houston, I couldn't stop my head from spinning as so many questions flooded my mind. What was I accused of doing wrong? How could this be happening? What was happening to my wife and our children back home?

I remember thinking about the crime shows I had seen on TV where anyone under arrest is advised not to say a word without their lawyers present. I had done nothing wrong, so I just kept talking and asking questions the entire way, desperate to understand what was unfolding around me. What crime was I accused of committing? Who was involved? When did this supposedly happen? The agents seemed as frustrated with my questions as I was with their lack of answers.

At the FBI processing center, I was fingerprinted, photographed, and swabbed for DNA—treatments usually reserved for criminals, not businessmen who have lived by the rules their whole lives. I was allowed to make

---

3 Honest services fraud is a law added by Congress in 1988 as 18 U.S.C. § 1346, making it a federal crime for someone to breach a fiduciary duty and deprive an organization of their intangible right of honest services.

one phone call. I called my assistant (because my wife Leslie was seven time zones ahead in Europe at the time) and asked her to inform Leslie the next day and my brother, a civil attorney, that the FBI had arrested me. I could only imagine Leslie's panic when she heard the news.

What came next felt like an out-of-body experience. The agents then drove me to a federal detention center in Houston—a towering fortress of security made of concrete and steel which looked like something out of a crime movie that would intimidate even a drug kingpin. Here, they shackled my ankles in addition to my handcuffs, forcing me to shuffle as I walked.

For a law-abiding father, husband, and businessperson, the experience was surreal. I had been to prestigious boardrooms and stood alongside multiple *Fortune 500* CEOs, US presidents, and even a Pope. Now I was nothing more than a number in the federal prison system, treated like a hardened criminal.

Inside the prison, the guards barked out commands: face the wall, don't look to your sides, don't speak to anyone, and so forth. It was humiliating. They ordered me to strip my clothes off and then proceeded to hose me down in a large common shower room. I felt less than human, more like an animal being processed through some cold, unfeeling machine.

The guards seemed incredulous when I told them that I had never been arrested before. One even sneered at me as if my statement was a lie and made me appear *more* suspicious. As they led me into the guard room, I also told them that no one could explain to me what crime I was accused of committing.

The guard room had large observation windows looking into a two-story cellblock with dozens of cells and inmates from the general population mulling about in a common area. It was just like a scene from a prison movie, except this was real life—*my life.*

One guard, sensing my fear was palpable and perhaps actually believing that this was my first time in prison, offered me some advice. He warned me, "Watch your back in there." He said, "Since you're an old white guy, they'll assume that you're a pedophile. And they *hate* pedophiles in here." I froze when he added matter-of-factly, "Someone might try to stab you with a shiv."

I was terrified and my heart was beating in overdrive. I asked if I could be locked in my cell, hoping to avoid the threat of violence and not have to worry about being attacked. "Lockdown isn't until much later," he gruffly responded. "And if you hide in your cell, the others will think you're a pussy and really f**k you up." He then gave me one more piece of advice. "Don't accept any favors from anyone, no matter how small." If I did, "then you'll owe them, and that won't end well either."

This was beyond my worst nightmare. I had never felt fear and confusion like this before in my life. I was in a cellblock with dozens of other inmates, yet I still had no idea what I was accused of doing wrong. I have been brutally beaten many times in my life (more on that later), but the thought of being stabbed and possibly killed at any moment by a total stranger for absolutely no reason was nearly paralyzing. Every time someone approached me in the cellblock, I feared an attack. I walked around with my back to the wall as much as possible so I could see an attack if one came my way. The guards had made it clear: I was on my own.

I shared an eight-by-ten-foot prison cell with one other inmate and a bunk bed. I didn't know anything about him or what he was in for, but I was bigger, and I insisted on taking the bottom bunk (so I couldn't be attacked from below). I was glad I got the bottom bunk without a fight and that there was only one person I might have to defend myself against during the night.

After nighttime lockdown, I remember thinking how strange it was that I actually felt relieved to be locked behind prison bars. I spent the entire night wide awake, praying and confused. The thoughts swirling around and around in my head sped up to what felt like 1,000 miles per hour as I still had no idea why I was even in that prison cell.

The next morning, I was handcuffed and shackled again as I was led, shuffling my legs to a secure meeting room. There I saw, through a plexiglass window, my brother and a Texas criminal lawyer he'd hired. This was the first time I began to understand what was happening. They mentioned Rick Singer, a college advisory consultant, and told me that dozens of other parents had been charged with fraud, bribery, and test cheating. My involvement with Singer had somehow put me in the crosshairs of a massive federal investigation.

It still didn't make any sense, and I said again this must be a case of mistaken identity. My children hadn't cheated on any college tests. I had never bribed anyone, and we never put any fraudulent information into any application. Our donations had gone to IRS-certified charities and university foundations, not to anyone's pockets. USC had given us receipts. Why was I being lumped in with people accused of committing these corrupt acts?

When the meeting was over, the guards took me back to the cellblock. Once again, I had to watch my back each time someone came near me. Several inmates came up to me offering food and even a pair of extra-large slippers. As I was forewarned, I declined each time and just walked away. I could tell they were testing me. I walked around on pins and needles the entire time.

Later that day, I was brought to a secure courtroom for a bond hearing. The Houston probation officer told the judge that since I had no prior record and was neither a threat to society nor a flight risk, he recommended I be released on bond. The Houston prosecutors were in the back of the courtroom getting their marching orders over the phone from their counterparts in Boston. That was when I first realized that the Boston prosecutors were in charge and just how extreme and brutal their tactics could be.

Shockingly, the Boston prosecutors demanded, via the phone, $1 million, *all cash* bail—an extreme demand that the Houston judge said was excessive. The Boston prosecutors said they had a right to appeal her decision and demanded that she put me back into prison for three days while they appealed.

The judge agreed to put me back into the cellblock until the end of the day, by which time they needed to provide *new* evidence about why such a large, all-cash bail was necessary. Otherwise, she told them that she would release me on a bond. I was returned to the cellblock, where I once again walked around fearing for my life.

The realization hit me hard: the Boston prosecutors were willing to put my life in danger, *not once but twice*, just to intimidate me. They knew I had no criminal record; I was a businessman, a father, and a thirty-year husband. Yet they treated me as if I was a hardened criminal, exposing me to potential violence (for some obscure charge the FBI agents didn't even know) as a scare tactic to get me to plead guilty.

At the end of the day, the Boston prosecutors didn't provide any new evidence, and the judge released me on bond. I later exited the prison, not knowing I was about to enter a different kind of hell—a place where the truth no longer seemed to matter, where I would have to fight for my freedom and my family's honor against a system determined to crush me.

This was just the first time (with many, many more horrific experiences we will share) that I felt what it was like to be a nail to the Boston prosecutor's hammer.

Being in the crosshairs of the US government, the most powerful and relentless prosecution force that the world has ever seen, is an emotional, physical, and financial nightmare that is impossible to fully describe. What made this horror even more unbearable is knowing, without a doubt, that I didn't commit a crime, and yet my innocence may be nothing more than a technicality to a prosecutor who just *didn't care.*

That's when I knew…this wasn't a mistake. There was something much bigger going on.

***

Once I was freed, the most pressing task was to reassure and comfort our three children. Our entire family was in shock. While *we* all knew that we had done nothing wrong and there were no allegations of my children cheating on tests or Johnny being a fake water polo player in his USC application, the mere inclusion of my name in the indictments painted a very different picture to the public and the media.

While our facts and even allegations were completely different from all the other charged parents, we were tried and convicted in the same court of public opinion and now guilty until proven innocent.

The Varsity Blues headlines lumped all the parents together and tarred everyone with the same dirty brush. It didn't matter that our children were all qualified on their own hard-earned merits or that we got receipts for our donations to USC on official USC letterhead, or that our family didn't cheat on college tests or give any false information to any college or that our son played on the USC water polo team. I still believed this had to be a case of mistaken identity. Yet it was "guilt by association" in the media before I even had a chance to defend myself.

Leslie and I needed to be strong for our children. We told them to hold their heads high and that the truth would ultimately prevail. That was our external, reassuring face. Inside, we were both shaken to our core. We were up against the full might of the United States government—the most powerful institution in the history of the world.

Every court document made it crystal clear;
this was no ordinary battle, this was:

The United States of America v. John Wilson.

Chapter 2

A BOY AND HIS WORLD RECORD

False Narratives Ignored the Truth

One of the most sensational aspects of the Varsity Blues college admissions scandal related to parents staging and photoshopping fake images and presenting their children as star athletes in sports they didn't even play. We thought it would be helpful to begin our story by setting the record straight about our son's athletic background and sharing the truth about his hard-earned credentials.

***

Few people are fortunate enough to grace the stage of *The Oprah Winfrey Show*, a platform seen by over 12 million viewers in the US and broadcast in 145 countries. Oprah has welcomed everyone from US presidents and European royalty to celebrities and everyday people with remarkable stories.

In 2006, when our son Johnny was just ten years old, he joined this prestigious lineup as a special guest on an episode featuring "Little People Doing Big Things."

Johnny on an episode featuring "Little People Doing Big Things" on The Oprah Winfrey Show

THE SCANDAL WITHIN THE SCANDAL

> Johnny was invited to the show to celebrate two incredible achievements: his world record swim from Alcatraz Island to the shore of San Francisco the previous year and the inspiring charity work he undertook when he transformed his amazing swim into a fundraiser for Hurricane Katrina victims.

***

In 2005, our nine-year-old son broke a world record, becoming the youngest person ever to swim the 1.4 miles from Alcatraz Island to the shores of San Francisco. This was no small feat for any swimmer, let alone a child. The waters of the San Francisco Bay are notorious for their frigid fifty-degree temperatures, choppy waves, and strong tidal currents, which can often make the actual swim distance in the water much longer.

Yet Johnny did it, raising, with the help of his fourth-grade classmates, over $53,000 for the Red Cross's Hurricane Katrina relief fund along the way. The swim not only highlighted his extraordinary athleticism but also his perseverance and compassion—qualities that continue to define him to this day.

The idea for this record-breaking swim came from a triathlete friend, Rick Murray, a member of the San Francisco Dolphin Club who regularly swam in the bay. Rick noticed our son's natural talent when Johnny was eight years old and suggested the Alcatraz swim. At first, Leslie and I thought the idea was insane, but with ten months of training and Rick's guidance, we realized it was possible.

We knew it would be a huge commitment for a young boy who already had schoolwork and year-round club swim practices. But Johnny's determination was unwavering, and his tenacity left us in awe; every day he trained, he wanted to go faster, further, and longer in the bay. Nothing was going to stop him.

A Boy and His World Record

Photo of nine year old Johnny swimming in the San Francisco Bay with Rick Murray

As the months passed and the devastation of Hurricane Katrina unfolded on TV, Johnny decided to turn his upcoming swim into a fundraising effort for the victims. He rallied his fourth-grade classmates, who helped raise pledges for each quarter mile he swam (ensuring that money would be raised even if he didn't finish the entire swim). But he did finish—and then some.

When it came to safety, we left no stone unturned. Thankfully, the Dolphin Club had a well-honed set of safety protocols from many years of sponsoring group swims from Alcatraz that we followed. Additionally, since the bay is a highly active shipping harbor, we had to get pre-approved time slots from the US Coast Guard vessel traffic control group.

Beyond the frigid temperatures, the cross-tidal currents in the bay can range from slack to five knots at their peak. Swimming during a strong cross-tide could increase the actual in-water swim distance to well over two miles. So we had to align the available shipping time slots with the tides to make it work.

THE SCANDAL WITHIN THE SCANDAL

We booked his swim for a 6:00 a.m. start on Monday, October 10, 2005, Indigenous Peoples' Day. We planned to leave the San Francisco shore in a small Zodiac boat at 5:00 a.m., making our way to Alcatraz Island in the dark. The Dolphin Club provided two adult safety swimmers and two kayakers to ensure that every precaution was in place. One of the kayakers would drift one hundred yards ahead to calibrate the speed of the cross-tide and adjust the swimming angle so that my son would be able to offset the currents and arrive safely at the Aquatic Park destination.

***

The night before the big swim, Katie Couric and the *Today Show* crew set up a live video interview with our son and his coach from our home at 3:00 a.m.—an hour before we were to drive into San Francisco. It was an incredibly early start, and everything went according to plan until we arrived at Alcatraz Island in our small Zodiac, when several surprises awaited us.

Screenshot of Johnny and Rick Murray with Katie Couric on The Today Show

First, the US Coast Guard radioed us to delay the swim by an hour because an unscheduled fuel tanker was entering the bay. This delay was significant because the tides would be stronger, and the true in-water swim distance would now be about two miles (versus the 1.4 miles we had planned for at slack tide).

Second, there was a group of Native American protestors who had camped out on Alcatraz for the holiday, and they were very irritated that our Zodiac came to the island on this important day.

Third, multiple helicopters hovered overhead, capturing the live spectacle for viewers across the world. Talk about pressure! It made all of us nervous—especially since the swim was now nearly two miles in the water. The extra distance was one thing; the extra time in the frigid water was another.

With helicopters above and news cameras on the shore, it seemed like the whole world watched live as Johnny made his audacious plunge. The cold ocean temperatures numbed his hands, feet, and face. Leslie and I were worried because Johnny was swimming further and longer than planned given the delay, but he persevered.

As he neared San Francisco, you could hear his classmates, reporters, and supporters cheering, "Go Johnny! Go Johnny!"

Just before he reached the shore, I jumped off the Zodiac and ran straight to him. I gave him a huge bear hug when he got to the beach, lifting his four-foot body high into the air in front of all the TV cameras. Leslie and I were overwhelmed with pride, and that moment is something none of us will ever forget.

Photo of Johnny's 4th grade classmates and supporters on the San Francisco shore

The swim was a triumph in so many ways. Not only did our son use his incredible swimming talents to raise money for Katrina victims, but also, the worldwide media coverage helped increase those donations

Photo of Johnny and me celebrating the completion of his Alcatraz swim

to over $53,000. Johnny was featured in live breaking-news broadcasts on major networks, including international TV coverage on the BBC.

One sweet moment from that day that still makes me smile was when the media asked him, "Now that you've broken a world record, what are you going to do next?" His reply: "I'm going to get breakfast." We all laughed hysterically. He had been awake since 3:00 a.m. and had had a modest breakfast before we headed out. He was now starving, and food was top of mind—that was our modest and *very pragmatic* son.

Photos of Johnny as he sets a new world record

Johnny received letters of recognition for his swim from President George W. Bush, Senator Edward Kennedy, San Francisco Mayor Gavin Newsom, and the Coast Guard Admiral Thad Allen, who oversaw Hurricane Katrina relief efforts. He was also featured in *Vanity Fair* and many other magazines.

Some of the recognitions Johnny received in honor of his Alcatraz swim

For the next decade, that talented and passionate little boy would go on to train tirelessly for 500 to 750 hours a year in swimming and water polo, accumulating many records and awards.

Johnny competed in regional and international swim championships and started on multiple top-ten-to-twenty nationally ranked Stanford Club water polo teams for six years. In 2012, his Stanford Club team won first place in the national Junior Olympics tournament, classic division, as shown in this photo.

Photo of some of Johnny's swimming and water polo awards

Photo of Johnny on the Stanford Water Polo Club team

Johnny was also twice selected for the US Olympic Team development program. When considering where to play in college, he was recruited by other top Division I teams—for example, the Air Force Academy (ranked a top-ten nationwide team in 2012 by the Collegiate Water Polo Association)[4], as shown in this email from Johnny's high school coach, Jack Bowen, to Leslie in December 2012.

From: Jack Bowen. [mailto:jbowen311@yahoo.com]
Sent: Monday, December 10, 2012 1:42 PM
To: Leslie Wilson
Subject: Re: Two Notes.

Hi Leslie,

Thanks for your note--and, wow, Christmas in Amsterdam sounds amazing! How nice for you guys to get some time over there.

Interestingly, I spoke to Johnny briefly at lunch. The Air Force Academy coach has expressed a real interest in Johnny. I didn't think Johnny would reciprocate that interest but when I asked him, he actually said that he'd like to follow up with them.

---

4 Collegiate Water Polo Association, Men's 2012 Varsity Top 20, week 13, November 28, 2012. The final rankings for 2012 listed the Air Force Academy as number ten in the nation.

Photo of Johnny during a high school water polo practice

Photo of Johnny in 2013 winning the Bay Area league championships

THE SCANDAL WITHIN THE SCANDAL

Jack Bowen was a 2-time water polo All-American and NCAA MVP while at Stanford University, and the alternate goalie on the 2006 U.S, Olympic Team. Jack has coached water polo at the Menlo school for 25 years, with over 500 team wins, including winning the league championships 19 times and California sectional championships 5 times (the highest-level achievement possible in California scholastic competition.) Over his career, Jack has supported over 65 players who went on to play water polo in college. Jack's inspirational motto that he uses while training his student athletes, "Be your best" still resonates with Johnny to this day.

Coach Bowen, trained Johnny for seven years throughout middle and high school and is the most qualified person in the world to comment on Johnny's abilities. In his expert professional assessment, he compiled objective data and facts to unequivocally set the record straight, stating in the text below: "Without a doubt, Johnny was legitimately in the group of Division I college-recruitable athletes."

Jack

Sat, Oct 12 at 19:49

John Wilson

I went through the Menlo Water Polo History which I've compiled and come up with the following .... hoping this is helpful in some way?
In my 25 years as the Head Coach at Menlo School, I have compiled very detailed and copious notes all as a part of our "History of Menlo School Water Polo," so I hope the following data can be helpful.

Johnny's junior year, against our strongest opponents (what we call "Tier I" teams) he was second on the team in steals, tied for second in assists, and third in goals scored. I
Johnny Earned First Team All-League in 2013, Honorable Mention All-League in 2012, and Second Team All-CCS DII in 2013.
As for his speed and swimming capabilities, Johnny tied for first his sophomore year in the team's 200 meter timed trial. His Junior and Senior year, Johnny finished first: the fastest player on an already fast, high level team. He was also 1st Team All-League Swimming on the Swim Team.

In my 25 years, 38 players earned a Varsity letter 3 years. Of those 38, 26 went on to play Varsity Water Polo at the college level. In addition, all but 6 of the athletes who earned at least All CCS Honorable Mention went on to play Varsity Water polo at the college level. Any chance that's helpful? Thanks for this. And yeah, that's what I was hoping to do when I sat down with the history books...just to compile objective data and facts which demonstrate without a doubt that Johnny was legitimately in the group of DI college recruitable athletes.

A Boy and His World Record

In 2013, when Johnny was a high school senior, Coach Bowen called the USC water polo coaches and recommended him to the USC team, the-then reigning national champions. As shown in the trial transcripts below[5], Coach Bowen testified that he was confident that Johnny's speed, work ethic, and water polo IQ could make him a starter on the national caliber USC team by his junior or senior year.

> 1 phone must have influenced the coach. Like, I said, "That call
> 2 must have done it."
> 3 Q. Okay. And that's because you thought Johnny had speed for
> 4 the high level of college play?
> 5 A. It's a combination of his speed, which you can't teach.
> 6 So the speed and the water polo IQ just by virtue of starting
> 7 for a team, a national caliber team for three years, that is
> 8 enough to confidently say by your junior year, maybe senior
> 9 year, you could contribute to a high-level program like USC.

As shown below, Johnny's certified swim times from his junior year in high school proved that he was one of the fastest players on USC's 2014 team—pretty impressive since USC was the then-reigning national champion.[6]

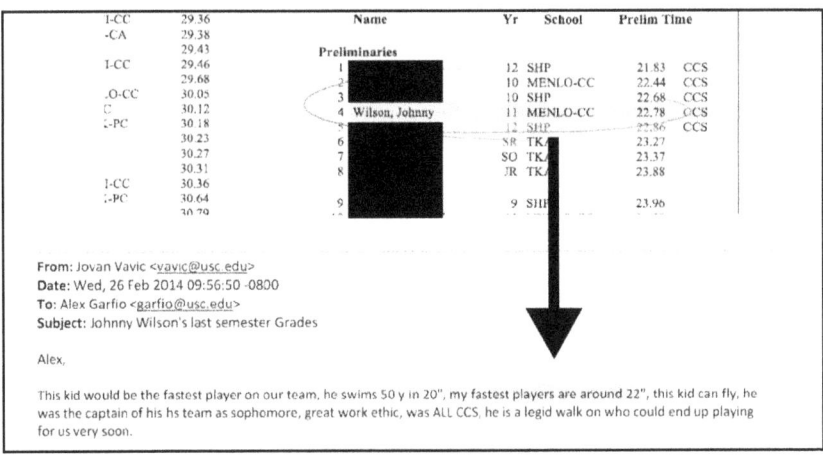

---

5 *See excerpts from trial transcripts, shown in chapter 15.*
6 *Hy-Tek's meet manager, 8:05 p.m. West Bay Area League Championships, May 1, 2013, page 1, and email from Coach Jovan Vavic.*

Unfortunately, as we will show later, Coach Bowen was not allowed by the prosecutors (and the trial judge the prosecutors hand selected) to share Johnny's actual swim times and other facts which proved that he was qualified for the USC team.

In fact, Johnny joined and officially participated on the USC team for the entire 2014 season and postseason (while training above deck for six weeks when he had a concussion) of his freshman year. Leslie and I traveled multiple times, thousands of miles each way, to watch Johnny at team practices and to cheer the team on with other parents at multiple USC matches throughout the season.

Official 2014 USC water polo team photo with Johnny circled

***

Despite all our son's incredible athletic accomplishments, he was maligned in the media as a "fake" or "alleged" athlete and someone who didn't play at the Division I level. The media purposely lumped him in with other families whose parents staged photoshopped images and presented their children as Division I athletes in sports *they* never even played.

Despite the fact that our son Johnny was a fully-qualified Division I level athlete who joined and participated on the USC team, he was falsely smeared by the media, Netflix and USC as being unqualified.

Shockingly, the public record and the government's own charging documents *never* said our son was a fake or alleged athlete or that he wasn't being recruited by other Division I colleges or wasn't qualified to be a walk-on player on USC's team. They couldn't put that in writing because it wasn't true!

The prosecutors had access to all of the information shared in this book and much more, which proved our son was more than qualified for a walk-on role on the USC water polo team. We know that they were aware of every bit of this evidence because (with the help of a highly supportive judge which they handpicked—more on this in chapter 10) they blocked the jury from seeing any of it. They objected to my defense motions an astounding 660 times during my trial.

The Boston prosecutors repeatedly worked behind the scenes to mislead the media about our son's qualifications to be a walk-on recruit for USC's water polo team. For example, in October 2021, the *New York Times* wrote, "He was not good enough to compete at the university, *according to the prosecutors* [7] *(emphasis added)*." These nonpublic statements to the media, in direct contradiction of the public record and the facts the prosecutors had, suggest that perhaps someone within the Boston federal prosecutor's office was leaking false stories about our son's qualifications in order to put pressure on me. Again, the prosecutors interviewed Johnny's national acclaimed middle and high school water polo coach (who trained Johnny for six years.) Coach Bowen wrote based on his extensive experience and compilation of, "Objective data and facts which demonstrate without a doubt that Johnny was legitimately in the group of DI recruitable college athletes."

---

[7] "The College Admissions Scandal: Where Some of the Defendants Are Now," New York Times, October 7, 2021.

THE SCANDAL WITHIN THE SCANDAL

I've worked and travelled to more than ninety-five countries during my career and seen many corrupt and disturbing things in my life. However, the thought that federal prosecutors, whose sworn duty is to seek the truth and justice and to protect the innocent, would falsely smear our innocent son to boost their own careers is perhaps the most morally depraved and despicable act that we have ever experienced.

***

We are extremely proud of Johnny's many talents and accomplishments. But what we are most proud of is his character. The best testament of how Johnny has maintained the same grit, determination, and kind heart as an adult that he had when he braved the frigid waters in his swim from Alcatraz Island is captured in his birthday note to me in 2022.

> Dear Dad,
>
> Happy Birthday Dad! Thank you for being the best dad in the world. I am so grateful to have an amazing role model like you who stands up for what is right no matter what. I appreciate everything that you do for me and our family and I am excited to see what the next untold chapter of our lives and more importantly your life has in store for us. The past several years of hardship have only made you and our family stronger and I know that if we can make it through this we can make it through anything. Thank you for never giving up.

Since Johnny inherited my poor penmanship skills, the note is also typed below.

Dear Dad,

Happy Birthday Dad! Thank you for being the best dad in the world. I am so grateful to have an amazing role model like you who stands up for what is right no matter what. I appreciate everything you do for me and our family, and I am excited to see what the next untold chapter of our lives, and more importantly, your life, has in store for us. The past several years of hardship have only made you and our family stronger, and I know if we can make it through this, we can make it through anything. Thank you for never giving up.

As we will recount in this book, no amount of false smear tactics by members of the Justice Department, Netflix, or USC can erase the truth: Johnny was a real Division I athlete who worked hard for everything he achieved and was a proud member of USC's 2014 water polo team.

Johnny's perseverance, talents, and grit define <u>his</u> story. His skills and years of hard-work clearly qualified him for a walk-on role on the USC team.

Chapter 3

ESCAPING THE PROJECTS

Rising from Hell to Harvard

To understand why I am willing to fight so hard to defend my family, it may be helpful to know where I came from and the source of my inner strength to take on the federal government. That strength wasn't born out of privilege; it was born out of hardship, pain, and a desperate struggle to rise above the circumstances I was born into.

***

"John, you dirty, rotten, no-good f***ing son of a bitch—get your ass in here *right now!*" My mother would yell that phrase verbatim with a seething rage whenever she called me in, starting when I was just five years old. While those ten words may sound harsh to outsiders, they were a near-daily ritual, screamed by my mother at the top of her lungs for the entire neighborhood to hear. The below photo shows one of the buildings in the Bowles Park housing projects of Hartford, Connecticut, the place I called home.

Photo of Bowles Park housing projects

THE SCANDAL WITHIN THE SCANDAL

> My mother never gave me a middle name, but for over a decade, those ten words were repeated after my first name so often that it felt like I had ten middle names. The humiliation was constant; even decades later, several childhood friends still remember it and tease me about it to this day.

***

My mother, Jeanette Soto, was the youngest child in a large, strict Roman Catholic family. Her father was a truck driver from Puerto Rico, and her mother was a second-generation Polish immigrant. At just fifteen, with only an eighth-grade education, she was kicked out of her house after becoming pregnant. She gave that daughter up for adoption, and to this day, I've never met that half-sister. I have no idea who my biological father is or if he's even alive. My mother never returned to her childhood home, and none of us half siblings ever met the only biological grandparents we knew of.

After a second brief marriage, my mother became a single mom, raising my older half-brother along with me and two half-sisters. This photo captures my family when I was three years old.

Photo of me and my family (I'm on the left)

My mother's harsh upbringing, combined with her severe mental health issues, left her poorly equipped to raise us. Even now, I can't help but think how different things might have been if my mother had gotten the love, support, and mental health care she needed when she was young. But life didn't give her those things, and she, in turn, inflicted extreme physical and emotional abuse on us.

Photo my older half brother and me in the Bowles Park projects

I quickly learned to avoid my mother as much as possible. The fields and woods surrounding the projects where I grew up felt like a refuge compared to what went on inside our apartment. Some of my earliest memories involve me and my brother exploring the neighborhood and nearby woods for hours, just to escape our mother. This photo was taken when I was two and my brother was five.

My mother's mood swings were extreme and unpredictable. While she could maintain her composure in front of visitors, the emotional roller coaster would start again the moment they left. When we were alone with her, there seemed to be an omnipresent mean streak that lurked just beneath the surface. The slightest misstep could trigger an explosive reaction, resulting in fits of rage and physical violence.

The beatings began when I was in kindergarten. Initially, she used her hands and fists, then a belt. As time went on, her methods grew more extreme. She started using cookware as a weapon, specifically the long-handled saucepan for boiling water and making instant coffee.

She would often hit me with that hot saucepan, leaving searing, painful bruises on my arms and back. In moments of extreme anger, she would throw boiling water at us. Thrown from a distance across the kitchen, the hot water hurt like hell and made us cry in pain, but it didn't leave permanent burns or scars. During one fit of rage, she poured boiling water directly onto my eldest sister's back, resulting in severe burns that required hospitalization.

To this day, I hate the thought of boiling water for coffee, and I've never had a single cup of coffee in my entire life. The very sight of a saucepan with boiling water brings back terrible memories.

In those early years, we lived on welfare, and putting food on the table was a daily struggle. My mother's oldest brother, Julio (whom we called Uncle Julie), and her oldest sister, Juanita (Aunt Nita), occasionally brought us food and secondhand clothes. Uncle Julie would deliver a gallon of fresh milk each month. My mother was resourceful, stretching that single gallon to last for the *entire* month while feeding five hungry mouths. She marked the glass jug at the midpoint, and we were never allowed to drink below that line—the consequences for doing so were swift and severe.

Each time the milk approached half-empty, she would fill it with water and sometimes a bit of powdered milk. The process was repeated until the original gallon became so watered down that it tasted like chalk water. The gradual dilution was clever, because each diluted batch tasted just a little worse than the prior batch, and the change wasn't shocking. But when a new gallon of "real milk" arrived at the beginning of the month, it sparked a frenzy over first dibs.

While the struggle for food had its downsides, it also taught me some valuable lessons. My mother's strict rules led me to learn how to track numbers, count, and multiply at an early age. Bologna sandwiches were a luxury, and my brother and I were limited to one slice of bologna per day. My brother preferred peanut butter, and he sometimes let me have his slice so I could have a sandwich with two slices.

My mother diligently wrote the purchase date and number of starting slices on the bologna wrapper and periodically inspected the package—to ensure we hadn't overeaten. I quickly learned to count the days, multiply that by two, subtract that from the starting number of slices, and compare that to the actual slices remaining. Basic math came in very handy to keep my brother honest and help me avoid a beating.

The math skills I gained tracking bologna didn't help me to learn to read or write. My early grades suffered due to my nearsightedness and severe dyslexia. We had no insurance, so we couldn't afford an eye doctor or glasses.

Dyslexia made school even more challenging; I wrote words backward and couldn't comprehend my mistakes. My teacher would slap me on the back of my head, calling me a wise guy for spelling my name backward—N-H-O-J. "Spell it the right way," she would snap as she hit me. I felt stupid and humiliated, and the public shame only muddled my already-confused mind. "I am," I would shout, not lying, because that was how I saw my name. My classmates teased me, chanting "N-H-O-J, N-H-O-J, N-H-O-J," which annoyed my teacher as much as it did me.

For the first few years, I hated school and skipped whenever I could. Instead of going home, however, I would roam the projects or explore the nearby woods.

One day, I noticed rising smoke from campfires in those woods and wandered up to a small shanty camp of twenty to thirty hardscrabble men. I was just five years old when I first approached them, and they barked at me to "get lost." But after several visits, one man, "Big Sam," took me under his wing. He allowed me to stay as long as I helped collect firewood. Scavenging the woods, dumpsters, and trash cans for firewood soon became my routine, as I avoided going home and wanted to hang out with these guys.

In the 1960s, these men were mostly World War II veterans who would do farm and construction work, and they proudly called themselves hoboes. They shared stories of riding trains and traveling across the country for work, living outdoors without the burden of paying rent.

They had amazing stories about various places in the United States and around the world from their time in the military. To a wide-eyed boy without a father, their tales of adventure captivated me, inspiring dreams of becoming a worldly adventurer like them. For years, I admired these men and wanted to be a hobo when I grew up.

I formed a special bond with Big Sam, who returned to the Hartford encampment for three consecutive years. A truck driver during World War II who served in Europe, he taught many life lessons that have stayed with me.

One of the first lessons was the importance of hard work. If I wanted something, I needed to earn it. Over the years, foraging for firewood became increasingly challenging. I had to be more aggressive, scouring trash cans and dumpsters and expanding the area of woods I searched. Dragging broken furniture, wood, or tree limbs over ever-greater distances was tough, but I welcomed the challenge to hear more of Big Sam's stories and stay away from my mother. From those early days, hard work became ingrained in me. For most of my life, I've worked seventy-plus-hour weeks, often while on "vacation."

Big Sam also taught me the value of moving around for the best-paying jobs. He said moving around could help you make more money *and* see more places. This mindset stayed with me; I've moved more than twenty times across the United States and internationally, which helped accelerate my career. I think even Big Sam would be proud, as I have been to every state in the US and more than ninety-five countries.

Another important lesson Big Sam taught me was the importance of fighting for what's right, no matter what life threw at me. He would tell me stories about the war and fighting against Nazis and the horrible things that happened. There were times when his unit was in impossible situations, and they all thought they were going to die. But they never gave up, no matter how hard they got hit or knocked down. They were fighting for what was right, and "You never give up when you are fighting for what's right." Big Sam never used the word *resilience*, but he taught me the importance of getting back up no matter how many times life knocked you down.

Big Sam's favorite topic, which I loved hearing about, was to dream big. He would say, "Anything is possible if you put your mind and back into it." I remember sitting for hours by the campfire, enraptured as he would describe the most amazing place in the world that he had ever seen—the Palace of Versailles. He described this palace to me over and over again, and I hung on every word each time.

"It was the biggest palace in the world," he would say. "The walls are solid gold. The furniture is solid silver. There's a hall of giant mirrors that was longer than two football fields, enough bedrooms to sleep thousands of people, a fountain big enough for real ships to sail in…" For three years, Big Sam regaled me with stories about Versailles. He described it so many times and in so much detail that I felt I could be a tour guide there someday. He never grew tired of describing it, and I never grew tired of listening.

Near the end of the war, Big Sam was stationed near Paris, tasked with delivering packages between the city and Versailles, the US Army headquarters. Big Sam pronounced it "Ver-sighhhhh," letting the end of the word linger, smiling widely each time he did. The way he said it gave it an almost regal quality. He emphasized that I could always remember how to pronounce it the proper French way, because when I saw it, I would sigh: "Ver-sighhhhh."

One incredible story Big Sam told me was about another US Army driver in Paris. This guy was the driver to General Eisenhower, the future president of the United States. This other driver, just an ordinary guy, was getting married to an army nurse, and to my astonishment, General Eisenhower allowed him to have his wedding at Versailles. I was shocked; could a *truck driver* really have his wedding in the most magnificent palace in the world? For a young boy living in poverty, the idea seemed more like a fairy tale than real life.

In many ways, Versailles was more than a palace to me; it was a symbol of dreaming big. My fireside chats with Big Sam offered a fantastic escape from my harsh reality in the projects with no father and no future, brief respites from the cycle of poverty and violence my poor mother had lived through and was now passing on to us. He taught me to dream big and believe that anything was possible.

Why couldn't I visit Versailles? Fly to France? See Paris? Walk down the Hall of Mirrors? These dreams danced in my head as a child in the public housing projects of Hartford. To an outsider looking at my situation in the mid-1960s, my chances of visiting Versailles seemed as far-fetched as me hitching a ride with Neil Armstrong on his Apollo 11 mission to the moon.

Who could have imagined that Big Sam's stories, wafting over the crackling sounds of a Connecticut campfire, would so profoundly impact my life? Yet those seeds he planted in my young mind took root, and visiting Versailles became a lifelong dream—and I made it happen. It was the first overseas destination I visited after graduating from college.

Growing up in poverty with an abusive mother made dreaming about something as grand as visiting Versailles a vital escape. Dreaming big became a part of my DNA both personally and professionally. But before I could book a flight to Paris, I first needed to learn to read and write.

By third grade, changes were happening on that front too. My mother married Tom Wilson, a sergeant in the Air Force who adopted my half siblings and me, changing our last names to Wilson. My new father moved us out of the projects into a modest house fifteen miles away in nearby Enfield, Connecticut. While it wasn't Versailles, it was a vast improvement over the projects. As we drove away, I never got to say goodbye to Big Sam.

My new dad was strict and disciplined, having spent his entire life in the Air Force and Air National Guard. He was unable to advance to officer level because he only had a high school diploma. He worked three jobs to make ends meet: during the day for the Air Force, evenings and weekends at a Friendly's restaurant, and graveyard shifts at a local motel.

Unfortunately, after this third marriage, my mother's violent tendencies escalated. Some of my most horrific childhood memories are of the physical fights between my mother and father. After he came home from a late shift, my mother would sometimes attack him with a large carving knife, screaming "I'm going to kill you" as she tried to stab him.

My half brother and I slept in a small room near the front door, and the loud noises of their fighting often woke us up. We would plead with our parents to stop, watching in horror as our mother kicked and attempted to stab our father. He would wrestle the knife from her hand onto the floor, and she would continue to lash out, screaming for us to "Give me the knife!"

Our father would shout back, "Don't give her the knife!" We were terrified—not only because of the violent fights, which occurred often, but also because of the inevitable punishment our mother would deliver the next day for not obeying her.

As much as the beatings hurt, those awful moments of pleading with my mother not to kill my father were far worse. Those were the moments that terrified me most.

Soon after my older half brother moved out, the violence turned toward me and my younger half sisters. My mother began attacking us with that same carving knife. I remember hiding in bedrooms with all of us lying on our backs on the floor with our feet up against the door, trying to hold it shut as our mother pounded and stabbed through the hollow-core door with the knife. I learned to lie on the floor to hold the door shut because I once got cut by the knife as it pierced the door when I was standing with my shoulder to it. It was like a scene from the horror movie *The Shining* with Jack Nicholson, but this was real.

This character reference letter, written by my sister Carol to the judge as part of my sentencing report, captures a small slice of our early childhood.

THE SCANDAL WITHIN THE SCANDAL

Dear Honorable Judge Gorton :

I am writing you as a character reference for my brother John Wilson. This is a difficult letter to write, as my brother John and our siblings did not have a very good childhood. On the contrary… it was one filled with both verbal and physical abuse.

We grew up VERY poor! My fondest memories would be making mud pies in the backyard and playing marbles. Our childhood was far from normal! In between the years of screaming and physical abuse, along with a lifetime of severe bouts of depression from our mother. Beatings that my brother took from my mother, had me counting the days till I turned of legal age to move out.

Most times while my mother would beat my brother John, I would hide under a table. Back then, there was no such thing as education for abuse in schools or an abuse hotline's to call for help.

What my brother John and I had to endure… along with my siblings growing up… is unfathomable to what the media have portrayed my brother John to be.

I moved out as a young teenager, what was a so-called home, when my mother came after me with a knife "when I told myself" for the last time, as I ran into my bedroom and the knife went through the door.

My brother John "SHOULD" be a success story with the media… who raised himself up through hard work, despite having dyslexia. He was made fun of in school… because he spelled his name backwards. All the neighborhood kids would make fun of my brother. JOHN spelled backwards, NHOJ was his nickname. If you try to pronounce it that way, it doesn't sound very nice. As we all know, KIDS CAN BE CRUEL!

My brother John overcame all his obstacles, along with a blessing of getting a scholarship to Harvard. This is what they call, the American dream, come true!

Instead of the, AMERICAN DREAM, I find myself having to write this letter… bringing up memories, I so hard tried to forget. This is NOT fiction, this is a non-fiction story of the American dream, of someone I personally know and grew

12/4/2021

up with. One that should be recognized as a beautiful, carring father, husband, friend and brother, who overcame, horrific obstacles in his life.

I personally, feel… I turn the negative into a positive… Being raised poor with abusive conditions, only made me MORE compassionate and MORE giving to others… People can choose to be one way or the other, from a terrible past.

I KNOW my brother John has most definitely done the same. Growing up, John worked very hard in the summers, several different jobs, including picking in tobacco fields for many years. He would come home filthy after working in the fields all day, only for me to yell at him for drinking out of the milk bottle.

It breaks my heart to read and hear all the accusations that are being said about my brother John. There has never been privilege or entitlement of any kind that came from my brothers bones. I know how hard my brother John has worked with integrity and all that he has done… giving to others. It's the exact opposite of what people are saying.

When I had a family of my own, my brother John was always there, whether it was a christening, a birthday or Christmas, John was there! Something you can't put a monetary value to… But also a giver financially. My brother who also opened a trust-fund for his nephews, that help them tremendously later in life.

My brother John's financial means, also afforded us to partake in many families memories, that were created as ADULTS, that we "NEVER" had as children. His financial means did not change the brother I grew up with, one with an unbelievable sense of humor. Teaching my boys how to drink soda through a straw with their nose. Funny, hard-working, with integrity and honesty… But has since stopped drinking out of a milk jug without a glass… Maybe not… But… Yep, that's my brother, who I love so very much to this day.

With the vile Social media… wanting, seeking, to see something that is not there. Judging before knowing…Something that has-not and is-not… my brother John.

With what my brother John and his family have been through already, definitely changed their entire lives upside-down. I humbly beg the courts… in my opinion any possible sentencing of time, would be… An injustice!

Sincerely,

Carol Rickless
John's sister
404-

12/4/2021

Looking back, I'm not sure which was worse—my mother's physical or emotional abuse. Her vicious streaks inflicted deep emotional wounds. When I did something she deemed particularly bad—like not completing a chore on time or eating more food than allowed—she would drive me to a nearby orphanage called Warehouse Point, 8.5 miles from our house (I recently looked it up on Google Maps).

I remember the terror I felt during those drives, crying and begging her not to leave me, pleading from the back seat of the car, while my two half sisters who she made go with us looked on in fear and confusion. "Please don't leave me; I promise I'll be good." But it was all in vain.

My mother would tell horrific stories about how much worse my life would be in that orphanage. Once we arrived, she would pull me out of the car and just leave me outside the property, saying I would have to live there because I could not follow her rules. Without even saying goodbye, she would drive off, leaving me there frightened and all alone. I remember running after the car, desperate to keep up, while my little half sisters cried and waved goodbye from the back window.

Thank goodness I have a decent memory and sense of direction. I knew the route home and had to make that five-hour walk back multiple times.

In terms of education, the biggest changes for me were driven by the smallest things. For example, my new father's medical insurance, which got me eyeglasses and help with my dyslexia, fundamentally changed my life.

Overnight, I could see and read better. Suddenly, school wasn't something to avoid; it was something I could actually do. I went from hating and often skipping school to a straight-A student. In high school, we moved to Windsor, a town closer to the Air National Guard base where my dad worked.

Throughout junior high and high school, I held onto my dream of someday visiting Versailles. I took six years of French classes and won the Alliance Française award; I was determined to pronounce Versailles correctly when I finally got the chance to go.

In 1977, I graduated as Windsor High School's top scholar and valedictorian of a class of just over 500 students and got this trophy.

Like many kids, I did odd jobs in the neighborhood to earn spending money. However, I had extra motivation to work longer hours and stay away from my home. At ten, I had two paper routes, mowed lawns, raked leaves, shoveled snow, and did many odd jobs. I had to give one-quarter of everything I earned to my mom to help the family make ends meet.

Photo of Top Scholar trophy and Valedictorian from high school

At twelve, I got my first W-2 job with Culbros Tobacco, a part of the General Cigar Company, which ran farms throughout the region. The Connecticut River Valley was famous for its shade tobacco, handpicked and used to form the wrappers for premium cigars worldwide. (This tobacco was vastly different from the broadleaf tobacco of the Carolinas, which was machine-harvested and ground up for use in cigarettes.) This was my first "real job," and I got pay stubs and payroll taxes withheld.

What picking tobacco lacked in glamour, it made up for with miserable working conditions and low wages.

Photo of Connecticut tobacco fields and drying shed

THE SCANDAL WITHIN THE SCANDAL

In the 1970s, twelve-year-olds could work full time on farms, and I was eager to make $1.30 an hour. (This farm wage for minors was an exception to the $1.65 general minimum wage for sixteen-year-olds.) However, the days were long, consisting of eight hours in the fields plus a forty-five-minute commute each way on a tobacco bus that made multiple stops from my town to the fields.

The work was hot, dirty, and backbreaking. Handpicking the tobacco leaves left a coating of tar and nicotine on my hands so thick that even scrubbing them with mud couldn't remove it. Summer temperatures soared into the mid-nineties (in the shade). With elevated water sprayers and mesh nets covering the fields to maintain humidity, it sometimes felt like working in a sauna.

The job was tough, but the most frustrating aspect was navigating the turf battles among several groups of workers on the farm. Local kids like me, aged twelve to sixteen, worked alongside older, out-of-state kids who stayed in bunkhouses. These out-of-state kids had to be sixteen or older and were naturally much bigger and stronger.

The largest group, from Texas, controlled every aspect of the farm, including the "straw boss" who ran the fields and the "bent keeper," the person who kept track of piece rate pay per "bent" (the distance between posts in the field). This group ran the operation with their own brand of injustice that was something you might expect to see in an episode of *The Sopranos*.

Photo of workers in the Connecticut tobacco fields

At twelve, I didn't know what the word *extortion* meant, but I'm fairly sure that what was happening in those Connecticut tobacco fields could easily be a case study for it.

On one of my first days, I was shoved around by some older Texas boys who berated me with their thick southern drawls as a "lowwwcol boyyeee." They pushed me to the ground, holding my face in the mud until I agreed to pay one-third of my daily earnings as "protection money" through the bent keeper. Just like that, my $1.30-per-hour wage was slashed to $0.88 per hour. To me, this was a big hit. I was now clearing only about $0.60 an hour after giving my parents 25 percent.

It was my first encounter with corruption, and it helped me to develop resilience. There was no one to complain to; the only thing I could do was pick faster and volunteer to work weekends to offset the losses. Those four summers picking tobacco taught me hard lessons about the value of a dollar.

I also recall calculating the basic economics of the tobacco farm, even though I was just twelve years old. For as long as I can remember, I've had a curious mind and knack for processing numbers and business models. While other kids were more focused on getting through the day, I found myself fascinated by how the farm business ran.

I asked a lot of questions, trying to understand how the pieces fit together, and soon grasped how the economic pie of the tobacco fields was divided. Each dried leaf of shade tobacco sold for seven cents, and each weekly round of picking yielded roughly two hundred leaves per bent. Each weekly harvest would generate $14 per bent in sales for the owner. To pick and drag those leaves out in baskets, I got paid a piece rate of $0.21 per bent (before paying protection fees). I estimated the people driving the tractors and sewing and hanging the leaves in the sheds to dry to be an additional $0.21 per bent at most. The total labor costs were less than 5 percent of what each leaf sold for. It astounded me that the owner of the land was getting more than 95 percent of the cash value. It was an early lesson for me in capitalism.

THE SCANDAL WITHIN THE SCANDAL

***

Education transformed my life and career path. My strengths were in math and science (I still couldn't read well), so I applied to several engineering schools in the Northeast. I chose Rensselaer Polytechnic Institute (RPI) in Upstate New York for its excellent engineering program and, most importantly, its generous financial aid package. RPI guaranteed 100 percent of my tuition and room and board would be covered through a combination of loans, work-study, and scholarships. I liked chemistry, so I chose chemical engineering.

I studied hard, earning straight As, and made the dean's list each semester. RPI offered a strong co-op program, allowing students to work as "engineers in training" in corporate environments. I received a summer job offer from Exxon during my freshman year with a salary of over $1,900 a month—a staggering figure compared to picking tobacco for $1 an hour two years prior.

What I didn't realize was how extraordinary this salary was compared to what my dad was making in 1978. I still remember seeing his eyes tear up when he read my Exxon offer—something I had never seen him do before or after that moment. He told me my offer was more than he earned from all three of his jobs combined.

Seeing my father well up with pride was one of the proudest moments of my entire life. My dad was a career Air Force sergeant and served in the Korean War; he never showed emotion and didn't impress easily.

Unfortunately, I unintentionally spoiled the moment by naively suggesting that I

Photo of my dad, Thomas Wilson

should quit school to save on the college costs since I had already landed such a high-paying job. In an instant, his sergeant instincts kicked in, and he immediately snapped to attention—as if a commanding officer had just entered the room. He scolded me, saying, "You can't quit! They won't give you a full-time job unless you finish your degree."

He told me that with my engineering degree I could earn more than he did with all three of his jobs combined. He told me to never forget that. He made me promise to finish my degree and said he was sorry he couldn't help me pay for college. He said that with my degree, I would be in a better financial position to make sure my future children also got a college education. I made those two promises to him in 1978.

For me, that day was one of the greatest aha moments of my life. My dad made sure I understood the importance of education, and I've never forgotten my promises to him or that moment.

***

That summer working at Exxon helped me realize that I wasn't just surviving anymore—I was beginning to thrive. I felt the distance growing between the life I had known and the new one I was building.

My curiosity about economics kicked in at Exxon and led me to ask the full-time engineers about the pay levels and backgrounds of the division leaders. When I learned the top people were making $100,000 per year (back in 1978), I was astonished. I probed further into the qualifications needed for those positions and discovered that all the top leaders held MBAs (in addition to their engineering degrees). Until then, I had never heard of an MBA, but in that moment, I was determined to get one.

I researched top MBA programs and found that most required two years of work experience before applying. I didn't want to wait that long, so I devised a plan to take eight engineering classes per semester, work at Exxon each summer, and skip a semester or two to work so I could get enough credits to graduate in four years *and* get enough work experience to qualify for business school right out of college.

I also read that top business schools valued leadership roles and unique experiences that would enhance my profile, so I added more extracurricular activities. I was already on the varsity wrestling team and had joined a fraternity where I was later elected treasurer and then president. I became a board member of the RPI student judicial board and took on leadership roles in several honor societies.

A fraternity brother, an aeronautical engineering student, told me that RPI had an airplane for training and heavily subsidized the cost of obtaining a pilot's license. I thought this would be a great lifelong skill and a standout point on my business school applications. I trained for months on a Cessna 150 and earned my pilot's license when I was nineteen.

My first solo flights were exhilarating, but my most memorable experience was when I flew from Albany, New York, to Bradley Field, the Air National Guard base in Windsor Locks, Connecticut, where my father worked. I received special permission to taxi close to the squadron of A-10s my dad worked on. It was a thrill to be greeted as a pilot by my dad and his colleagues. Whether my pilot's license helped my applications, I'll never know, but it's still a skill I cherish.

At twenty-one, I was accepted into Harvard Business School (HBS), the youngest student in a class of 850. It was a moment of triumph but also one of intense pressure. I knew that everything I had worked for—from the promises I had made to my dad to the dreams I had started from those campfire chats with Big Sam—were depending upon me succeeding at Harvard.

I knew I was in a whole new league, but I also worried I just might be out of my league.

Chapter 4

SHARING THE WEALTH

But No Good Deed Goes Unpunished

As I entered HBS and the business world, I began to learn and appreciate the complexity of the systems that govern success and opportunity. It wasn't just hard work, skills, and intelligence that opened doors—relationships, networks, and family status sometimes mattered even more. That reality shaped my thinking about how donating could help our children as they pursued their own paths.

***

> The phrase "No good deed goes unpunished" is a sarcastic expression that suggests kind acts can sometimes backfire on those who perform them. The phrase traces back to Walter Map, a prolific twelfth-century writer and royal servant to King Edward II who was known for his wit. While the statement may not be literally true, it can feel painfully accurate when kind actions lead to harsh negative consequences.
>
> **Walter Map**
> "No good deed goes unpunished."

> Ironically, our own experience in the Varsity Blues case embodies this very sentiment. We never imagined that making donations to IRS-certified charities to support college programs and help our highly qualified children's admission prospects could lead to profound devastation for our family. In the opaque world of federal prosecutions and higher education, things are not always as simple as they appear.

***

Getting into Harvard Business School was one thing; *fitting* into Harvard Business School was quite another. I was one of only a handful of HBS students who started out living on welfare. From college onward, I realized I lacked the social or communication skills necessary to thrive; I often felt I didn't belong. My early upbringing certainly didn't equip me with an understanding of the unwritten rules or social nuances of elite institutions—the things you're supposed to know but aren't taught in any class.

Fortunately, throughout my life, I was able to date remarkable women who were far more socially adept than I was and who were willing to help and take the time to teach me. I often wondered what they saw in me—was it sympathy, or a nurturing instinct? I like to think it was my work ethic, integrity, and sense of humor; it certainly wasn't my good looks or charm.

Reflecting on those relationships, I realize now how much I learned from them—important lessons in social skills and more that I foolishly never even appreciated enough to thank them for at the time. Without their guidance, I might not have succeeded in the business world.

My college girlfriend came from a wealthy family, a world completely foreign to me. She introduced me to social etiquette and the subtle habits of upper-class society, things I didn't even know that I was *supposed* to know.

Many things that may seem outdated in today's world, like holding the door for a woman, standing up when a woman entered a room, rising to help with the chair whenever a woman joined or left a table, always walking with my date positioned furthest from the street so my body would block a splash from a passing car, and so forth. These gestures seem small, but they really mattered in high-level social situations.

From a business perspective, she also guided me on which topics were proper to discuss with a boss or interviewer and what to wear to a job interview. She also taught me how to dress and helped upgrade my wardrobe.

I was so fortunate to have her guidance and I soaked it all in like a sponge.

***

Early in the first semester at business school, I vividly recall walking into a black-tie dance hosted by the European Club of Harvard and being mesmerized. I watched these sophisticated guys wearing tuxedos and dancing swing and foxtrot with such elegance that I knew it was something I wanted to learn.

Luckily, one of my study group members was a competitive ballroom dancer from Texas. He too was an engineer, and we became lifelong friends. I asked him if he would teach me to ballroom dance. Our study group consisted of him, me, and two female classmates. He really liked one of the women in our study group, so when we asked him if he could teach us all ballroom dancing, he volunteered with gusto.

He ended up teaching our study group once or twice a week, and we would go out and practice dancing at clubs. (He went on to marry that study group partner.) I practiced enough to hold my own at parties, but I also became good enough to help him teach ballroom dancing lessons during our second year. Setting up a business to teach ballroom dancing to other students was a fantastic opportunity to further improve my dancing skills *and* make money.

Given that the business school was 70 percent male at the time, I invited Wellesley College women to join as paying students and give us more couples. It turned out to be a tremendous success. The Wellesley women enjoyed dancing with the business school guys, and the HBS guys were delighted to have more female dance partners. We instructed multiple groups of twenty to thirty students each, and it was a win-win-win—I made good money (enough to buy a tuxedo and fund my social life), improved my dancing skills, and got quite a few dates. The black-tie dances at HBS are still some of my fondest lifelong memories.

***

Harvard wasn't just about social life. The case study method at HBS was very demanding. It involved interactive questions and discussions between students and teachers, which forced you to prepare your analysis the night before and be quick on your feet to formulate real-time persuasive oral arguments during class. Over two years, we studied nearly 800 different cases, each covering different companies, different industries, unique business problems, and functional areas like finance, marketing, and strategy.

It was a fantastic learning environment that helped hone my pattern-recognition skills and prepare me for the real-world challenges in business. I loved every minute of it. I graduated in 1983 at the age of twenty-three, the youngest in my class with an MBA, with exactly $50,000 in student loans—I was told this was the maximum loan balance allowed by Harvard at the time, so the school gave me scholarships for everything above that loan amount. For someone who just seven years earlier was sweating in the hot tobacco fields counting every penny, this debt weighed heavily on my mind. But I knew it was an investment in my future.

Following the advice of Big Sam from all those years ago, I sought a job that involved global travel. I landed a position in General Motors overseas product planning division based in Detroit. GM had operations in more than 145 countries, and many of them struggled much of the time. I quickly advanced and was transferred to the New York treasurer's office, where I took on a variety of leadership roles in worldwide financial planning.

By twenty-four, I was traveling across six continents analyzing major projects, negotiating joint ventures, and restructuring failing businesses. Big Sam would have been proud. The wide-eyed boy who had dreamed of worldly adventures was now living it.

After several years, I moved on to Bain & Company, a management consulting firm in Boston, where I met my future wife, Leslie Quartermain. At this time, I began paying attention to the relationships that my dates had with *their* parents, because the last thing I wanted to do was marry someone who came from a dysfunctional family like my own. I had lived that nightmare already and didn't want to repeat it.

I was thrilled to learn that Leslie came from a very loving family. From the first day we met, Leslie has shown me again and again that I couldn't have chosen a better life partner, wife, mother to our children, and soulmate. Her parents were wonderful role models, and when her father passed away, we invited her mom to live with us. That's the kind of family Leslie had—the kind that made me feel safe, something I rarely felt growing up.

My mother-in-law ended up living with us for over a decade; that says a lot about what a great role model my spouse's mother was. Leslie and her mom taught me invaluable lessons about proper parenting, which were as significant to my overall life as my formal education.

My education, geographical flexibility, and strong work ethic were all extremely helpful in my professional success. However, what truly set me apart was my willingness to get my hands dirty to learn about each business I was involved with from the ground up.

This hands-on approach likely stemmed from my early experiences, such as spending forty-hour weeks picking tobacco or scavenging for firewood from dumpsters and the nearby woods. Because of these early experiences, I felt equally comfortable working in offices or corporate boardrooms as being a cashier in a store, picking items in a warehouse, or serving colleagues in breakrooms.

THE SCANDAL WITHIN THE SCANDAL

After becoming president of a company, my starting routine began by spending several weeks working in entry-level roles across warehouses, stores, factories, call centers, and operational areas. This approach gave me firsthand insight into what was truly happening on the ground, often revealing opportunities for improvement, and earned me credibility at all levels of the organization.

As president of Staples Europe, I immersed myself in the day-to-day operations by working in multiple entry-level positions across several countries. During a week I spent picking items to fill customer orders in a German warehouse, I found several significant opportunities to improve our business processes. For instance, I learned that a quarter of this warehouse was being used exclusively to store and pick customized items for our larger clients—an arrangement unknown to anyone at headquarters.

Photo of me working in a Staples store in the UK

There was an entire mezzanine floor in this warehouse dedicated to stocking thousands of different customized items, things like individual sheets of preprinted stationery for a major bank client rather than full reams. Each sheet featured the address of a specific branch, allowing hundreds of different branch locations to individually order quantities as small as seven sheets or even a single sheet of preprinted paper for free delivery the next day to their branch. Despite the inefficiency, we were charging the client less than a penny per sheet, individually wrapped and delivered. This practice was quickly revised by implementing minimum order quantities and adjusting pricing accordingly.

As a consultant at Bain, I also did deep dives and never shied away from ground floor work. For instance, while conducting a competitor cost analysis for a potential new manufacturing client, I spent a week in the competitor's town gathering firsthand insights. I visited the local building department to obtain blueprints of their headquarters and manufacturing facilities. These drawings often included labeled offices and desk counts by department (e.g., vice president of marketing and marketing staff cubicles or CFO and accounting department cubicles). This approach provided valuable data to quantify rent costs and headcount for overhead and headquarters functions, offering a clearer picture of their overhead costs.

I would park across the street from their headquarters, manufacturing plants, or warehouse facilities for several days and nights to observe operations firsthand. By counting cars and employees entering and leaving during each shift, I could estimate the operating headcount by day and shift, including weekends. At factories, by supplier name, I also tracked the number of raw material supply trucks and finished product trucks arriving and departing, which helped me estimate production volumes and which suppliers were selling them raw materials.

Public equipment financing filings, known as UCC filings, offered valuable insights into competitors. These records revealed the equipment vendors, specific types of equipment at the facility, and the prices paid by competitors for the equipment. By combining building square footages with local lease rates, the building's lease date, and local commercial utility rates for power, water, and other services, I could accurately estimate their fixed facility costs.

I would analyze local hiring advertisements to find pay rates for various roles at each competitor site. By combining this data with headcount estimates and insights provided by the potential client, I could create highly accurate cost estimates for each competitor at specific locations.

I was thoroughly prepared when presenting our competitor cost analysis to the client CEO. If the CEO questioned how we obtained specific insights, I could confidently reference the facility blueprints, employee counts by hour, advertised pay rates, or UCC filings. This level of detailed evidence instantly bolstered the validity of the analysis, and my credibility skyrocketed.

I quickly became an integral part of several new client development teams where we were often competing for this new business against several other consulting firms. Each of the teams I was on won the new client business 100 percent of the time. At twenty-nine years old, I earned the distinction of becoming the youngest partner in Bain & Company's history.

As I climbed the corporate ladder, I purposely kept a low public profile. I became the senior vice president of strategy and planning for Northwest Airlines. I then joined Staples as the chief financial officer (CFO) and head of strategy, where I helped develop and execute a growth plan that helped Staples become the fastest company in history to make the Fortune 500 list—less than ten years after its first store.

At thirty-seven, I became the chief operating officer (COO) of Gap Inc., managing over 85,000 employees across all major functions outside of product design and merchandising. I spearheaded a transformation program that dramatically increased our sales and profits; sales nearly tripled, and profits surged by more than 500 percent. During my tenure as COO, Gap Inc. became the first specialty retailer to achieve a stock market equity valuation of $50 billion.

After my time at the Gap, I launched a consulting firm and small private equity fund to make investments in start-up companies and commercial real estate.

In 2012, I returned to Staples as the president of Staples International and the head of the company's global strategy. Staples's international operations were primarily in Europe, which required relocating my family to Amsterdam. It was during this time that our son remained in California to finish his senior year in high school (staying with close family friends).

***

Leslie and I have a thirty-year history of donating both our time and money. As I achieved greater financial success, we donated increasing amounts of money. To date, we have donated over $2 million to various causes, including cancer research, autism support, hospitals, and education. We've always kept our donation history private. We're sharing it now, not to boast, but to provide context for our donations to colleges.

Given the profound impact that education had on my life, our most frequent charitable giving was to public and private schools. Education transformed my life and was my ticket to escape the projects. It opened doors that poverty had slammed shut and enabled me to create a future for my family which I couldn't have imagined as a child. Giving back to the educational institutions that helped shape me was not just a duty—it was an act of deep personal significance.

Our children attended public schools until middle school, as we believed a public-school foundation was crucial. Leslie and I weren't just donors; we actively volunteered our time as chaperones on field trips, homeroom parents, and library aides, and we helped organize bake sales and other fundraisers. I coached Little League for our son and soccer for our daughters for six years, was a Cub Scout den leader, and attended father-daughter dances.

Photo of me as coach for one of Johnny's Little League teams

THE SCANDAL WITHIN THE SCANDAL

Photo at father-daughter dance

Every holiday season, I got dressed up as Santa Claus and brought presents to all the classrooms in our kids' grammar schools. Christmas always gives me such a great feeling of joy, and I loved seeing those young faces light up, knowing that I was creating memories for them that I never had as a child. This photo is from my son's first-grade classroom.

Photo of me as Santa Claus

We also made significant donations to the public-school systems to fund extra science, language, and arts teachers. We wanted to do all we could to help other kids have access to the resources that could help them dream bigger and reach higher.

Beyond education, Leslie and I hosted multiple fundraisers that raised millions for causes like autism and cancer. We both served on several non-profit boards and committees. I was a board member of Cure Autism Now and its successor, Autism Speaks, for over fifteen years, despite being one of the few board members without any family or extended family members affected by autism.

Our involvement in autism advocacy began in the late 1990s when we attended a fundraiser hosted by a neighbor to support children on the spectrum. We learned how devastating and increasingly prevalent autism was and how underfunded it was, prompting us to get involved to help make a real difference.

Several board members and I played key roles in the merger of Cure Autism Now and Autism Speaks, which created a stronger voice for autism in fundraising, government relations, awareness, treatment programs, and family services. Mark Roithmayr, the former CEO of Autism Speaks and the current CEO of the Alzheimer's Drug Discovery Foundation, wrote this letter on my behalf during my sentencing. It gives some independent perspective on my efforts and impact in the field of autism.

Alzheimer's Drug Discovery Foundation

November 2, 2021

Nathaniel M. Gorton
Judge, U.S. District Court, District of Massachusetts
John Joseph Moakley U.S. Courthouse
1 Courthouse Way, Suite 2300
Boston, Massachusetts 02210

Dear Honorable Judge Groton:

I am writing you as a character reference to John B. Wilson. I first met John in 2005 and worked directly with him through 2012. Since then I have kept in touch with John following his business, philanthropic and personal (family) endeavors.

I was first introduced to John in my capacity as President of the charity Austim Speaks. At the time of our first meeting John was a Board Member in good standing with Cure Autism Now (CAN). It was in his capacity as a CAN Board Member that John initiated talks to merge the two largest autism charities in the United States. He was designated by the CAN Board to approach me and the Autism Speaks Board. For a process that took the better part of a year John led the negotiations.

While he did not have a family member with autism, John nevertheless took it upon himself to donate and raise funds, spearhead advocacy and awareness and expand services for families. His unique passion was based on having many friends and associates who had family members on the spectrum and seeing the struggles of individuals with autism as well as their parents, siblings, extended family members and caretakers.

John's unique business acumen led him to believe a merger between the two largest organizations would deliver more funds, more awareness and more services with more efficiency to those in need. As a CAN Board Member he first had to persuade that organization's founders (parents of a son with severe autism) and Members loyal to the founders that the vision of a merger was clearly in their best interests. That more research, stronger state and federal laws supporting services, greater awareness and more local community grants could be forwarded through a merger. Given that the majority of the Board were all parents of children with autism, I always found it a tremendous testimony to John's character that they would not only trust his vision on the merger but then appoint him their lead negotiator to get the merger done.

Sitting opposite John at the merger table I quickly understood why he was chosen. Throughout twelve months of up and down negotiations he never lost sight of subsuming ego while always staying focused on what was best for families with autism.

John negotiated a tripling of private funds dedicated to research into the genetic causes and environmental triggers of autism from the Autism Speaks Board. Additionally, the advocacy framework he negotiated ended up ensuring both national and local support resulting in over $1B of NIH research dedicated to autism as well as the ultimate passage of 50 separate state mandates providing insurance covering services for children with autism nationwide. The successful finalizing of the merger created the largest Autism nonprofit not only in the United States but the world and led to the United Nations declaring World Autism Awareness Day celebrated in perpetuity every April 2nd around the globe.

Once the merger was complete John was invited to sit on the Board of Directors of Autism Speaks continuing his involvement with the cause. He helped to create an annual $1M event in Northern California while also personally contributing to numerous Autism Speaks events in New York City throughout the years. Additionally John was one of the Board's most generous philanthropists through his annual major gift giving.

Generous, philanthropic, doing for others less fortunate than himself, leading, a visionary selfless to his own plight. This is the John Wilson I had the honor and pleasure of getting to know while serving the Autism community and continuing to know to this day.

Thank you.

Sincerely,

Mark Roithmayr
Chief Executive Officer

Conquering Alzheimer's Through Drug Discovery
57 West 57th Street, Suite 904
New York, New York 10019
T. 212 901 8000
www.alzdiscovery.org

THE SCANDAL WITHIN THE SCANDAL

By 1998, I had saved enough to cover our son Johnny's college education (he was just three at the time) as well as any of our future children's educations. I then set up five trusts of $20,000 each to support my nieces and nephews' college educations. Back then, tuition at most state schools was about $5,000 per year. This is an example of one of those five trusts that helped my niece, Whitney Wilson.

For the kid who started out netting less than a dollar an hour picking tobacco, this $100,000 in 1998 was a large down payment on the promise I made to my stepfather exactly twenty years before.

That's how important education was to me.

THE WHITNEY WILSON 1998 TRUST

ARTICLE ONE

CREATION OF TRUST

1.1. Parties. This trust agreement is made by John B. Wilson (the "settlor") of San Mateo County, California, as settlor, and Clifford Wilson, the settlor's brother, as trustee (the "trustee"). The settlor hereby transfers and assigns to the trustee certain property (the "trust estate"), in trust, to be held, administered, and distributed as provided in this instrument.

1.2. Name of Trust. The name of the trust created by this instrument shall be the Whitney Wilson 1998 Trust.

1.3. Effective Date. This agreement shall be effective immediately on execution by all the parties.

In 2000, I also committed to give back to the universities that helped shape my career. In this will, completed a decade before our son even started high school, I pledged $2.5 million to Harvard and $2.5 million to RPI, along with substantial donations to autism and cancer research.

We specifically aimed these donations to help students like me, "whose parents did not have the opportunity to receive a college education." I wanted to repay some of the scholarship support I had gotten as a student at RPI and Harvard.

> (ii) The sum of Two Million Five Hundred Thousand Dollars ($2,500,000) (as adjusted as provided in Paragraph 2.12.) shall be distributed to **HARVARD UNIVERSITY**, Cambridge, Massachusetts, to establish a fund which will provide scholarships to students in the schools of engineering, science and business administration whose parents did not have the opportunity to receive a college education. Such scholarships will provide for up to one-half (½) of the educational expenses (including room and board) of the recipients. Each recipient must maintain a grade point average of at least 3.0 to be eligible to receive and/or renew any such scholarship.

I worked hard to earn every dollar and knew firsthand the possibilities that those funds could open for future recipients—especially in breaking the cycle of poverty for first-generation college students.

Skeptics of the Varsity Blues scandal have suggested that my $500,000 donations to Harvard and Stanford were bribes, implying that my children were unqualified for admission. But that wasn't the case at all. We were moving a portion of the existing donation commitments to colleges (included in my will) forward to give 25% to the universities before I passed and to improve our daughters' chances of admissions.

The donations we were making were through a third-party foundation to an IRS-certified charity set up by someone introduced to us by our trusted, long-term Goldman Sachs advisor, and positioned as a "United Way" for college giving. This approach to giving would help us reduce future requests for donations from the development offices at the schools.

This may seem strange to someone who doesn't have experience making large donations. However, if there is a downside to making frequent donations, it is this: you get on the development team's donor list, and you seem to get perpetually hounded for even more donations.

THE SCANDAL WITHIN THE SCANDAL

We still get multiple requests from our children's schools and colleges and other charities. Donating through a third-party, IRS-certified charity was a way to reduce those future requests.

***

The government was aware of our planned donations to Harvard and RPI in our will from the year 2000 and encouraged us during the recorded setup calls in 2018 to move about one-quarter of those commitments ($1 million) forward to support our twin daughters' admission. All our contributions were directed toward college programs, not individuals. Before we made this donation, we verified with the IRS website and our Goldman Sachs advisors that these foundations were in good standing. Unbeknownst to us at that time, the government confiscated this $1 million donation.

We had seen others successfully donate large sums to colleges or hospitals and get onto their VIP lists, which improved their family members' admissions chances or gave concierge access to medical services. We never considered that donating to a college through IRS-certified organizations could be viewed as illegal. We went to USC to verify in person with two senior leaders that donating through a third-party organization was common and acceptable for the school. USC gave us official receipts for our donations through this third-party organization and sent us a "Thank You" letter from USC written on official USC letterhead signed by USC's Associate Athletic Director. The Thank You letter also copied Coach Vavic and the development office. To this day, they have kept our donations.

Giving a donor's qualified child a boost in admissions has been a common practice at many universities for generations. Data from the recent Supreme Court case *Students for Fair Admissions v. Harvard*[8] showed that donor family members experienced a 1,200 percent increase in admissions

---

8 "Legacy Admissions at Harvard and Other Elite Institutions," Forbes, July 7, 2023. The overall acceptance rate was 3.2 percent, while the admit rate for donors was 42 percent.

chances, (from 3.2% to 40% admissions rates for donor families) and USC data in the *LA Times* showed a 600 percent average boost for donor children, with an 85 to 90 percent acceptance rate for donor families compared to the 15 percent average at USC.[9]

Unfortunately, all the USC admissions data and policies were improperly blocked during my trial, a critical factor that would later contribute to the appeals court overturning all my core convictions.

Looking back, it is still shocking that making donations to colleges could be so twisted by the prosecutors and misconstrued in the media. We genuinely believed that moving a portion of the commitments in our will forward was a positive thing for the colleges and our daughters.

Donations and full-tuition-paying families are a key source of funds for universities to help pay for scholarships, school facilities, and important programs. Without donations, many schools would have to cut back on many programs and the scholarships they offer to less-well-off students.

We followed USC's rules and multiple university officials assured us our donations were proper.

---

[9] Harriett Ryan and Matt Hamilton, "She Went to Prison in Varsity Blues Admissions Scandal. Now She Says She Was a Scapegoat," LA Times, December 16, 2024.

Chapter 5

THE CROOKED SINGER

The Bernie Madoff of College Consulting

The greatest mistake of our lives was trusting Rick Singer. This didn't happen overnight. He came highly recommended to us by a trusted, long-term advisor from Goldman Sachs in 2010. He told us Singer was a college consulting expert who worked with many Goldman clients and Silicon Valley icons. Singer turned out to be a confessed con artist who lulled us into trusting him by providing legitimate tutoring, community service, and college counseling for over eight years.

***

> The term "con man" is short for "confidence man," referring to someone who cunningly gains the trust of a victim for a hidden agenda. Con artists have likely existed since humans began interacting with strangers. The longevity of a con artist's schemes varies greatly; some masterful con men deceived thousands of very smart people for decades by playing on their hopes and exploiting their fears.
>
> **Abraham Lincoln**
> "You can fool all of the people some of the time; you can fool some of the people all of the time, but you can't fool all the people all the time."

THE SCANDAL WITHIN THE SCANDAL

> As Abraham Lincoln famously said, "You can fool all the people some of the time … but you can't fool all the people all the time." Infamous con man Bernie Madoff defrauded some of the smartest people in the world for more than twenty years. Singer, like Madoff, performed legitimate services while duping 1,700 families into believing his business was entirely legitimate for fifteen years.

***

Singer had embedded himself in our lives as an ally, a college coach, and a trusted resource. Looking back, what became painfully clear was he had been grooming us all along like a skilled predator. He convinced us he could help our children make the most of their futures, when in reality, he was only fortifying his own. The government then exploited our trust in Singer in 2018 as they tried to entrap me by scripting innocent sound bites during those recorded calls which could be misconstrued when taken out of context.

Singer began his career as a high school basketball coach before starting his college consulting business. In the early 2000s, he began cultivating relationships with some of the world's leading financial institutions to gain referrals to *their* clients. Singer expanded his firm to become the largest on the West Coast, providing legitimate consulting and tutoring services to over 1,750 students and over 3,000 parents. According to government filings, Singer raised more than $25 million in donations from his clients.

He started engaging in fraud with a small fraction of his clients sometime before 2007. By early 2018, he had several dozen parents, who were explicitly discussing cheating, bribery, or fraud (less than 2% of his total.) After the government caught Singer discussing bribery and test cheating with a soccer coach from Yale, he agreed to cooperate and become a confidential informant.

The Crooked Singer

Singer was such a highly skilled con artist that an FBI agent who worked with him closely on this case testified under oath that the government trusted Singer—up until they discovered he had double-crossed them too by getting a burner phone to warn some of his clients.

Prior to the Varsity Blues case, we had only heard of con artists. Apart from some false credit card charges, neither of us had ever been defrauded. Our closest encounter with a con artist had been through acquaintances who were defrauded by Bernie Madoff [10] years ago. Interestingly, the more we learned about Singer, the more he resembled Madoff, except Singer's marks were in the college consulting realm, while Madoff's marks were in the investing realm.

As the Varsity Blues story unfolded, *USA Today* interviewed Joel Margulies, a forty-year colleague of Singer. He described Singer's business as having two distinct sides: a "wholesome side" for innocent clients and a "dark side" for those engaged in wrongdoing who openly crossed ethical lines.

Wholesome Clients	Dark Side Clients
Innocent Victims	Knowing Co-conspirators

Margulies said that "None of the people who were involved in the wholesome side [of his business] knew anything about the dark side."[11] Prosecutors recognized this duality too. They charged only thirty-three

---
10 Bernie Madoff was an American financier who orchestrated one of the largest Ponzi schemes in history.
11 "The rise of Rick Singer: How the mastermind of college admissions scandal built an empire on lies, exploited a broken system," USA Today, June 19, 2019.

parents—less than 2 percent of Singer's 3,000 parent clients, indicating that most of his clients were unaware of his fraudulent activities. Like Madoff, most of Singer's families didn't know anything about his "dark side." We were one of Singer's "wholesome" families.

> In an exclusive hour-long interview with USA TODAY, Margulies said he knew nothing about Singer's criminal activity. And while he doesn't take the prosecution's case at face value – Margulies has had his own run-in with federal prosecutors, facing unrelated securities fraud charges – he acknowledged that Singer has pleaded guilty to the charges.
>
> "None of the people who were involved in the wholesome side (of his business) knew anything about the dark side," he said. "I had nothing to do with celebrities, and I don't have any children."

In the FBI-recorded calls, Singer claimed his organization made over 730 donations annually to more than fifty colleges. We believed these donations were legitimate, especially since we received official receipts from USC for the donation we made through Singer's organization back in 2014. We never imagined he was bribing anyone.

Besides, how could it be plausible that one man would be able to bribe over 730 individuals across fifty colleges each year without any rumors or leaks occurring? That would mean Singer was making an average of nearly fifteen bribes every week, year-round, spread across fifty colleges. That's absurd.

Instead, it's far more reasonable that his organization made hundreds of legitimate donations—ones that helped the colleges and students like our children get tiebreaker help in the college admissions process. It was credible for Singer's staff to make 730 legitimate donations each year on behalf of his clients, not bribes.

The recorded call transcripts shown below included a segment where Singer told me that he was meeting with the president of Harvard. Singer said that the Harvard president wanted to coordinate the millions of dollars that his foundation was giving to the school each year through the president's office.

The Crooked Singer

Singer's conversation with me about working with Harvard's president to coordinate the millions he was donating each year reinforced his credibility as a top-level college consultant and the legitimacy of his foundation. The government and the media ignored this transcript since it didn't fit their narrative.

```
23              you know, make a contribution kinda thing.
24   SINGER:    Yeah so we we're--that's why I'm goin' to Harvard
1               next Friday, because the president wants to do a
2               deal with me because he found out that I've
3               already got four already in, without his help, so
4               he's like, how 'bout--why would you go to
5               somebody else if you could come to me? I said
6               well I didn't know I could come to you. [laughs].
```

If we were truly co-conspirators, knowingly bribing college officials, why would Singer feel the need to fabricate a story about working directly with the Harvard president? Clearly, we didn't think that Singer was bribing Harvard's president.

Like Madoff, Singer knew how to play his role well. The overwhelming majority of Singer's clients were honest, wholesome accounts—people who knew nothing about his fraud—that he kept in the dark.

Just as Madoff had a few corrupt supporters, Singer had a few dozen "dark side" clients and associates. Thirty of Singer's "dark side" parents confessed to knowingly taking part in some combination of test cheating, bribery, and fraud. However, these parents were a tiny fraction of Singer's total clients.

Singer and Madoff both conned many highly regarded, intelligent, and wealthy parents. Madoff exploited his clients' desire for strong financial returns. Singer preyed upon parents' anxiety about the hyper-competitive college admissions process and their desire to help their children get into top colleges. Madoff's marks included Steven Spielberg, Jeffrey Katzenberg, and Larry King. As noted in the *Palo Alto Daily Post*, Singer's marks included innocent, well-known people like Steve Jobs, John Doerr, and Joe Montana.

Daily Post — No. 1 in Palo Alto and the mid-Peninsula

ARCHIVES ABOUT SPOTLIGHT OPINION LETTERS CONTACT AWARDS

HOME › IN THE NEWS › Big local names linked to college admissions fraudster

Big local names linked to college admissions fraudster

© March 14, 2019 12:30 am

JOBS DOERR MONTANA

Both Madoff and Singer skimmed substantial portions of their clients' money and used it to fund their own lavish lifestyles. Government records show that Singer stole half our donation; he gave half of our donation to USC but stole the rest for his personal use. We were shocked to learn this truth, which only came to light after I was charged.

Both con men cultivated relationships with some of the world's largest and most trusted financial institutions and used them to get warm referrals to their high-net-worth clients. Government records showed that Singer got multiple client referrals from firms like Goldman Sachs and Morgan Stanley.

Singer was referred to us in 2010 by our trusted financial advisor, who worked for a unit of Goldman Sachs. We had worked with this Goldman advisor since the late 1990s, and he had a long history of introducing us to high-quality professional resources for legal services, estate planning, and so forth.

He introduced Singer to us when our son was a freshman in high school. He told us that Singer was highly regarded and ran one of the largest college consulting businesses in the United States and that his clients were a "who's who in Silicon Valley."

We trusted this Goldman advisor and relied on him, as we had in the past, to recommend only the highest-quality service providers. Since he told us that Singer was also working with multiple other Goldman clients, we assumed that they had fully vetted Singer and his organization. We had no reason to question it. In our eyes, the Goldman Sachs endorsement alone was a testament to Singer's legitimacy.

We hired Singer to assist with our son's college preparation, test tutoring, prioritizing and recommending colleges that would be a good fit, and helping with the application process. Singer began by coming to our home and meeting regularly with us and our son. He charged a $6,000 annual fee, plus hourly rates for tutoring. These tutors were recent graduates from Stanford and other top universities.

Singer made a strong impression from the beginning. He came over to our house wearing coach-type tracksuits and was into sports—which fit well with our son. He was highly knowledgeable about many colleges and dozens of top high schools across the country. He seemed like an encyclopedia of facts about this college or that high school whenever we asked him a question.

He impressed us with his deep knowledge of water polo, especially since it wasn't a very well-known sport. He knew all the top colleges, high schools, and nationally ranked club teams in water polo. We had firsthand knowledge of the top high schools and club water polo teams in the country from going to years of national Junior Olympics water polo tournaments. Singer's knowledge of the top national water polo programs led us to believe that the other information he was sharing was also correct and truthful.

At the time, it seemed like a fortuitous match. Singer's depth of knowledge about top water polo teams nationwide was reassuring. We believed that we had found someone who could help guide us through the overwhelming and stressful process of college admissions.

Singer's approach was structured, and he ran his meetings with us in three parts: first, he met with Leslie, me, and our son together; then he met with our son alone; then he would meet with Leslie and me alone. Over the next two years, we developed a routine and grew more trusting of Singer, believing he genuinely understood our family's values aspirations and our son's potential.

We would discuss colleges, test scores, grades needed, and sports or other differentiators to help improve our son's chances of admission, making it seem as if he truly cared about Johnny's development and future. He knew about Johnny's world-record Alcatraz swim and how fast and strong he was in water polo. He knew that Johnny's Menlo School and Stanford Club water polo teams were ranked among the top ten to twenty in the country.

Singer's tutoring services went on in parallel. The tutoring made a real difference for our son as his practice test scores got progressively better. Singer also had community service programs he ran in Sacramento and Los Angeles. In Sacramento, our son taught inner-city children math and reading skills. I drove Johnny to Sacramento on weekends, three hours each way, because I liked the idea of him helping inner-city kids—kids like I was growing up in the projects of Hartford decades before.

We later hired Singer's company to help tutor our twin daughters and find their best college options. By this time, we had worked with Singer for eight years and trusted him. In hindsight, little did we know,

Singer was grooming our entire family as part of his long-con scheme. His polished façade was just that—a façade, carefully designed to deceive families like our own.

Everything our family did with Singer over those eight years was legitimate. Singer published books about getting into colleges, which enhanced his credibility. His company also created real workbooks and other tools to help students practice for their college exams. This image is one three-hundred-page workbook that Singer's company gave to our daughters. The tutors we hired through Singer were solid and helped each of our children in their college test preparations.

Singer told us several times that college admissions were getting tougher and tougher, even for highly qualified kids. He said that there were multiple categories that schools gave preferred admissions status. These preferred groups included legacies, political VIPs, faculty children, dean recommendations, board of trustee referrals, athletes, donors, full-tuition-paying families, non-faculty children, and so on. The list was long, and the percentage of preferred slots in each category would vary depending on the college.

He said that these preferred groups could sometimes get an allocation as high as 50 percent of total admissions slots. He said that when half the slots went to these preferred categories, your child's true odds of being accepted could be half the published acceptance rate.

He told us that each of the preferred categories existed because they served a specific purpose for the schools, from encouraging alumni to donate to perks to improve faculty retention to helping attract board members and trustees to generating goodwill with politicians to raising funds for facilities or scholarships to getting more full-tuition-paying families, and so forth. These were carefully architected programs. Singer said the colleges were concerned about the possible negative public perceptions of these preferences, so they deliberately kept these practices opaque.

In early 2012, Singer began discussing the possibility of us making donations to the colleges our son was interested in to improve his odds for admission. He told us there were two broad categories of donations: he called them the "back door" and the "side door." There was nothing nefarious with either category; he described them as common practices at many colleges that differed in size of donation and scale of benefits the schools gave.

In fact, Singer spoke about these types of side-door and back-door donations openly and publicly in many forums, including in a recorded presentation to a group of executives at Starbucks corporate headquarters. This image is a screenshot of Singer's presentation. It was one of several examples where Singer told large audiences that both types of donations were legitimate.

Singer's presentation at Starbucks' headquarters

This sample email below to another parent (another exculpatory piece of evidence the prosecutors blocked) shows how Singer positioned his side-door program. Singer wrote, "OK, side door is not improper, nor is the back door; both are how all schools fund their special programs." Contrary to the prosecutor's spin, these donations were not positioned to us as corrupt or illegal. This was how Singer positioned the side door and back door to his "wholesome clients."

> **From:** ▮▮▮▮▮▮▮▮▮▮▮▮▮▮▮▮
> **Sent:** Wednesday, February 5, 2014 9:50 PM
> **To:** Rick Singer <rwsinger@gmail.com>
> **Subject:** Re: Hello Rick/college visits
>
> ok, but should we mention it to him?
> On Feb 6, 2014, at 4:49 AM, Rick Singer <rwsinger@gmail.com> wrote:
>
>> Ok side door is not improper nor is back door both are how all schools fund their special programs or needs. Nevertheless we can apply to some of his top choices that are above his qualifications but the chances of getting in would be limited.
>>
>> Sent from my iPhone

Singer frequently talked about the two types of donations and that each type of donation would give donor family members help in the admissions process. It wasn't a guarantee, but a donation could offer a tiebreaker boost for a *qualified* child. Singer said that colleges have been giving donors' children admissions help for generations. This chart summarizes how Singer described the primary differences between the two types of donations to us.

	BACK DOOR DONATIONS	**SIDE DOOR DONATIONS**
• DONATION SIZE	$10 - 20+ MILLION	$100K TO $1.0 MILLION
• NAMING RIGHTS	VALUABLE QUID PRO QUO	NONE
• VIP STATUS	LIFETIME	ONE-TIME
• ADMISSIONS HELP	EXTENDED FAMILY FOR GENERATIONS	ONE CHILD

Back-door donations were much larger ($10 to 20 million or more, depending upon the school) and would give the donor lifetime or even multigenerational VIP status. This lifetime VIP status often included valuable building naming rights as well as admissions preferences for the donor's extended family—even admissions support for future generations. According to Singer, back-door donors got more admissions support than side-door donors, and if the donation were large enough, the donor could even get an unqualified student accepted at many colleges.

Singer said side-door donations were much smaller ($100,000 to $1 million, depending upon the school) and would give the donor one-time VIP status. These donations would go to the departments or teams with the greatest needs, often loss-making sports programs (sports like crew, sailing, water polo, and so forth) that needed funding. Singer said that many schools encouraged their coaches to actively help in fundraising. He said some coaches were allocated one or two slots for walk-on, non-scholarship players, and some had team manager roles for non-athlete children of major donors to help them fundraise.

Contrary to the public statement Singer made after he agreed to cooperate with the government, the side door was not a guarantee. Donations to college programs could get you on a coach's recommendation list, and it made a difference, but it was not a guarantee. Many examples showed that donations at USC could improve the odds from 15 percent for the average applicant by 6 times to an average of roughly 90 percent for donors' children.

As mentioned previously, data from the recent Supreme Court case *Students for Fair Admissions v. Harvard* showed that donor families at Harvard got a 1,200 percent boost in admissions rates to 42 percent, versus 3.2 percent for the average applicant. Donations *could* give qualified students from donor families a tiebreaker boost, but they weren't guarantees.

In this email exchange with Singer from February 10, 2013, he told us that donations to USC would give our son a 95 percent chance, while a donation to Boston College (BC) would improve our son's odds to 50 percent. Our son had a ninety-third-percentile ACT result, which was strong for both schools. Singer explained that the difference in probabilities was because BC didn't have a water polo team and that our son's strong water polo credentials made him a great walk-on recruit for USC. Clearly, a 50 percent chance for side-door donations to BC wasn't a guarantee.

> Sent from my iPhone
>
> On Feb 10, 2013, at 12:19 PM, "Rick Singer" <rwsinger@gmail.com> wrote:
>
> USC and BC by mid July. USC 95 percent chance- BC 50 until I have a face to face and his test scores are in, Georgetown need very good grades and no more than one B this semester and 1950+ by mid June then depending on commitment 90 percent if all in -
>
> Sent from my iPhone
>
> On Feb 10, 2013, at 2:01 AM, "John Wilson" <john@hyannisportcapital.com> wrote:
>
> Rick
>
> What is the deadline to decide on side door for USC or BC or Georgetown etc this year? (Also pls confirm for which schools is side door option really viable)
>
> A4210
>
> USAO-VB-01708116

In fact, Singer had our son apply to multiple backup schools because our donations did not guarantee acceptance. Why would we waste the time and money applying to multiple colleges if our donation to USC were a guarantee of admission? We also emailed Singer multiple times during our son's senior year asking him for updates on the USC decision. Why would we email Singer multiple times asking about the USC decision if the side door were a guarantee?

The only time we heard Singer say that side-door donations were a guarantee was *after* he agreed to cooperate with the government, and he made public statements to that effect. Singer's post-cooperation public statements suggested that side-door donations were a guarantee and that much larger back-door donations just improved your chances of admissions.

These post-cooperation statements were clearly inconsistent with both common sense and Singer's own emails. How could a $20 million donation to a college give you a lower chance of getting help in admissions than a $100,000 donation? In hindsight, perhaps these public statements by Singer were scripted talking points to mislead the public to assume that all side-door donations were bribes.

Singer told us that the Key Foundation (his charitable foundation created around 2012) would be a sort of United Way of college donations. He said his foundation would help parents navigate across all the different donation possibilities across multiple colleges and programs to identify the school programs in greatest need and the best fit for each child.

Singer also said donating through his organization would help insulate his donors from being hounded by college development departments for more donations. He also said this would give his company more clout with the schools while the parents would eventually get a donation receipt from the school.

This is indeed precisely what happened with us and USC back in 2014. It was also consistent with our experience of making donations to schools and other charities. Once we donated and got on their radar, we found ourselves bombarded regularly with calls, emails, and printed literature seeking even more donations. In fact, we still get donation requests from our kids' schools.

When our son said he liked USC, and because his water polo fit was so strong, we began to have serious conversations with Singer about visiting the school and potentially donating to USC. Singer said he knew many senior people at USC, including the athletic director and the head water polo coach. He also said USC was in the middle of a huge campaign to raise $6 billion.

***

In 2012, I had taken a new job with Staples Europe based in the Netherlands. The entire family was originally going to relocate to Amsterdam. However, because of differences between the European International Baccalaureate program and US high school programs, our son would have had to repeat a year of high school if he moved to Europe. This extra year, coupled with Johnny's desire to stay in California to finish his senior year and graduate with his classmates, led us to let him stay with a close family friend in California while the rest of the family moved to Europe.

Singer said he would support our son's college application process while we were in Europe. Being nine time zones away made it extremely difficult to talk regularly. For example, when our son finished practice at 5:30 p.m. California time, it would be 2:30 a.m. for us in Europe. Similarly, when he was getting ready to head to school at 7:00 a.m., it was 4:00 p.m., the middle of my workday. Singer said he could help make sure our son's college applications were completed and submitted on time.

As we became more serious about donating to USC in 2014, Singer said that our $200,000 donation would be divided into two equal parts. $100,000 would go to Singer's foundation, the Key Worldwide Foundation, to fund the team's trip to Europe the following summer in 2015. Singer said that this could cover the cost for twenty to twenty-five people to fly to Europe and stay for several weeks, including airfare, hotels, meals, and ground transportation. We agreed and received a receipt for this donation from Singer's IRS-certified foundation.

The second $100,000 would fund an immediate donation in 2014 to the USC Athletic Fund for water polo. Since Singer's foundation was still in the IRS's final approval process, this donation would be made through his company. His company would give us a "placeholder" invoice to my company for consulting (his company was a for-profit organization, so it couldn't give us a charity receipt for this $100,000). However, Singer assured us we would eventually get a receipt from USC for this donation amount to use in our tax returns—and we did get this receipt from USC.

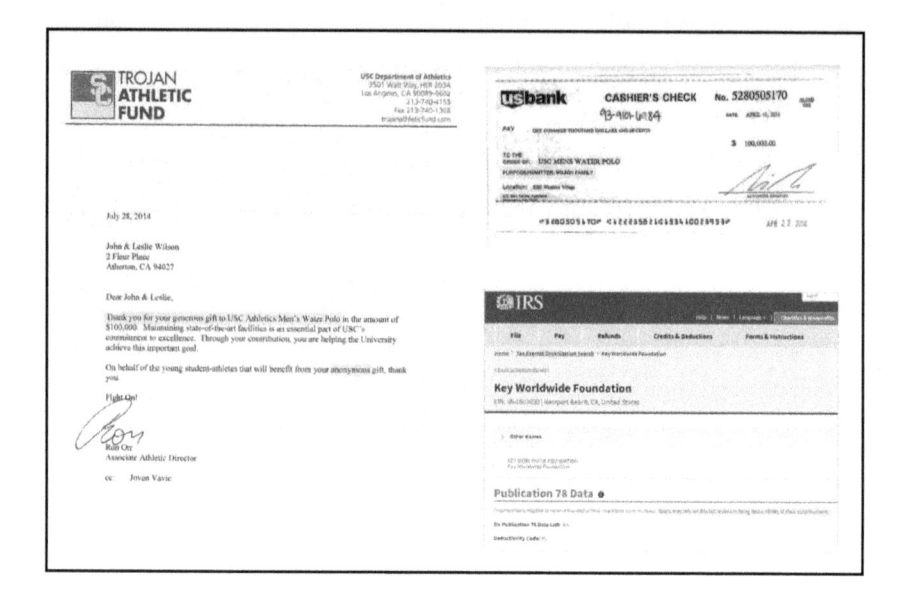

Unfortunately, the original invoice from Singer's company was used in my tax return instead of the USC receipt. Deducting this expense using Singer's consulting invoice instead of the USC charity receipt resulted in a $1,425 difference in the taxes we owed. This honest mistake on our taxes is one of two bases for the tax conviction for filing a false tax return.

The second basis for the tax charge was the government's argument that any donation to a college that gave the donor's family help in admissions was illegal and therefore not tax deductible. According to multiple FOIA (Freedom of Information Act) requests to the IRS, the government has never taken that position with anyone else either before or after my trial.

***

For eight years, Singer groomed us as part of his long-con scheme, and we trusted him enough to let him meet with our son alone while the family moved to Europe for my work. At the time, nothing seemed strange. Singer did nothing but legitimate work with us like his other "wholesome" accounts.

Our emails showed we trusted Singer and recommended him to multiple friends and even one of my former bosses, who was a lawyer. If we were co-conspirators with him in some grand criminal enterprise, these recommendations would have increased our risk of getting caught enormously. We would never knowingly refer a criminal to anyone.

Like many of the 3,000 parents who worked with Singer, we believed every aspect of his business was 100% legitimate—not knowing he was a con-man or anything about the corrupt acts of the thirty-two parents who were arrested.

__Trusting Singer was clearly the biggest mistake of our lives; what we didn't realize was just how enormous a mistake it was.__

Chapter 6

GUILT BY ASSOCIATION

A Media Firestorm Scorches Everyone in Its Path

After we returned home to Boston from Texas, we did our best to reassure our children. Our twin daughters were juniors in high school, and we could comfort them directly, while our son was finishing his degree at USC in Los Angeles. We were all in shock, grappling with the painful reality of being innocent and falsely accused, while the media smeared us through guilt by association.

***

> "Repeat a lie often enough, and it becomes the truth"; this is what modern-day psychologists call the "illusion of truth" effect. It's a highly effective and long-standing technique used since ancient Roman times. Grouping people together and tarring one person with the bad acts of others is known as "guilt by association." This phenomenon can transfer negative attributes of one group to an unrelated third party.
>
> **Mark Twain**
> "A lie can travel halfway around the world while the truth is still putting on its shoes."

THE SCANDAL WITHIN THE SCANDAL

> Combining these techniques is a powerful means to spread and turn false narratives into accepted beliefs. As Mark Twain noted 150 years ago, when a story's elements are salacious and repeated often enough, "A lie can travel halfway around the world while the truth is still putting on its shoes." Today, social media can turn false narratives into perceived truths at the speed of light.

***

The Boston prosecutors ignited a media firestorm that scorched everyone in its path. They certainly knew how to leverage press coverage to their advantage. The Varsity Blues narrative was sensational because it included Hollywood celebrities and other wealthy parents bribing, cheating, and committing fraud to get their unqualified children into top schools. The unfairness of rich people abusing their privilege and bumping more deserving, less well-off students from admissions understandably stoked public anger.

Although our facts and allegations were completely different from all the other charged parents, the truth was obscured by being grouped with the corrupt acts of dozens of other parents that were being splashed across headlines and newscasts everywhere.

My experience in the Houston prison hit me like a bolt of lightning from a clear blue sky. The media coverage we experienced back in Boston was more like a growing category-five hurricane—a superstorm fueled by prosecutors who falsely accused me and spoon-fed salacious sound bites and out-of-context email fragments of other parents' misdeeds to the media with a seemingly insatiable appetite for scandal.

***

As *Vanity Fair* magazine noted on March 12, 2019, the day after the scandal broke, "The scam has everything: TV celebrities, elite colleges, photoshopped images, parental overreach, the theft of places from more deserving students, and several forms of alleged fraud."

The media focused on Felicity Huffman and Lori Laughlin and the egregious actions of other parents who were caught "red-handed" in various audio tapes. The headlines were devastating. The guilt by association and out-of-context sound bites overshadowed our children's actual qualifications, my actual dialogue, and facts. It was a firestorm that distorted our reality beyond recognition.

We had not committed any of the acts attributed to others, nor was it even alleged that we had committed the same acts. Yet we were smeared with the same dirty brush. We asked our children to avoid the news and social media, but that was futile for teenagers.

The negative coverage was relentless. Every newspaper, every TV channel, and every online search featured the story, prompting us to stop consuming news altogether for a few weeks. Instead, family and friends provided us with informal verbal updates.

The news reporting lacked nuance, and the media ran with the narrative that everyone charged was guilty from the start. The innocent-until-proven-guilty standard, at least as it related to our facts, seemed to go out the window. Three major false narratives quickly emerged as accepted truths through relentless repetition.

The first false narrative: Singer's business was entirely corrupt. The media ignored the legitimate services his company provided for two decades to thousands of clients. Singer's company provided bona fide tutoring, college counseling, and community services.

The second false narrative: all of Singer's clients were corrupt. No one questioned why only thirty-three—less than 2 percent of Singer's 1,750 families—were arrested. While some guilty parents may not have been charged, 98 percent of Singer's clients were never charged, likely "wholesome accounts" like us, unaware of his fraudulent dealings, not coconspirators in cheating, bribery, or fraud.

The third false narrative: this case was a "single nationwide conspiracy" across all parents. Charging everyone as coconspirators was critical to getting media attention. Had they charged dozens of separate, one-off cases, the story would not have garnered the same national coverage. The spectacle of arresting dozens of individuals at once, especially Hollywood celebrities, amplified media interest.

For us, it was surreal. Catching a glimpse of *Desperate Housewives* twenty years ago or a rerun of *Full House* was the closest that we had ever come to Ms. Huffman or Ms. Loughlin. We never had a single interaction with either of them, nor did we know anything about other parents cheating or conspiring to bribe coaches or school officials. Singer kept us completely in the dark about any of his illicit activities as he did with all of his other "wholesome" accounts.

Ultimately, this false conspiracy allegation was overturned by the appeals court, where Chief US Circuit Judge David Barron noted, "You have to pile on inference on top of inference to believe the parents knew they were participating in a nationwide fraud conspiracy."[12] Unfortunately, this commonsense perspective came far too late to offset the wildly false story the prosecutors were feeding the media.

> "You have to pile inference on top of inference" to believe that the parents knew they were participating a nationwide fraud conspiracy, Chief U.S. Circuit Judge David Barron said at oral arguments this afternoon in Boston.

By the time the appeals court overturned the false conspiracy charges, the damage was done. The guilt-by-association strategy worked extremely well with both the media and the public.

***

---

[12] Thomas F. Harrison article in *Courthouse News Service*, November 7, 2022.

We understand the public outrage against wealthy parents abusing their privilege and bribing, cheating, and committing fraud to get their unqualified children into college and bumping more deserving students. This unethical behavior tapped sensitive nerve endings on broader issues of class warfare and populist outrage.

For the prosecutors, it was also the gift that kept on giving. Each time new charges were added or a defendant pleaded guilty, was sentenced, or went to prison, the prosecutors seized upon the opportunity for media exposure, further stoking anger and keeping the spotlight focused on their version of events. These sound bites were repeated throughout the twenty-four-hour news cycles.

The story was front-page news for months and became a sensationalized spectacle for tabloids, who exploited celebrity faces to frame narratives about wealth, entitlement, and fraud. The damage extended to social media platforms, where internet trolls were quick to add their own venom to the toxic atmosphere.

The media piled on while the story was white-hot, in many cases without adequate fact-checking. For instance, on March 12, 2019, the *Boston Globe* published a front-page article mistakenly linking me to an earlier felony conviction for fraud belonging to *a different* John Wilson from the Boston area. This error not only misled readers but also reinforced the public perception of *my* guilt.

There are approximately 350 people named John Wilson in Massachusetts alone and nearly 15,000 John Wilsons nationwide. One would hope a national newspaper would do some basic fact-checking before blasting a front-page story about one John Wilson with the criminal convictions of a different John Wilson.

When the *Globe* issued a correction many days later, it was a small blurb buried deep in a back section of the newspaper. Once again, the damage had already been done. The retraction seemed as useful as holding one of those small toothpick-and-paper umbrellas you sometimes get with a tropical drink against the category-five media hurricane we were now facing.

The intrusions into our personal lives were outrageous. Our home address became public knowledge, leading reporters to show up at our house seeking comments and even trying to interview our minor children when Leslie and I weren't home. One reporter tracked down and contacted my brother's ex-wife in Tennessee, asking her for any "dirt" on me. The intensity of the negative coverage was overwhelming.

***

On March 15, 2019, just three days after the case was announced, Boston's NPR station WBUR went scorched-earth on my background with a story that exemplified the media's mindset in the early days of this scandal. The headline read, "Mass. Businessman Charged in College Admissions Case Has a Résumé on LinkedIn. So, We Fact-Checked It."

The entire article was a mockery, treating me like a liar and totally aiming to discredit me. It mischaracterized honest statements and misstated the time periods I used to calculate growth rates in sales or profits at the companies I had worked *and* consulted for. The article even noted a missing-word mistake on my résumé, inferring this was somehow equal to criminal fraud.

Beneath the sarcastic headline was a team photo of the 1980 RPI varsity football team. My résumé correctly states I was a member of the varsity wrestling team at RPI. I never claimed to be on RPI's varsity football team. My son's bio on the USC Trojan's roster mentioned that I was an athlete—a wrestler in college and a football player at RPI.

I did play Inter Fraternity Council (IFC) football at RPI for two years, and my son's statement on his USC background page was correct. The WBUR false assumption that he somehow implied I played football on RPI's varsity team was the source of their "we got 'em" moment. Again, it wasn't something that was even on my résumé—the résumé that they were supposedly fact-checking.

WBUR dedicated six paragraphs to this topic. Within just two days of my arrest, they researched and interviewed a member of RPI's 1980 football team, who claimed, "I have no memory of a John Wilson on our team." I was being smeared over a claim I never made. I wish they spent as much effort checking my son's actual water polo credentials. These were the lengths that "journalists" were going.

The article also scrutinized an award from my résumé from the 1990s which said I was "named a top-fifty CFO by *CFO* magazine." Sometime over the past thirty years, the word "a" had been dropped; it should have read, "named a top-fifty CFO by *a* CFO magazine." It was *Global Finance* magazine that recognized me as a "top-fifty global CFO superstar" in their June 1995 edition.

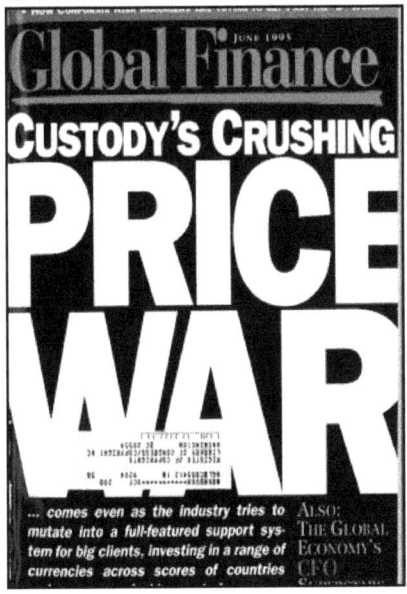

These magazine editions are so old, they aren't available online. It took me, with the help of some research assistants, a month to find one of the few remaining hard copies in existence at the Library of Congress in Washington, DC. How did WBUR find all these decades-old magazines or get magazine editors to track down these decades-old editions (which were only available in hard copy), verify and analyze the information, write it up, and review it with their editorial staff in just two days?

Over the decades, I had shortened titles, job descriptions, activities, and awards on my résumé to allow more space for new roles. This led to shortening "*Global Finance* magazine's global economy's fifty CFO superstars" to "top-fifty CFO by a CFO magazine." This difference from twenty-five years ago somehow became "proof" that I was a fraudster. WBUR also dedicated paragraphs to this subject, trying to "catch" me in a lie over a twenty-five-year-old résumé bullet point.

WBUR also recalculated every growth rate mentioned in my résumé for sales and profits for each company I worked at for over thirty years, adjusting for stock splits and acquisitions and so forth. Again, how could they do all this in just two days?

They used my full-time employment dates and ignored my transitional consulting with each company (I did consult before and after my full-time employment at each firm). This resulted in WBUR using incorrect time periods in their calculations. Years later, I hired Marcum LLP, a global accounting firm, to verify my figures with the consulting periods included, and they confirmed the growth rates used in my résumé.[13] How did WBUR do such extensive research, confirming decades of education, work history, awards, and growth rates and tracking down an RPI football team player from 1980, all within days of my arrest? It took me months with expert help and knowledge of my own information just to get some of the documents. It certainly raises the question of whether WBUR was improperly tipped off by the Boston prosecutors prior to the public announcement of the arrests, allowing them to smear me as the story broke.

These examples illustrate the prosecutors' aggressive media tactics and the extreme public scrutiny I faced. Some media outlets became cheerleaders

---

13 *Full written report available from Marcum LLP.*

for the government's smearing of me and our children and seemed hellbent to sensationalize my culpability beyond the vague allegations contained in the public record.

Imagine having every detail of *your* life over the past fifty years, including every email and every text message for the past decade, combed through by more than a dozen federal prosecutors and FBI agents. (And the best they could come up with were some quotes of me asking for details on the timing of payments and invoices for write-offs for USC donations, given that it was a 501(c)(3) nonprofit.) This was in addition to the hours of carefully scripted setup calls and text exchanges specifically designed to create sound bites from Singer that sounded innocent to me and potentially incriminating to the public and a jury when taken out of context.

That was my new reality.

***

The Boston prosecutors (and the media they misled) also seemed determined to denigrate our children's hard-earned accomplishments—despite the facts and allegations against me and our children being radically different from the fake athletes and test cheaters from other families.

The prosecutors repeatedly and falsely told the court and media that there "was zero exculpatory evidence" for any defendant. The positioning and message were crystal clear: *all* the Varsity Blues parents were guilty, and their children were undeserving.

The actual allegations against me in the charging documents that the government filed stated that Singer (allegedly with my concurrence) fabricated some awards and overstated my son's swim times on a one-page profile that Singer created for my son. This government filing never said by how much (8 to 12 percent on one swim time) or that many statistics on this profile actually understated our son's qualifications.

The government never said that our son's verified swim times proved he was indeed one of USC's fastest players, nor did the prosecutors disclose that the water polo photos were true and accurate, not photoshopped.

Shockingly, the public record and the government's own charging documents never said our son was a fake athlete or alleged athlete or that he didn't play at the Division I level or that he wasn't good enough to be a walk-on player on USC's team. The prosecutors couldn't put that in writing because it wasn't true, and they knew that.

Instead, the media lumped our children in with the photoshopped images of celebrity children rowing on machines, posing as fake crew athletes for a sport they didn't even play, or parents paying people to cheat on their children's tests, creating a sensationalized media frenzy. The social media trolls piled on to the deafening chorus of negativity.

At the time, our twin daughters were juniors in high school, vulnerable to social pressures like most teenage girls. The emotional toll of being publicly ridiculed for something they had no part in was as overwhelming as it was unfair.

They didn't cheat on their college tests; in fact, they studied hard and achieved a perfect 36 and near-perfect ACT scores. Yet our daughters were branded as unqualified, test cheaters, and frauds.

The *New York Times* reported that our son was admitted to USC as a walk-on water polo player "[d]espite the fact that he was not good enough to compete at the university, according to prosecutors."[14]
These and other similar statements in the media were in direct contradiction of what was included in the charging documents and the public record. The prosecutors had all the evidence and knew the truth about our son's qualifications; we know the prosecutors were aware of all this evidence and much more because they actively blocked it all, hundreds of times, item by item, during my trial. (More on that in later chapters.)

For a reputable newspaper like the *New York Times* to make those

---

14 "The College Admissions Scandal: Where Some of the Defendants Are Now," New York Times, October 9, 2021.

statements, "according to prosecutors" there had to be some unwritten communications from the prosecutors. That would suggest, since there are no allegations that Johnny was a fake athlete (or that our daughters for that matter would be presented as fake athletes and not team managers), that someone or some group within the Boston federal prosecutor's office may have been actively leaking false stories to the press about our son's qualifications to falsely smear him and put pressure on me to plead guilty.

No one in the media asked this critical question: What were the facts and evidence supporting the statement that our son wasn't qualified for a walk-on role on the USC team, especially since none of this was ever stated publicly or included in any charging document? What expertise did the Boston prosecutors have to assess a Division I water polo athlete? Did they coach or play Division I water polo in college? More importantly, what specific knowledge did they have about *our son* to somehow know that *he* wasn't qualified?

The prosecutors shared a single out-of-context email exchange I had with Singer from our son's junior year in high school as their "proof" our son wasn't qualified. The concerns I expressed in this email were *before* we visited the USC team and the coach.

It related to our son's fit versus twenty-five-year-old Eastern European "freshman" players that Singer told us were a major part of USC's recruiting strategy—men who Singer told us qualified as freshmen under NCAA rules since they didn't have any prior college and were less than twenty-five years old.

The prosecutors knew that our son's nationally acclaimed high school coach called the USC coaches and recommended our son to the USC team. The prosecutors interviewed this coach as well as several of our son's water polo teammates at USC and his high school—each of whom publicly stated that our son was qualified for the USC team, just like all the other redshirt players on the team. In fact, they all said that our son was one of the fastest players on the USC team.

THE SCANDAL WITHIN THE SCANDAL

The prosecutors knew that he had trained for 500 to 750 hours a year for more than a decade, competing on multiple top-ten-to-twenty nationally ranked water polo teams, and that he was invited twice to join the US Olympic team development program. They knew our son joined the USC team and that his certified swim times proved he was one of the fastest players on the team. They also knew that he trained outside the pool for six weeks at USC when he had a concussion. This was crystal clear from the emails between the water polo team training staff and USC hospital (which the prosecutors explicitly objected to and blocked from being shown to the jury).

Did the prosecutors share any of this with the media? No. Despite having all this evidence, it seemed that someone within the Boston prosecutor's office repeatedly fed false, nonpublic statements to the media that led them to write that our son was "unqualified" and an "alleged athlete."

It was heartbreaking to watch our son suffer as the prosecutors deliberately misled the media about his true athletic abilities and accomplishments.

***

As parents, we were devastated to see our children suffer due to these knowingly false accusations. The most disturbing thing about these brutal attacks is that they didn't come from some jealous schoolyard bully but rather from federal prosecutors who deliberately misled the media. We always thought that senior government officials had a duty to protect innocent children, not falsely attack them to help make a case against their parents.

To exert more pressure on us, the Boston prosecutors also gave access to over eight years of my private and work emails to two-hundred-plus people: the entire prosecution team, all the defense lawyers, and the fifty-plus total defendants (including Singer's organization, coaches, etc.) associated with this case. This material included intimate messages to my wife, our family's personal medical records (the government told us the HIPAA privacy laws didn't apply), and hundreds of photos, including vacation shots of our teen and preteen daughters and son in swimsuits.

These personal emails were outside the scope of the search warrant and were doubly protected under something known as spousal privilege. We warned the prosecutors in writing about this, and they ignored our warnings and circulated all these emails. We then filed an added motion to have these emails taken off the shared website.

The prosecutors opposed our motion to take down access to these personal photos and medical records, and the judge ruled that these records must remain accessible to all. For the prosecutors, it may have been just another high-pressure tactic, but to us, it felt like a significant violation of common decency.

The thought of intentionally sharing vacation swimsuit photos of our twelve-year-old daughters with two hundred people still makes our skin crawl. The prosecutors' tactics went from unethical to outright disturbing as they stripped us of any sense of privacy and exposed our family to a kind of scrutiny that felt invasive, vindictive, and disturbingly personal.

Plus, who else might these photos have been shared with? To share photos of our preteen daughters in swimsuits with two hundred people was reprehensible and very, very creepy.

All these actions and many more seemed to suggest a level of moral depravity which we had never experienced firsthand before. It also seemed to indicate the extreme measures that prosecutors could take to pressure and coerce people into pleading guilty.

The guilt-by-association locomotive had officially left the train station, and we were now being smeared before we even had a chance to share the truth and defend ourselves.

Chapter 7

AGAINST ALL ODDS

Deciding to Fight the Federal Government

Being scorched by the media firestorm was extremely depressing. Researching the statistics about federal criminal trials made things even worse. It was shocking to learn that the federal government wins 99.6 percent of their cases. I had fought and beaten long odds throughout my life, but the stakes here were the highest I had ever faced; our entire family's honor and my personal freedom were at risk.

***

> For centuries, British and American systems of criminal justice have been structured to prioritize protecting the innocent from false charges over punishing the guilty. In modern times, prosecutors seem more focused on media attention and maximizing conviction rates. Ninety-five percent of cases don't ever go to trial because the accused lack the financial resources, emotional grit, and family support to fight, forcing many innocent people to plead guilty.
>
> > **Federal prosecutors have a 99.6% conviction rate**, according to a 2019 Pew Research Center study. As such, federal investigations result in more pleas and avoid trials altogether. Jun 14, 2024

THE SCANDAL WITHIN THE SCANDAL

> While many charged people are undoubtedly guilty, it is unlikely any system subject to human error gets it right 99.6 percent of the time, especially when prosecutors can sometimes be motivated by outside factors. Conviction rates in the US have increased for decades to the point where "[i]n fiscal year 2022, only 290 of 71,954 defendants in federal criminal cases, about 0.4 percent, went to trial and were acquitted."[15]

***

Charging over fifty defendants simultaneously created chaos in Boston legal circles as most defendants wanted some local counsel (either regional firms or national law firms with a Boston footprint and local knowledge), and each firm could only represent one defendant. Those first few weeks felt to us like a combination of speed dating and musical chairs between all the defendants and Boston law firms.

We had the truth on our side—but would that be enough to beat these nearly impossible odds? To become part of the 0.4 percent, we needed to find the best legal representation possible to make sure that our facts and the truth prevailed. We interviewed eight different law firms and nearly two dozen lawyers (recommended by friends and colleagues) before making our final selection.

As we learned more about the legal process and the government's conviction rate, we began to understand the media and public's presumption of guilt. Instead of being innocent until proven guilty, it seemed everyone charged was presumed guilty. Additionally, most people assume the government wouldn't charge an innocent person (at least without some clear ulterior motive or prejudice). If you were charged, then you're probably guilty, and 99.6 percent of the time, you will be convicted.

---

15   *Pew Research Center reports from 2020 and 2023.*

This same logic caused me to immediately lose my corporate board roles and consulting work with McKinsey and major clients. All my insurance policies, credit cards, checking accounts, savings accounts, investment accounts, ATM cards, etc. were canceled. Professional clubs like the Young President Organization and social clubs also cancelled me. The knock-on effects of being charged were very broad.

The government's playbook seemed to be three parts: accuse someone, smear them in the media, and then use their unlimited resources and the threats of piling on more and more charges (and potential prison time if you don't take a plea) to bury you and force you to plead guilty. That's the brutal reality of our legal system today.

***

There was a silver lining to being unemployed; it gave me more time to gather the facts which helped prove my innocence. As we pulled together our evidence, it became even harder to understand why we were grouped with families who had cheated on tests, bribed school officials, and committed fraud. We had done none of those things. Our children were all highly qualified for admissions to each school they applied to based on their own hard-earned merits, and they were each qualified for the roles on the teams we were discussing with Singer and the schools.

Facts matter. For example, our twin daughters scored near-perfect and perfect 36 ACT test scores—an accomplishment only achieved by 4,879 students out of 1.8 million test takers worldwide in 2019. [16]This placed them among the top quartile of students attending universities like Stanford and Harvard.

---

16 *Annual ACT statistics*, www.act.org

THE SCANDAL WITHIN THE SCANDAL

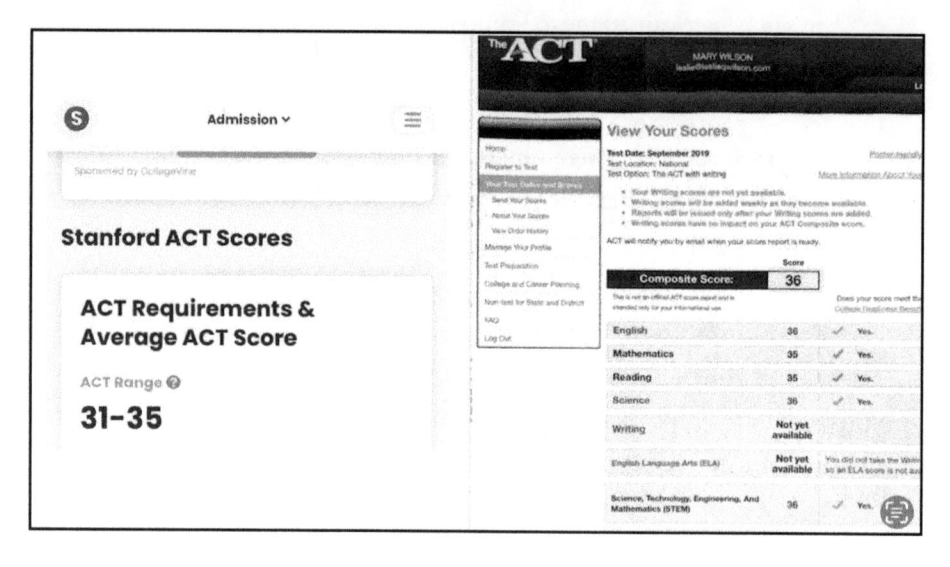

Collegevine.com 2020 report for Stanford (left) and our daughter's ACT exam results (right)

They also won multiple awards in World Scholar's Cup competitions in Europe. One daughter placed third and fourth in European-wide math competitions held in Switzerland and Germany each year.

They were both all-around athletes who played multiple sports (instead of one year-round sport like our son), including basketball, volleyball, swimming, and water polo in high school. They excelled in swimming, winning many medals and certificates for breaking league records in northern European championships (covering six countries). They are the two on each end of this photo. One daughter was also captain of her high school water polo team.

the World Scholar's Cup®
2017 Amsterdam Round
Certificate of Achievement

Courtney Wilson

1st Place - Top Writing Teams	10th Place - Champion Scholars	2nd Place - Top Challenge Teams
3rd Place - Debate Champions	2nd Place - Top Debate Teams	3rd Place - Scholar's Bowl
Honor Medal - Challenge History	Honor Medal - Challenge All Subjects	Honor Medal - Challenge Science
Top 25% - Challenge Literature	Honor Medal - Writing Champions	

Senior Division
15 December 2016

Daniel Berdichevsky
Alpaca-in-Chief

---

the World Scholar's Cup®
2017 Amsterdam Round
Certificate of Achievement

Mamie Wilson

2nd Place - Top Challenge Teams	1st Place - Top Writing Teams	2nd Place - Top Debate Teams
8th Place - Writing Champions	3rd Place - Scholar's Bowl	9th Place - Champion Scholars
Honor Medal - Challenge History	Honor Medal - Challenge Arts	Honor Medal - Debate Champions
Top 30% - Challenge Science	Top 30% - Challenge All Subjects	Top 35% - Challenge Literature
	Top 50% - Challenge Special Area	

Senior Division
15 December 2016

Daniel Berdichevsky
Alpaca-in-Chief

THE SCANDAL WITHIN THE SCANDAL

Photo of our daughters on their Dutch middle-school swim team

Both girls were Red Cross–certified lifeguards who worked on ocean beaches and had been sailing and power boating on Cape Cod for years. They each had their Massachusetts boating safety certifications and were able to solo captain powerboats in the ocean since they were fifteen.

Singer knew about our Cape Cod home and our daughters' years of boating and lifeguard experience. He said these would be helpful credentials for team manager roles in sailing or crew programs. He said they could drive training boats or committee boats during regattas, videotaped races, and so forth. We never discussed them being Division I players on any team.

***

As noted in an earlier chapter, our son was a year-round water polo player for six years and a starter on multiple top-ten-to-twenty nationally ranked Stanford Club water polo teams. His high school coach, Jack Bowen, called the USC staff and recommended him to the team.

We shared that we had discussed Johnny's fit on the USC team with Coach Bowen, who told us back in 2013 that he called and recommended our son to the USC staff. Coach Bowen told us Johnny was a good fit for USC from a speed and work ethic perspective. He also said a redshirt role would be good for Johnny because he needed a couple more years to develop to be a contributor on a team as high caliber as USC but that he was confident Johnny could be an impact player at USC by his junior or senior year.

Coach Bowen repeated these things to the FBI agents and under oath at my trial as shown in the trial transcripts below.[17] The Q's are the questions and the A's are Coach Bowen's answers.

```
13  Q.  Mr. Bowen, I think when you were under examination you
14      said he had A plus speed?
15  A.  Yes.
16  Q.  Did you also say he had an A or A plus work ethic as a
17      grinder?
18  A.  Yes.
```

```
                                                              115

1       phone must have influenced the coach. Like, I said, "That call
2       must have done it."
3   Q.  Okay. And that's because you thought Johnny had speed for
4       the high level of college play?
5   A.  It's a combination of his speed, which you can't teach.
6       So the speed and the water polo IQ just by virtue of starting
7       for a team, a national caliber team for three years, that is
8       enough to confidently say by your junior year, maybe senior
9       year, you could contribute to a high-level program like USC.
```

---

17 *Trial Court of Massachusetts, case no. 1-19-CR-10080.*

Coach Bowen's email to Leslie, shown below, proved that Johnny was also being pursued by other Division I teams like the Air Force Academy (a top-ten nationally ranked team in 2012).[18]

From: Jack Bowen. [mailto:jbowen311@yahoo.com]
Sent: Monday, December 10, 2012 1:42 PM
To: Leslie Wilson
Subject: Re: Two Notes.

Hi Leslie,

Thanks for your note--and, wow, Christmas in Amsterdam sounds amazing! How nice for you guys to get some time over there.

Interestingly, I spoke to Johnny briefly at lunch. The Air Force Academy coach has expressed a real interest in Johnny. I didn't think Johnny would reciprocate that interest but when I asked him, he actually said that he'd like to follow up with them.

Our son was one of the fastest water polo players in the country. His certified swim time for the fifty-yard freestyle was 22.78 seconds, faster than the 23.00-second Olympic gold medal time of Johnny Weissmuller of Tarzan fame.[19] Johnny's official time was from a Northern California swim championship event during his junior year in high school. (Unfortunately, Johnny's official swim time wasn't allowed to be shown to the jury—more on this later.)

For those unfamiliar with water polo, faster players have a significant advantage in both offensive breakaways and in defending against counterattacks. This email from USC's water polo coach, Jovan Vavic, said that his fastest players were around twenty-two seconds, showing that our son's

---

18 Collegiate Water Polo Association, Men's 2012 Varsity Top 20, week 13, November 28, 2012. The final rankings for 2012 listed Air Force Academy as number ten in the nation.
19 Weissmuller held sixty-seven world records, including the fifty-yard men's freestyle of 23.00 seconds, according to www.johnnyweissmuller.com.

actual swim time from high school made him one of the fastest players on USC's team, a team that won the national championship in 2013.[20]

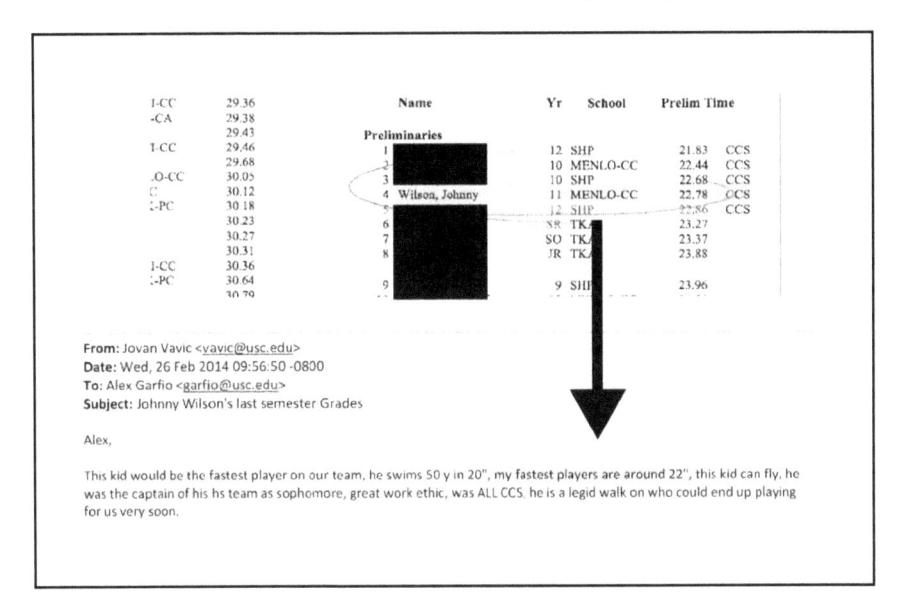

```
1-CC    29.36           Name              Yr  School      Prelim Time
-CA     29.38
        29.43       Preliminaries
1-CC    29.46           1                 12  SHP          21.83   CCS
        29.68           2                 10  MENLO-CC     22.44   CCS
.O-CC   30.05           3                 10  SHP          22.68   CCS
        30.12           4   Wilson, Johnny 11  MENLO-CC    22.78   CCS
:-PC    30.18           5                 12  SHP          22.86   CCS
        30.23           6                 SR  TKA          23.27
        30.27           7                 SO  TKA          23.37
        30.31           8                 JR  TKA          23.88
1-CC    30.36
:-PC    30.64           9                 9   SHP          23.96
        30.70
```

From: Jovan Vavic <vavic@usc.edu>
Date: Wed, 26 Feb 2014 09:56:50 -0800
To: Alex Garfio <garfio@usc.edu>
Subject: Johnny Wilson's last semester Grades

Alex,

This kid would be the fastest player on our team, he swims 50 y in 20", my fastest players are around 22", this kid can fly, he was the captain of his hs team as sophomore, great work ethic, was ALL CCS. he is a legid walk on who could end up playing for us very soon.

Our son was one of ten redshirt players on the USC team, and he played for the entire season and postseason of his freshman year. He even trained above deck and helped the team with equipment and videography for six weeks during concussion protocols (after he was taken from the water polo pool to the USC hospital and diagnosed with a concussion). After his concussion protocols were complete, he rejoined team practices in the pool every day.

Leslie and I also both flew back and forth multiple times from Europe to California to attend several games and watch team practices during the year. Why would we repeatedly fly thousands of miles to attend team practices and games if this were a fraud and our son was a fake athlete?

We had the receipts from our donations to Singer's Key foundation and USC for our contributions, and to this day, USC has kept our donation.

---

20 *Hy-Tek's Meet Manager*, 8:05 p.m., West Bay Area League Championships, May 1, 2013, page 1, and email from Coach Jovan at USC.

THE SCANDAL WITHIN THE SCANDAL

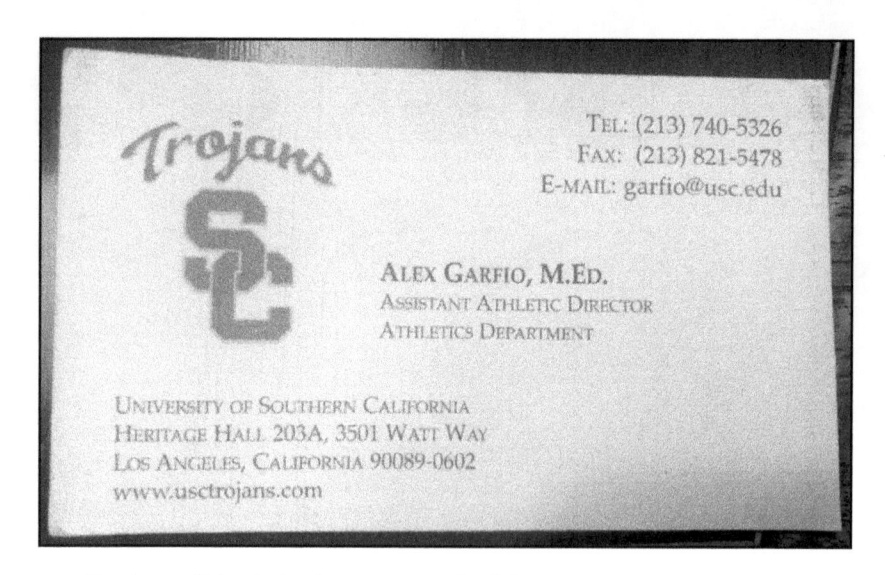

[Business card:]

Trojans

Tel: (213) 740-5326
Fax: (213) 821-5478
E-mail: garfio@usc.edu

ALEX GARFIO, M.ED.
ASSISTANT ATHLETIC DIRECTOR
ATHLETICS DEPARTMENT

UNIVERSITY OF SOUTHERN CALIFORNIA
HERITAGE HALL 203A, 3501 WATT WAY
LOS ANGELES, CALIFORNIA 90089-0602
www.usctrojans.com

We also still had the business card of the Assistant Athletic Director, Alex Garfio, who was the development person working in athletics. We met with him in person at USC to verify our donations to the school through Singer's organization. He told Leslie and I that a donation and Coach Vavic's recommendation would be very helpful and improve Johnny's application prospects and was consistent with USC's fundraising in athletics. Mr. Garfio also told the us that other parents of athletes had donated to USC through Singer's organization in prior years. We followed all the rules and policies that multiple senior USC officials had outlined to us.

The only inaccuracies that we could find in any material or in our email exchanges with Singer came from a one-page profile of our son that Singer created and gave to USC, not an email from us. We never sent any false information to USC or any college, nor did we agree to commit any fraud. Singer and his team made the changes to our son's profile without our knowledge.

Importantly, we didn't read this profile until *after* I was arrested, when we meticulously went through every email Singer had sent us. The profile, which did include some inaccuracies, was an attachment to an October 19, 2013, email which Singer forwarded to me from a total stranger named

Joel Margulies. This email, shown below, simply said "fyi." There was no request to read to get back to Singer with edits or feedback.

At the time, I was receiving hundreds of emails and texts each day for work and personal accounts, which were combined on my phone. I would skip unimportant or suspicious emails without opening any attachments. This email was forwarded from a stranger and had no message in the body, just an attachment; it looked just like the phishing emails that I was trained at work not to open.

Forwarded Email From Unknown Source

From:	Rick Singer <rwsinger@gmail.com>
Sent:	Saturday, October 19, 2013 7:30 PM
To:	John Wilson <john@hyanrisportcapital.com>
Subject:	Fwd: WILSON
Attach:	WILSON.pdf

fyi

---------- Forwarded message ----------
From: Joel Margulies <M@mandyang.com>
Date: Sat, Oct 19, 2013 at 4:26 PM
Subject: WILSON
To: Rick Singer <rwsinger@gmail.com>

Only after my arrest did we find this old email from Singer and open the attachment to reveal the profile Singer had created. In this profile, Singer changed our son's swim time by about 12 percent, or two seconds. This made no sense, since our son's actual swim time at seventeen years old proved that he was one of the fastest swimmers on USC's team. This lower time would have made our son two seconds faster than every player on the USC team. It's stupid and totally unnecessary for a redshirt walk-on position.

In fact, when we scrutinized our son's verified profile versus what Singer gave to USC, we found several inaccuracies that actually *harmed* our son's credentials. We later created this side-by-side comparison of the two profiles to show those differences.

103

THE SCANDAL WITHIN THE SCANDAL

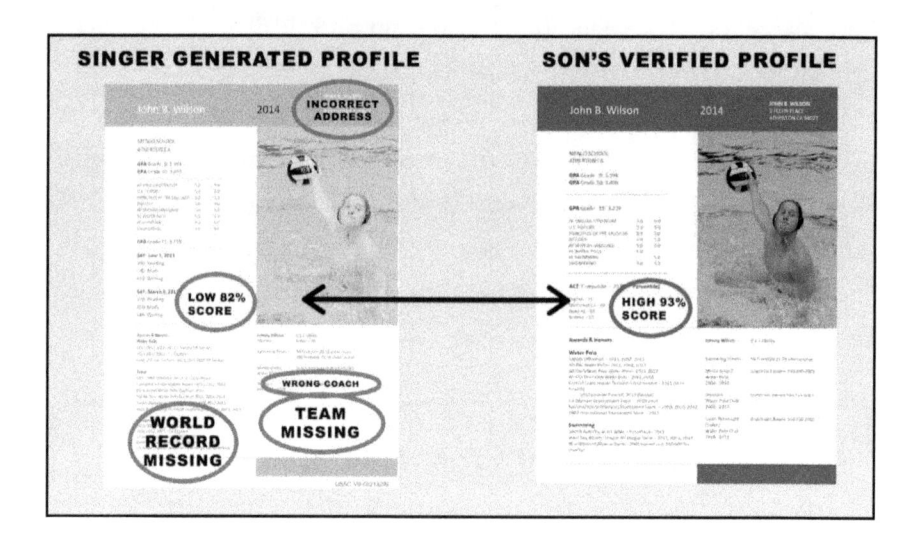

[Figure: Comparison of "Singer Generated Profile" (John X. Wilson, 2014) with annotations — INCORRECT ADDRESS, LOW 82% SCORE, WORLD RECORD MISSING, WRONG COACH, TEAM MISSING — versus "Son's Verified Profile" (John B. Wilson, 2014) with HIGH 93% SCORE.]

For example, Singer used our son's lowest 82 percentile SAT score rather than his highest 93 percentile ACT score. The eleven-point difference in percentile score is significant, especially when applying to top schools. Some of our son's top club teams and coaches were missing, as was his world record.

There were also stupid mistakes like not having our correct home address—why would I put an incorrect home address on the profile? This was all strong evidence that I hadn't read the profile.

If I had colluded with Singer to falsely boost our son's profile, why would I put in all these things that made our son look worse?

Armed with unassailable facts about our children's many qualifications and accomplishments, it was painful to hear the horrific lies circulating in the media. Radio talk shows, social media trolls, and others made egregious claims, such as that our son had never even been in a swimming pool in his life and that our daughters couldn't get a job at McDonald's because they couldn't count or make change.

The stark contrast between the facts we could easily prove versus the false public narrative was painful to endure.

Another point of confusion and frustration for both of us was the government's novel theory that donating money to a college foundation for an athletic program that could have the potential of getting admissions support was somehow bribing the coach. The government was trying to criminalize a practice that had been going on for generations at many institutions.

Yes, colleges giving admissions help to donor families is arguably unfair. As noted earlier, it's one of many distinct categories of preferences unavailable to the wider applicant pool. Such categories include legacy families, faculty children, other employee children, political VIPs, dean recommendation lists, board of trustee referrals, athletes, full-tuition-paying families, and so forth.

While these policies clearly disadvantage students outside a preferred category, they are not illegal. Schools keep these practices opaque to avoid the public appearance of being unfair. The reality is that many schools have endowments in billions because secondary education is, in part, a big-money enterprise.

In fact, the 2023 Supreme Court case *Students for Fair Admissions v. Harvard* showed that from 2014 through 2019, the children of Dean's List donor families were admitted 42.2 percent of the time, over 1,200 percent of the overall admission rate of 3.2 percent.[21] If receiving admissions support related to donations was now a felony, many Americans could find themselves in legal trouble. According to the Council for the Advancement and Support of Education (CASE), roughly nine million people donated almost $60 billion to American colleges in 2022, with nearly sixty thousand of those donations exceeding $100,000.[22]

***

Family, friends, and acquaintances who were knowledgeable about the law repeatedly told us we hadn't broken any laws—even if all the government

---

21 "Payoff-based College Admission," Students for Fair Admissions, January 7, 2023.
22 "2022 Key Findings," CASE Insights on Voluntary Support of Education.

allegations against me were true. Everyone who took the time to dissect the government's allegations against me came to the same conclusion each time. First, we were never alleged to have cheated on any college test. Had we done that, it would be a crime.

Next, the bribery charge was an unprecedented contortion of the law. None of my money went to enrich any college employee. All our donations went to college foundations and IRS-certified charities.

For the government to call this a bribe to the coach was illogical and a total distortion of the law (and truth). It would be the first time in history that the victim of a bribe (the colleges) were the ones who got the money (more on this in later chapters). Everyone was surprised that USC gave us a receipt for the money and were allowed to keep the money. How could that be a bribe? If it was a bribe, why wouldn't the government confiscate the "ill-gotten" gains?

Third, there was the fraud charge related to fake athletes and fake profiles. Our son was a legitimate Division I athlete who joined and played on the USC team the entire season and postseason of his freshman year. Singer changed our son's swim times by 8 percent to 12 percent and added some awards (and omitted some of his best ACT scores and awards that hurt my son's credentials) to our son's profile.

Even if I had agreed to change our son's credentials (and I didn't), our son's certified swim times proved he was one of the fastest players on USC's 2014 team—a team that was the reigning national champion. Our son's high school coach even called the USC coaches to recommend him to the team. How could a few inaccuracies in a one-page profile (some that helped and some that hurt) for someone who was qualified and actually joined the USC team be a federal felony?

Lastly, the eventual tax allegations also defied common sense. The government alleged I was not allowed to deduct my donation to USC (despite being given a receipt from the school) because I got help in the admissions process. This had never happened before or after to any college donor in America.

Additionally, the government alleged I purposely used the invoice from Singer instead of the receipt we got from USC on my tax return. Why would I go through all the trouble to get a receipt from USC for my donation and then deliberately not use the receipt in my tax return? This deduction on the wrong line of my tax return was an honest mistake which ended up saving me $1,425 in a year where the government acknowledged that I actually overpaid my taxes by $120,000.

We could not comprehend how the prosecutors swept us into this storm, considering that even if all the government allegations were true, none of my actions were a felony in the real world. It was painful in the extreme.

Despite our strong facts, our research into this legal process revealed the sheer brutal reality of what lied ahead. Fighting would feel like being in intensive care, filled with pain, hardship, and expense. Even if we beat the odds and won, our reputations would suffer. Fighting would cost millions of dollars and consume years of our lives.

Many people acknowledged that we had extremely strong facts on our side but cautioned that fighting the federal government was risky; our facts could be distorted or even blocked by unethical prosecutors, and the jury pool could be poisoned by pretrial publicity. The government has unlimited resources, every conceivable home-court advantage, an unmatched win rate, including convictions against many innocent defendants, and prosecutors who can tilt the playing field to their advantage in every way imaginable, even being unethical.

Each firm gave us cost estimates in the millions. White & Case, the firm we eventually selected, estimated the total costs between $1 million and $2 million dollars. They were right about the one and the two, but they whiffed on placing the comma. Given COVID delays and the prosecutors repeatedly piling on charges and dragging this case out for years, the total legal-related costs (including the appeal and forfeiture cases) was over $10 million—more than our total life savings and retirement accounts accumulated over a highly successful career.

I admit that the nerd in me once calculated how many years of picking tobacco (after adjusting for inflation) it would take to pay those legal bills; it would take four thousand years to earn that much money (excluding any protection money paid to the boys from Texas).

The first big decision we had to make was whether to fight or negotiate a plea deal. Suddenly, the philosophical question I raised at the start of this book became very real: How far were we really willing to go to defend our family's honor?

This was truly one of the most crucial decisions of our entire lives. There was no halfway or "wait and change our minds later" scenario that made any sense. The prosecutors told us they would keep piling on charges and prison time if we did not plead now. (They did pile on eight new charges four more times over the next year, all related to the same alleged crime of donating to colleges and getting a boost in admissions.) We were told it would get worse over time.

We didn't realize then, but I would eventually face not one but *nine* total felonies and 180 years of potential prison. Even if I were to be convicted for just one or two charges, I could end up spending multiple years in federal prison!

Deciding to plead guilty later was always worse than taking a plea deal now; it meant fighting *more* charges, incurring *more* legal costs, and accumulating *more* potential prison time in a future plea deal. If you thought you might plead guilty, it was best to do it up front.

There weren't any good outcomes. Our choices ranged from disastrous to horrific. We knew all too well that we were up against a ruthless, vindictive, and uncaring Goliath that won 99.6 percent of the time.

We also knew that fighting would deplete our life savings. If we fought and lost, I could end up in prison for multiple years. If we won at trial, it would be a Pyrrhic victory, as the cost of clearing our children's names would destroy their inheritance. Plus, there were the emotional and reputational trauma and scars.

Everyone reminded us that there was an easier path: to confess to a single felony and negotiate a plea deal (the prosecutors were adamant that each defendant had to plead guilty to a felony, no exceptions). That path would save millions in legal fees and require me to confess to something I didn't do, serve a few months to a year in prison, and then try to move on with our lives as best we could. That's what 95 percent of people did.

Leslie and I talked about the worst-case scenario—losing at trial and then going to prison. It would be extremely hard, harder than either of us could imagine. In many ways, my tough childhood helped prepare me for these types of worst-case scenarios. I was more worried about Leslie and our children; she needed to be strong for them if that day ever came.

For me, the hardest thing about this case was how a confession would not only stain *my* reputation but that it would also permanently label our children as unqualified. My confession would reinforce the government's false narrative that we had to bribe, cheat, and use fake credentials because our children weren't qualified for admissions. That false confession would leave a stigma of shame on our children for the rest of their lives.

These were profound, life-altering choices.

***

In the end, we chose to fight for three reasons.

First, we wanted to do everything we could to clear our children's names. Confessing would scream to the world that our children were unqualified. Even if the odds of winning were just 0.4 percent, I would rather go down swinging defending our children's reputations.

Second, I couldn't live with myself publicly confessing to crimes I didn't commit. It would destroy my personal integrity that I spent a lifetime building. Additionally, making a false confession instead of fighting for what was right would set a terrible example for our children.

Third, what the government did to us was absolutely wrong and should never happen to anyone. I was fortunate to have the financial resources, support of family and friends, and the grit to choose to fight. Many innocent people don't have that choice and are coerced into taking a plea deal. We wanted to do what we could to call out this misconduct and help make sure it didn't happen to anyone else.

***

There would be no plea deal.

I would not take a deal, even if that meant I could end up broke and in prison for years. We decided our family's honor was worth far more than money.

We were up against impossible odds, and if we were going to win, we had to go all in with everything we had. This was no longer *The United States of America v. John Wilson*; this was *John Wilson v. The United States of America*.

Fighting was the _only_ path where we could all hold our heads high.

Chapter 8

BECOMING COLLATERAL DAMAGE

The "Hook" to Bring All the Trials to Boston

Although we faced long odds, we had overwhelming facts that proved our innocence. After we presented our facts, each firm shared insights about the public facts of the other charged parents that they were researching and meeting with. The stark contrast between our situation and all the other defendants quickly became clear and made us question why *I* was charged in the first place.

***

> Robert H. Jackson was the only person in history to be a former attorney general, solicitor general, and Supreme Court justice of the United States. His distinguished career included a famous 1940 speech to a conference of US attorneys from the entire United States, where he cautioned, "The prosecutor has more control over life, liberty, and reputation than any other person in America." He continued, "when he acts from malice or other base motives, he is one of the worst [forces in our society]."
>
> **Robert H. Jackson**
> "The most dangerous power of the prosecutor: to pick people that he thinks he should get... and then searching the law books, or putting investigators to work, to pin some offense on him."
>
> - Former US Supreme Court Justice

> Jackson admonished federal prosecutors to exercise extreme caution before deciding to make a charging decision and to prioritize justice over winning cases. He warned, "The most dangerous power of the prosecutor: to pick people that he thinks he should get ... and then searching the law books or putting investigators to work to pin some offense on him."[23]

***

Remarkably, none of the eight law firms could understand why I was charged. From what I read in the public charging documents and records and what the various law firms told us, the other indicted parents were alleged to have cheated on tests, bribed school officials with payments to their personal accounts, and photoshopped fake photos depicting their children as star athletes in sports they didn't even play.

We were not alleged to have cheated on any college entrance exams, nor to have made any payments to the personal accounts of any school official, nor to have taken any fake photos of our children. The allegations against me were that I agreed to have Singer exaggerate some awards and swim times for our son. This comparison chart, based on court filings and case and public documents about the other charged parents, shows how profound those differences were. The contrast was impossible to ignore.

---

23 Robert H. Jackson, "The Federal Prosecutor," address delivered at the second annual Conference of United States Attorneys.

KEY DIFFERENCES BETWEEN THE WILSON FAMILY AND OTHER FAMILIES' FACTS

To the best of our knowledge, based on court filings, case and public documents and other materials.

QUALIFICATIONS DIFFERENCES	WILSON FAMILY FACTS	OTHER FAMILIES' FACTS
Children Academically Qualified for Each School:		
Children didn't cheat on college admissions tests. His twin daughters had perfect and near perfect ACT test scores. His son had top 93% score.	✓	✗
Children's test scores placed them in the middle or top quartiles for each of their targeted schools: Harvard, Stanford and USC.	✓	✗
Children Athletically Qualified for Roles Being Pursued:		
Child played for 7 years on multiple top 10-20 nationally ranked teams, with email from coach showing he was being pursued by another Top 10 Division I team.	✓	✗
Nationally recognized high school coach called USC coaches to recommend child, testified he was D I level player and could be starter on USC team in later years.	✓	✗
Child joined and participated on the USC team for entire Freshman season and post season, even working above deck for weeks while he was injured with a concussion.	✓	✗
Child had a world record and verified swim times, from high school that proved he was one of the fastest players on USC's 2014 water polo team.	✓	✗
Other children were explicitly discussed during the recorded set-up calls for non-player roles—such as team managers or in other team support roles.	✓	✗

PROCESS DIFFERENCES	WILSON FAMILY FACTS	OTHER FAMILIES' FACTS
Singer groomed family for eight years with real college coaching, charity work and tutoring, not test cheating nor submitting any fake admissions information.	✓	✗
Parents had 30-year history of donating millions to charity, including to public and private schools; and prior commitment in their will to give millions to first generation scholarships.	✓	✗
Family met with USC Water polo coach and attended team practices during son's junior year in high school to ensure he was a good fit with the team.	✓	✗
Family verified that donations through Singer's organization were acceptable with USC coach and separate USC development person and got donation receipt from USC.	✓	✗
Son was NCAA registered member of USC team played on the team as one of 10 freshmen "red shirts." Parents traveled to USC to watch multiple practices and games.	✓	✗

KNOWLEDGE & INTENT DIFFERENCES	WILSON FAMILY FACTS	OTHER FAMILIES' FACTS
Parents agreed to and paid someone to cheat on their child's college tests.	✗	✓
Parents staged and submitted fake "athletic" photos of their children to Singer.	✗	✓
Parents knowingly provided false information to Singer or universities.	✗	✓
Parents agreed to bribe coaches or lie to colleges or the IRS in FBI recordings.	✗	✓
Parent volunteered and passed multiple polygraph tests — administered & separately QC checked by the former national chiefs of the FBI's and CIA's polygraph divisions.	✓	✗

Each law firm we met with was shocked that I was charged with a crime—even if the allegations were true (and they weren't). No one could understand how our son's swim time being changed by a small percentage or some of his high school awards being overstated was a federal felony.

This became even harder to understand when the FBI's own notes about Singer's discussion regarding me with the government were included. The FBI and prosecutors were specifically told by Singer, as they recorded in their own notes, that "RS [Rick Singer] unsure if dad [me] knew of inaccuracies."

Singer only said that I was aware he was going to help my son with his profile and to embellish it with details and qualitative information (like "strong work ethic, strong leader, team player," etc.) to make it as powerful as possible—not to commit fraud.

SINGER'S FBI DEBRIEF NOTES
"unsure if dad knew of inacuracies"

This one-line FBI note (one of only seven total lines the FBI purportedly ever wrote about me in the months and months they worked on this case) must have been taken very seriously, because the government never once had Singer make any statements about any inaccuracies in my son's profile during the dozen scripted setup calls Singer made to me.

The government's entire case against me was that I allegedly agreed to exaggerate some statistics on a one-page profile (and I didn't) for my son. Yet their own star witness against me told them that he wasn't sure if I even knew of the inaccuracies in that very profile. And the government never scripted Singer to make any statement about these inaccuracies (like they did with every other parent) during the six months of recorded setup calls—where my reaction could have irrefutably proven my guilt or innocence. Why didn't they script Singer to do this?

***

We understood why the Boston prosecutors opened an investigation into our family. In 2018, I was discussing making side-door donations to colleges through Singer's foundation on the wiretapped calls, just as we had donated through Singer's organization legitimately to USC in 2014.

The government had the daunting task of sorting through Singer's 1,750-plus families to identify "wholesome" accounts versus coconspirators in one or more of his corrupt schemes. Like the adage that to a carpenter with a hammer, everything looks like a nail, to a government agent listening to wiretapped calls with a con artist like Singer, everything sounds like a bribe.

Without further evidence, it was reasonable to investigate anyone linked to Singer, me included. But why ignore all of our overwhelmingly exculpatory facts to continue their prosecution of me?

***

For example, when the prosecutors learned that none of our children cheated to earn their ACT scores and were all extremely well qualified for admission on their own hard-earned merits, they should have paused and said, "This family had no motive to cheat or bribe or commit fraud."

But the prosecutors didn't.

When they saw our emails showing our son was pursued by other top-ten Division I water polo teams like the Air Force Academy and that he was invited to and joined the US Olympic team development program for

two years, they should have said, "This young man really was a Division I–level water polo player and clearly not a fake in any way, shape, or form."
But the prosecutors didn't.

When they learned our son had played year-round on multiple top-ten-to-twenty nationally ranked water polo teams for years and that his nationally acclaimed high school coach called the USC coaches to recommend our son, they should have asked, "Their son's coach called the USC coaches; how can this be fraud?"
But the prosecutors didn't.

When they knew our son's certified swim times proved he was one of the fastest players on the 2014 USC team and that his teammates confirmed this, they should have said, "This wasn't a fake athlete; he was one of the fastest players on a reigning national championship team."
But the prosecutors didn't.

When they saw NCAA records, team photos, schedules showing our son joined the USC team, and emails from the USC coaches to the medical staff asking when our son would be cleared of his concussion protocols, they should have said, "Their son actually participated on the USC team."
But the prosecutors didn't.

When the bank records showed our donations through Singer went to USC's Trojan Athletic Fund, that we got donation receipts from USC, and that none of our money went to any university employee, they should have asked themselves, "How can this be bribery?"
But the prosecutors didn't.

When they knew I was the only defendant driving past their offices twice a week and that they could have easily interviewed me to determine

if I were one of Singer's "wholesome" clients or a "dark side" account, they should have said, "Let's bring Wilson in for questioning."
But the prosecutors didn't.

When the FBI's own case notes quoted Singer as saying our son was "a real water polo player" and that he "wasn't sure if the dad ever saw any inaccuracies in the profile," they should have said the Wilsons didn't knowingly give false information or commit fraud and stopped.
But the prosecutors didn't.

When Singer was under the government's full control and making scripted setup calls, they could have had him make explicit statements to me about fraud, lying, or bribing to generate irrefutable evidence of my guilt or innocence—like they had Singer do with the other charged parents.
But the prosecutors didn't.

In fact, instead of seeking justice, whether that meant proving my guilt or innocence as Robert H. Jackson had admonished US attorneys, these Boston prosecutors ruthlessly ran roughshod over all my exculpatory evidence. Trials are intended to be searches for truth, and the criminal justice system is supposed to take all reasonable measures to avoid wrongly convicting innocent people.

Yet each time we tried to introduce evidence supporting the abovementioned facts supporting my innocence, the prosecutors opposed our motions. In fact, the prosecutors opposed our defense motions an extraordinary 660 times during my trial.[24] This was an average of fifty-five objections per day (to my evidence and other sound motions) during the two and a half weeks of substantive hearings.

Their handpicked, highly supportive judge sustained their motions an astounding 98.3 percent of the time during my defense. Although all of this

---

24 Trial transcripts, US District Court of Massachusetts, case no. 1-19-CR-10080.

evidence was in the public record, we were not allowed to share it with the jury (more on this egregious imbalance in trial rulings in later chapters).

Given how different our facts were versus all the other charged parents, how and why did we make the cut of thirty-three parents charged out of Singer's 1,750-plus families? We asked that question over and over.

We explored every plausible reason. Did the Boston prosecutors feel they needed one more defendant to bring the total up to fifty-three from fifty-two to hit some tipping point for national media coverage? No one believed that could be the case.

Was it the number of children or amount of money that we donated that set us apart? No; other parents had more children involved and donated more money than we did.

Was it the fact that we had worked with Singer for over eight years that set us apart? No; there were other charged families that had worked with Singer even longer.

We went through every plausible reason, but only one logical answer came back each time: geography—or in legal terms: venue.

***

Some context will help clarify why geography plays a critical role in our story. The Boston-based federal prosecutors first came across this case from an unrelated criminal case in Connecticut where the defendant tried to plea bargain by providing a tip about a corrupt soccer coach from Yale. This coach led the Boston prosecutors to Singer and his test cheating, bribery, and fraud schemes with multiple Hollywood celebrities and other wealthy California-based clients.

The outrageous behaviors of multiple celebrity defendants made this a case with obvious national media potential. Such high-profile cases can be a once-in-a-lifetime opportunity for ambitious government prosecutors. For government lawyers, prominent cases like Varsity Blues can help launch a career in politics or lead to million-dollar partner roles in national law firms.

There was just one big problem for the Boston-based prosecutors: geography.

As shown in the map below, 90 percent of the parents accused in the Varsity Blues case were from California.[25] Singer and his company were based in California; Singer's charity was based in California; USC and Stanford, two of the primary universities involved in the case, were located in California.

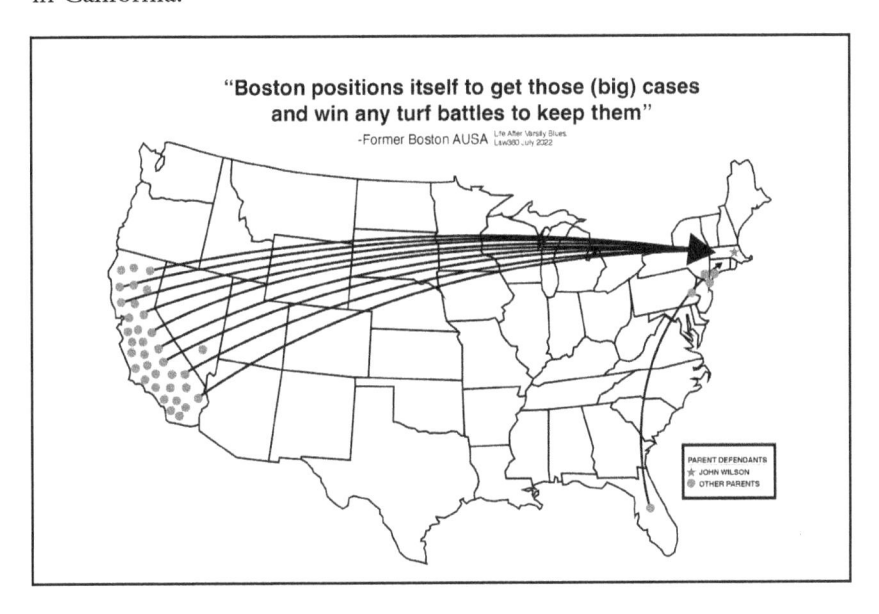

"Boston positions itself to get those (big) cases and win any turf battles to keep them"
-Former Boston AUSA, Life After Varsity Blues, Law360, July 2022

PARENT DEFENDANTS
★ JOHN WILSON
● OTHER PARENTS

Under federal law, a defendant has the right to a trial in the state where the alleged crime was committed or where the defendant lives. Ms. Huffman, Ms. Laughlin, and the dozens of other California defendants lived *and* committed their confessed crimes in California.

Federal statutes on the proper venue for a criminal case state that "[t]he court will consider factors like convenience of the defendant, witnesses,

---

25 United States Attorney's Office, District of Massachusetts, *Investigations of College Admissions and Testing Bribery Schemes and related filings*

and the efficient administration of justice when deciding where to hold the trial."[26] The California defendants all had the legal right to have their trials take place in California, where they lived and where they were alleged to have committed their crimes.

For the Boston-based prosecutors, that would mean losing this career-making case to their colleagues based in California. To avoid this transfer, the Boston-based prosecutors needed a plan to justify the extra costs, travel time, and inefficiencies of forcing more than two hundred people—including dozens of defendants, FBI agents, prosecutors, university officials, other witnesses, lawyers, and so forth—to repeatedly fly back and forth three thousand miles between California and Boston.

***

The Boston-based prosecutors implemented a two-step approach to justify bringing all the trials to Massachusetts.

Step one: falsely allege a single nationwide "conspiracy" of parents so they could combine all the parent and celebrity trials into one giant case. Never mind that most of these parents had never met, let alone conspired together, or that the First Circuit Court of Appeals would later unanimously reject this false conspiracy theory. The mere allegation of a nationwide conspiracy was enough for the Boston-based prosecutors to combine all the parents into a single trial.

Step two: show that the crimes being committed in California were either taking place in Massachusetts or have at least one defendant in the conspiracy who lived in Massachusetts and therefore committed their crime in Massachusetts.

Only one of Singer's 1,750-plus clients lived in Massachusetts: *me*.

I was that critical venue hook. The Boston-based prosecutors needed

---

26   US Department of Justice, Federal Rules of Criminal Procedures, rule 18.

to charge me to help win any turf battles and justify bringing all the trials to Boston. It didn't seem to matter how different my facts were or how much exculpatory evidence they discovered in my case; my family simply became collateral damage.

Prosecutor turf battles were part of the Varsity Blues cases. David G. Lazarus, former assistant US attorney from the Boston office, told *Law360* in a July 2022 article entitled "Life After Varsity Blues," "Boston positions itself to get those [big] cases and win any turf battles to keep them."

Years later, I called and asked Mr. Lazarus about this quote. He confirmed that it was accurate, and he said at the time, he received blistering criticism from his former colleagues about his statement. He told me that his reply to his former colleagues was, "It's the truth!" It was refreshing to hear a former Boston prosecutor so adamant about telling the truth.

Imagine this map if there were no defendant named Wilson who lived in Massachusetts. Think how the turf battles between Massachusetts and California might have gone for the Boston-based federal prosecutors without a single defendant in Massachusetts.

The Boston prosecutors may have wanted to do whatever they could to try to win those turf battles to keep the venue (and the career-boosting media spotlights) in Boston. I understand how tempting it can be to go from a $150,000 government job to a private-sector partner role with a $1 million earning potential.

There were several other indirect data points which corroborated why charging me, despite the overwhelming facts supporting my innocence, was important to the venue for this case.

A former FBI agent told a mutual friend, "[The Boston-based prosecutors] wanted [our] case to get venue in Boston, and they had a very friendly judge who would be extremely helpful." This agent also said there was "no way they were going to let the 'Boston guy' off; they needed [me] to keep the venue in Boston. If [I] fought, they would ramp up charges to pressure me to plead guilty. If [I] didn't plead, they would do whatever it took to win at trial."

Additionally, two former assistant US attorneys from the Boston office told a lawyer friend that "the reason [the Boston prosecutors] went after [me] was to get venue. The conspiracy, bribery, and fraud charges in [my] case were BS. But that didn't matter because they needed [me] to get the cases to be in Boston."

Bringing all the trials to Boston may have been inefficient, inconvenient, and high cost to the taxpayers footing these bills, *but* it brought the media spotlights to the Boston office. The Boston-based prosecutors deflected the few questions they did get from the media about why all the trials were held in Boston by suggesting Boston had a unique ability to handle these types of cases.

It's devastating to think that geography was the reason I was falsely accused and my family was ensnared in this case. Each time I share the defendant map with any fair-minded third party, one undeniable truth emerges: unlike some prosecutors, geography doesn't lie.

Falsely accusing me and abusing our family as collateral damage for personal career gains was the *exact* type of abuse that Robert H. Jackson warned against. It appalls and disgusts us to think that federal prosecutors may have been willing to destroy a family and smear innocent school-aged children to try to cover up their false allegations and boost their own careers.

Yet with the mountain of evidence the prosecutors had which proved my innocence and the extreme actions they took over six years to cover up their misdeeds, it was the only explanation that made sense.

We realize that just stating this hypothesis runs the serious risk of further retaliation by a very vindictive set of prosecutors. To us, at least, the truth matters, and federal prosecutors who deliberately overreach should be held accountable.

If this hypothesis were correct, the prosecutors would take five separate actions related to my case which would help prove the theory.

1. They would carefully script Singer's entrapment calls to me to create sound bites that would sound innocent to me but when taken out of context could sound incriminating. These calls would be significantly different from the explicit calls he would make to other parents.
2. All Singer preparation and debriefing notes with the FBI and government lawyers related to *my* case would need to be carefully sanitized and, if necessary, deleted.
3. To enable their novel theories of honest services fraud, bribery, and conspiracy as well as their extremely aggressive tactics at trial, they would need to handpick a favorable judge—a highly supportive judge with a long track record of favoring the prosecution.
4. They would take extreme steps to pressure me to plead guilty. (A guilty plea would cover up any questions about falsely accusing me for venue.) Piling on more charges against me versus any other parent would drain us financially and intimidate us with decades of potential prison time.
5. If I did not succumb to their extreme pressures and take a plea deal, the prosecutors would need to railroad me through a show trial (with the help of a preferred judge) and do whatever it takes to ensure a conviction.

For the prosecutors, my case seemed to be less about the truth and justice and more about winning at all costs.

Chapter 9

PROSECUTORIAL OVERREACH

The Long Arm of the Federal Bureau of Entrapment

If the prosecutors needed me for venue but were concerned about creating exculpatory evidence, they would need to carefully script Singer's setup calls to sound innocent to me while creating sound bites that could be taken out of context to sound nefarious to the public and a jury. Singer couldn't say anything explicit to me, as he did with other parents—I could spoil their case and ask, "What are you talking about?"

***

> Taking someone's words out of context to undermine them in a court of law is an age-old dirty tactic. This dastardly strategy was masterfully employed in the 1600s by Cardinal Richelieu, chief minister to King Louis XIII of France. Richelieu often disposed of his rivals through sham trials. His infamous quote shared how he destroyed foes by taking their words out of context: "If you give me six lines written by the hand of the most honest of men, I will find something in them which will hang him."
>
> **Cardinal Richelieu**
> "If you give me six lines written by the hand of the most honest of men, I will find something in them which will hang him."

THE SCANDAL WITHIN THE SCANDAL

> As the top advisor to a French king with absolute power, he could openly say this harsh truth. Richelieu also pioneered the use of mass media to smear people, setting up France's first newspaper, the *Gazette de France*, to spread damaging pamphlets about his enemies. His corrupt tactics helped Louis XIII become the wealthiest and most powerful monarch in Europe, setting the stage for the king's son, Louis XIV, to build the magnificent palace of Versailles.

***

Today, the FBI and federal prosecutors have adapted Richelieu's proven playbook to the twenty-first century and put it on steroids. Modern technology enables them to surreptitiously script and record setup calls or meetings and sift through vast quantities of emails and messages to extract out-of-context quotes or splice quotes to defame and feed a narrative which fits their agenda. This narrative can then be disseminated instantly through the internet and amplified by twenty-four-hour news cycles.

The magnitude of the government resources committed to this case was enormous. The Boston office alone had ten high-level assistant US attorneys or above and seven FBI agents assigned to this case (plus dozens of supporting field agents in California and elsewhere and scores of support personnel).[27]

This group of prosecutors received awards for their "heroism" and supporting "the principal that we do not have a two-tiered system of justice in this country."

The irony of calling out this group for not having double standards is particularly rich. Later chapters will show how these same prosecutors (mis)handled the corruption case of one of their own (the former top US attorney who led the Boston office) who was forced to resign for corruption while the DOJ declined to file any charges against that US attorney.

---

[27] News release from the US attorney's office, District of Massachusetts, February 1, 2024, about US Attorney General's Awards in Washington, DC.

***

I estimate that the total cost to taxpayers (across all the FBI offices and prosecutors and administrative teams) for all the Varsity Blues cases is likely to have exceeded $100 million, and the meter is still running. After seven years of government activity on this case (they started working on this well before the public announcements), the Boston prosecutors are continuing to pursue appeals cases against a coach and other parents who are contesting their plea agreements.

The sheer volume of documents in this case was enormous. We were given millions of documents and far more pages of materials covering all fifty-three defendants. These materials included emails, phone transcripts, texts, tax records, and so forth. Some of these documents themselves were hundreds of pages long.

If each of the roughly 2.5 million documents required various people in the government to spend a combined total of thirty minutes per document (to get the search warrants, obtain the documents, access, scan, read, review, and analyze them, then sort for relevance, note any important pages and facts, have supervisors and lawyers review and analyze each important page, organize and catalogue each document in some hierarchy, prepare some materials for public release and important pages for trial, and so forth), that alone would require 1.25 million hours of work spread out over seven years of investigation and prosecution for this case.

If the average FBI, legal, and support staff are paid $45 per hour, plus benefits costs of 35 percent of wages, the data collection and analysis costs alone would be $76 million. Travel costs, office space costs, and supervisory costs could add another 15 percent to those figures, making that subtotal $87 million.

Additionally, one FBI source indicated that the government investigated upwards of 350 of Singer's other clients who were not ultimately charged. The investigation costs for 350 other parents (assuming several man-months of investigation for each) could add another $18 million to the totals.

Trial costs, sentencing preparation and hearing costs for fifty people, appeals court costs, etc. could add a further $5 million, making a grand total well over $100 million.

As a cross-check, this would equate to just under $2 million cost per defendant. According to some knowledgeable former government experts I spoke with, that didn't seem unusual for a large white-collar criminal case going into its eighth year (the Boston prosecutors began this case in 2018, and it is continuing into 2025).

Given their virtually unlimited budget and fifty-three defendants (fifty of whom pleaded guilty with highly incriminating emails and recordings), the government had everything they needed to create the public image of a toxic swamp of corruption. Then, each time any defendant pleaded guilty, was sentenced, or began serving time, they got to dunk *me* into that toxic swamp with the media.

The *other* parents' facts were extremely explicit and incriminating (and there were plenty of those for the other parents), and as each domino fell, the media assumed that all the parents charged were guilty. No one questioned the motives of the government nor thought any of the remaining parents might be innocent.

FBI guidelines for the dialogue between a confidential informant and suspects require them to be explicit—to prove or disprove each given suspect's guilt (or innocence) beyond a reasonable doubt. The FBI setup calls with all the other parents (released to the public) had explicit dialogue between Singer and others discussing test cheating, bribery, and fraud. They also set up three explicit ruses which Singer used with the other parents—not with me.

One ruse included Singer calling parents and saying that the USC athletic committee was being audited and that parent X's child profile was being checked. Singer went on to say that they both knew that their child's profile was a fake, and he asked the parent (on the setup call) to agree to lie in the event USC called them. That was explicit confirmation that Singer and the parent had knowingly falsified their child's athletic credentials. Those parents were caught agreeing to lie to USC on the recorded calls, and they pleaded guilty.

Singer never mentioned the "USC audit" ruse to me and never discussed with me falsifying my children's actual college applications to appear to play sports they did not play.

A second ruse was Singer saying to parents that the IRS was auditing his charitable foundation and that they both (Singer and the parent on the call) knew his foundation was a sham. Singer asked these parents to lie if the IRS called them. Those parents agreed to lie to the IRS on the FBI setup calls and pleaded guilty.

Singer never mentioned the "charity audit" ruse to me and never discussed with me lying to the IRS about anything at any time.

A third category of ruses with other parents included agreeing to explicit lies—for example, agreeing to fake injuries for students who never showed up for a sport, agreeing to have made-up learning disabilities to get kids more time on tests, or agreeing to falsely state a child's ethnicity to get special consideration as a minority applicant. Those parents agreed to these lies on the recorded calls or in emails and pleaded guilty.

Singer never discussed with us falsifying our children's actual college applications. We never would have agreed to it if he had. Johnny was a real water polo player who applied to USC as one. Our two daughters *never* applied to *any* college through Singer, as they were juniors in high school in 2019 when I got swept up in the maelstrom of indictments.

Finally, Singer explicitly discussed bribing coaches with multiple other parents, explicitly using the term "bribe" repeatedly. Those parents agreed to bribe coaches or other university staff members on the recorded calls and pleaded guilty.

Singer never used the word *bribe* or any derivative of the word *bribe* with us in any conversation, recorded or unrecorded by the FBI. Singer told us that every payment we were making was a donation to his IRS-certified charity to fund things like team travel to Europe or donations through his organization to college foundations to fund facilities or programs.

***

In all Singer's calls with me, he used vague language that would sound innocent to me. For example, Singer asked me if I was OK "giving a check to the coach." Prosecutors knew that in 2014, we had made a donation to USC through Singer, who gave a check—made out to USC—to the water polo coach. It was a check made out to the school, not to the coach (as shown in chapter 4).

The prosecutors had a copy of this check and the receipt we received from USC's Trojan Athletic Fund for our donation through Singer's organization back in 2014. We always gave the check to someone; we wouldn't just tape it to a door or leave it by the pool. In prior years with other charities, we had given checks (made out to the school or program) to coaches or administrators, who would then get credit for helping raise the funds.

We assumed Singer was referring to a similar action in 2018. Giving a check to the coach didn't mean making a payment to the coach's personal account. We never gave any money to a coach's personal account. When I agreed for Singer to give a check from his foundation to the coach during the FBI setup calls, I assumed it would be a check made out to Harvard or Stanford, just as we had done back in 2014 at USC. This was nothing nefarious.

The fact that neither the FBI nor the government lawyers scripted Singer to use the word *bribe* or say "make a check out to a coach's personal accounts" or "bring a brown bag filled with cash" as they did with him and other parents is very telling. If I were really agreeing to bribe a coach or other school official, why not have Singer say so on any of the dozen scripted calls with me?

It would have been incredibly easy and consistent with FBI policies to be explicit with me about any past criminal activity. Singer did in fact say that when he spoke with other parents.

Had Singer done that with me, I would have objected immediately. That was something the prosecutors could not allow to happen. Instead, my innocent agreement to give a check to the coach was spun by the media into something sinister; my willingness to give a check to the coach must have been a bribe.

***

The final setup call Singer made to me in 2019 is particularly disturbing. On this call, Singer asked me not to meet with the development staff of Harvard or Stanford or discuss giving money. I trusted Singer and agreed. If the conversation is excerpted at that point, as Cardinal Richelieu would suggest, I can be seen to have a potentially guilty mindset, falsely implying I agreed to keep this a secret for corrupt reasons.

However, in this guilty-mindset ruse, the falsifying party must omit the next sentences in that same 2019 call, which disproved any suggestion of a nefarious intent on my part in agreeing not to discuss donations with Harvard or Stanford. When I immediately asked Singer, "Why not?" he replied, "Because the schools will then come after you for more donations." Singer used the word *donations*, not *bribes*. The full conversation accurately described my intentions and the meaning of the exchange in its entirety.

If we were indeed bribing coaches, how could the development offices of Harvard and Stanford come after me for more "bribes"? Sharing only the first part of this conversation would be deliberately misleading; the complete dialogue proved that I believed I was making legitimate donations, not bribes.

There is an email exchange that occurred between Singer and me that I need to address that occurred back in 2012 during our son's junior year in high school. This exchange followed a conversation where Singer told us our son wasn't going to get any playing time because he was going to be a redshirt.

Singer explained that the only freshmen who played in games at USC were much older recruits from Eastern Europe. He told us these older players, often from semipro clubs or military teams, were in their mid-twenties but qualified as freshmen under NCAA rules since they were less than twenty-five years old and had not yet gone to college.

The idea of our teenage son going up against freshman males from Eastern Europe in their mid-twenties was deeply unsettling. These weren't just seasoned athletes; they were grown men, with years of experience, physical maturity, and a level of aggression well beyond our 17-year-old son's fit both socially and physically. We scheduled a visit to the school to meet with the coach and see for ourselves.

Before we met with the coach, Leslie, Johnny, and I watched the USC team practice for about thirty minutes from the deck, a few feet from the edge of the pool. When we saw the team up close, we were immediately relieved. During our time by the pool, we saw several older players, but there were also several teenage players comparable to our son in age and size. In fact, Johnny even recognized several players he had competed against in previous years' tournaments, alleviating our concerns about his fit on the team.

When we met with Coach Jovan, he asked Johnny about the teams and coaches that he had played for. Our son highlighted his long-standing role as a starter since his sophomore year for Coach Bowen and how he was a sprint-off player on every team he played for. Our son also told Coach Jovan about the multiple coaches he had on the different Stanford Club teams he played for over the prior five years. Jovan knew the teams and the coaches and said our son would be a great candidate for a walk-on spot.

The topic of Johnny's fit on the USC team never came up again—not once. We knew he was well suited for the team, and he proved to be just that. Importantly, the issue of his fit on the USC team was not raised in any of the six months of FBI-scripted setup calls that Singer made to me in 2018.

If the prosecutors genuinely believed our son was a fraudulent Division I athlete, they could have scripted Singer to explicitly mention that we had created a fake profile or claim our son "wasn't a Division I player" like he did with other parents. They did not, because that assertion was untrue. More importantly, I would have reacted negatively to such claims during the recorded conversations. And that could spoil their case against me.

In fact, Singer's FBI interview notes said, "John Wilson—dona[t]ion to USC program for real [water] polo player." The FBI also interviewed Coach Bowen, along with my son's high school and USC teammates, and received the same descriptions. Coach Bowen told the government that Johnny was "an A-plus by USC standards for speed and work ethic" and he testified under oath that he was confident Johnny "could contribute to a high-level program like USC" by his junior or senior year—not bad for a walk-on.

The government was aware that our son was a legitimate Division I–level water polo player who was an "A-plus" for speed by national championship team standards and that he was being recruited by the Air

THE SCANDAL WITHIN THE SCANDAL

Force Academy, a top-ten nationally ranked water polo team in 2012.[28] Yet someone secretly fed the *New York Times* and other media outlets false narratives about our son that was opposite the facts and the written allegations in the official charging documents. The *New York Times* reported that our son "wasn't good enough to compete at the university, *according to prosecutors*" (emphasis mine).[29]

We believe that some unnamed prosecutor deliberately and repeatedly misled various media outlets to smear our son and me in the court of public opinion in order to apply additional pressure on me to plead guilty.

As we gathered our facts, it was painful to hear the horrific lies circulating about all three of our children. Radio talk shows, social media trolls, and others made egregious claims. The wave of public resentment grew against us and our children, despite the glaring differences between our facts and the other parents.

Cardinal Richelieu would have been impressed with the handicraft of the Boston federal prosecutors.

***

During the FBI setup calls in 2018, Singer also persuaded us to move a part of the donations in our will forward. (Since our daughters' college applications were not due until January 2020, it was surprising that no one in the media questioned how my donations to IRS-certified charities in 2018 could be bribes.)

The prosecutors publicly claimed that even if all the money went to the colleges and not the coaches, the donations were still bribes if we got quid

---

28 Email exchange from Johnny's high school coach about the Air Force Academy interest and the Collegiate Water Polo Association 2012 Men's Varsity Polls (week 13: November 28/final).
29 "The College Admissions Scandal: Where Some of the Defendants Are Now," New York Times, October 9, 2021.

pro quo admissions help. This new definition of bribery confused many legal experts; how could the alleged "victim" of a bribe (the colleges) be the ones receiving the money?

Moreover, how could the widespread and long-standing practice of giving donor families admissions help now be bribery? The government was trying to criminalize a practice that had been accepted for generations at many institutions.

If this precedent were upheld, other donations that resulted in some unquantifiable benefit to the donor could also be criminalized. For instance, donating to a hospital and getting on a VIP list for preferential access to key doctors or personalized care might also now be considered a bribe to the doctor.

It also struck us as bizarre that the IRS continued to publicly certify Singer's foundation as legitimate while prosecutors were simultaneously trying to set up individuals for donating to that very same foundation. The IRS website for Singer's foundation, kept online until 2020, explicitly stated that "users may rely on this list in determining the deductibility of their contributions."

Why didn't the prosecutors push the IRS to retract its endorsement of Singer's foundation when they first learned of his fraud in early 2018? Were they using the IRS's seal of approval to help set up innocent people like us? It's hard to believe we were explicitly told on the IRS's own website that we could rely on this list to make our donations deductible while I was arrested for doing just that.

The prosecutors also took extreme steps to pressure me into pleading guilty and cover up *their* misdeeds. They piled on *nine* total felonies in four rounds of superseding charges over the next year—with 180 years of total potential prison time. These additional charges were not related to any new criminal acts the prosecutors uncovered; they all related to the same alleged crime of donating to colleges and getting help in admissions.

THE SCANDAL WITHIN THE SCANDAL

We learned the hard way that these coercive tactics were a common form of legal extortion which prosecutors often use to deplete a defendant's financial resources and will to fight.

The chart below puts these nine felony charges into perspective. I faced twice the charges against Singer—the criminal mastermind at the center of this scandal (who confessed to stealing tens of millions from his clients)—and more than four times the charges against the other parents in the Varsity Blues case.

The charges against me were also more than Sam Bankman-Fried and just slightly less than Bernie Madoff, who were both convicted for misappropriating billions in investors' funds and sentenced to decades in prison. That's how extreme and disproportionate the charges stacked against me were.

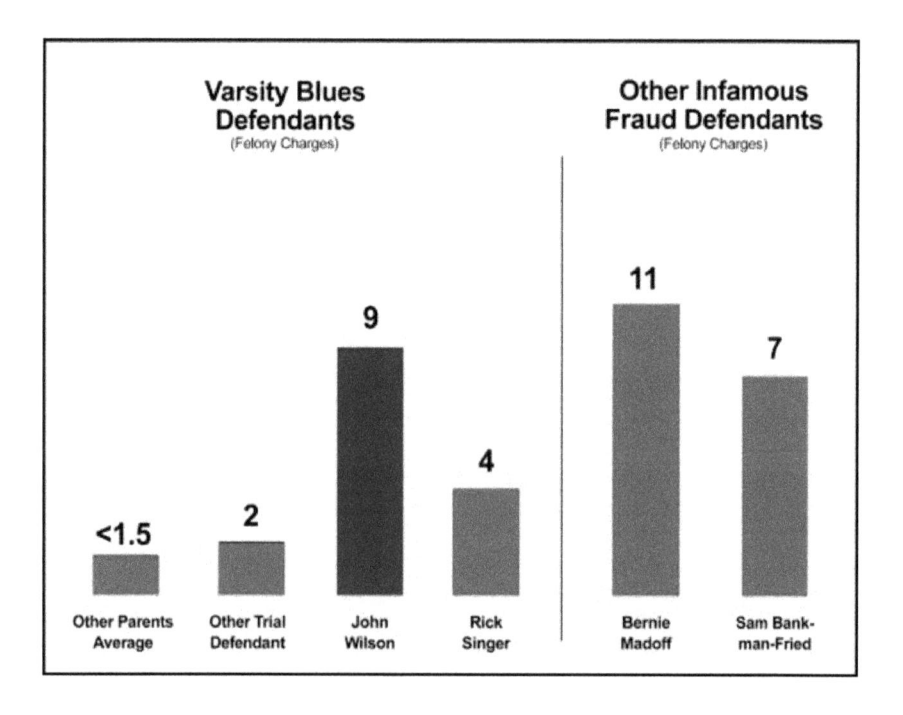

Varsity Blues Defendants (Felony Charges)

- Other Parents Average: <1.5
- Other Trial Defendant: 2
- John Wilson: 9
- Rick Singer: 4

Other Infamous Fraud Defendants (Felony Charges)

- Bernie Madoff: 11
- Sam Bankman-Fried: 7

Each felony charge was so serious (and the sentencing penalty that prosecutors recommend if you refuse to take a plea deal could be so severe) that even if I were convicted of just a single charge, I could end up spending years in prison. The prosecutors knew that doing this would cost the taxpayers a lot of extra money, but it was a way to exert maximum financial, psychological, and media pressure against me.

Additionally, multiple studies show that the odds of being convicted rise substantially if the government stacks multiple charges against a defendant. As the *Harvard Law Review* said in March 2023, "Charge Stacking Worsens Defendants' Chances."[30] Most people, me included, assume that federal prosecutors wouldn't charge an innocent person with nine felony charges, the accused must have done at least something wrong—the legal equivalent of "Where there's smoke, there must be fire." It was just one more dirty tactic in the long line of dirty tactics that the prosecutors used in my case.

It still seems hard for me to believe, even as I write this years later, that I faced nine federal felony charges and 180 years of potential prison time. For what? Making donations to colleges and IRS-certified charities (where the college gave me a receipt and they have kept my donations to this day) and getting admissions help for children who didn't cheat and who were each highly qualified academically and athletically for the schools and team spots they applied for?

Is the widespread and long-standing practice of giving donor families help in college admissions really now a federal felony?

---

[30] "Stacked: Where Criminal Charge Stacking Happens—And Where It Doesn't," *Harvard Law Review*, March 2023.

Chapter 10

CRITICAL EVIDENCE VANISHES

How Proof of My Innocence "Disappeared"

Once we understood the prosecutors' potential motives for charging me, the pieces of the puzzle began to fit together. It wasn't a pretty picture, but the prosecutors' actions started to make sense. The abuses of power we experienced were very disturbing, especially when key evidence supporting my innocence, a thirty-four-minute call Singer made to us from the government's own offices, somehow "disappeared."

***

> The potential for law enforcement officials to abuse their authority and power for personal advancement or other questionable motives is both shocking and devastating for any defendant. A stark historical example of such abuse of power is Lavrentiy Beria, the notorious Soviet police chief under Joseph Stalin, who infamously said, "You bring me the man, I'll find you the crime."
>
> **Lavrentiy Beria**
> "You bring me the man, I'll find you the crime."
>
> - Stalin's Former Secret Police Chief

THE SCANDAL WITHIN THE SCANDAL

> The strategy to smear me through guilt by association and set up scripted, out-of-context sound bites to incriminate me was a critical first step. Step two was to avoid creating any evidence that could exonerate me. This meant a critical thirty-four-minute FaceTime call, which proved our innocence, had to be erased, or as they claimed, never recorded. The only FBI records for this call (the longest Singer made to me during his cooperation period) were just seven words: "Good first call with the Wilson daughters."

***

During the six months the prosecutors had Singer under their control, they could script his calls, dictate his emails and texts, and direct all his actions. According to Singer's sentencing report, he worked with the government for over one thousand hours during this six-month period. The agents were scripting and debriefing everything he said or wrote. Nothing was left to chance.

After my arrest, we went through all our phone records, texts, emails, and calls we had with Singer. The FaceTime call with Leslie and me introducing our daughters stood out because it was the first call with our daughters, and we recalled that it was extremely helpful and could prove my innocence. We repeatedly tried to obtain the transcripts, knowing they would exonerate me. Despite multiple requests, this critical evidence was somehow made to "disappear."

We later learned that Singer made this call from the FBI's own offices in California while he was meeting for three full days with four FBI agents and two senior federal prosecutors. The government acknowledges the FaceTime call occurred. (Since we had the phone bill and texts to verify it, they couldn't deny it.) It just somehow disappeared, or as the government said, it was never monitored or recorded.

Critical Evidence Vanishes

According to sworn government trial testimony, six government agents inexplicably left Singer and his attorney alone, *in their own offices*, for the exact thirty-four minutes that this call took place. Incredibly, before they left the room, they all forgot to execute the most basic task in a high-profile wiretap operation with a confidential informant speaking with their key suspect: press the record button.

They could have easily recorded this call using one of Singer's multiple cell phones, any of their own cell phones, or one of many recording devices in the FBI offices. The call was crucial, yet it vanished like a magic trick.

Here, again, context is important. Singer agreed to cooperate with the government when he was confronted by the prosecutors in mid-September 2018—just before we were to meet him at our home near Boston. He canceled this in-person meeting at the last moment (when, unbeknownst to us, he was nabbed by the government). We then arranged to meet him a few days later at a hotel at Boston's Logan airport. We later learned that this hotel meeting room was wired with surveillance cameras and microphones.

On our way to that meeting, Singer called once again to cancel. The government may have been apprehensive about how Singer would interact with us—their critical hook for Boston venue. If he treated us, as he always had, as honest and "wholesome" clients, he might inadvertently create exculpatory evidence. To allow more preparation time and avoid the possibility of generating exculpatory evidence, the agents may have had Singer cancel this second meeting.

THE SCANDAL WITHIN THE SCANDAL

The following week, government records show six government officials spent three full days meeting with Singer in person in their offices in California, debriefing and prepping him.

On the second day of their in-person meetings, Singer scheduled a third attempt at an introduction meeting with our daughters through texts with Leslie. Singer set up this call with Leslie (on Thursday at 11:39 a.m. California time) while he was in the middle of his meetings with the government.

According to the prosecutors, Singer deleted all his texts arranging this call. Amazingly, they said they had no copies or records of any of these texts. Fortunately for us, my wife saved her texts.

The FBI agents should have been fully aware of Singer's activities since he was sitting right there with them in their own offices when he set up this call. With his phones tapped, they monitored every text and call he made or received. It is highly unlikely that they would allow him to sneak a text to their key suspect, someone crucial to their venue goals, under the table with six government agents in the room.

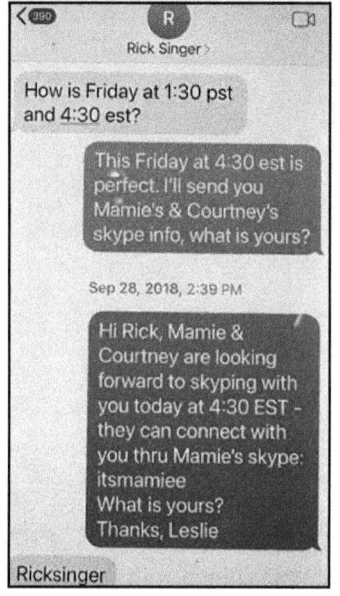

The call was scheduled for Friday, September 29, 2018, at 1:30 p.m. PST (4:30 p.m. Boston time). This call had the potential to be a game changer for me—if they had only recorded it (or perhaps didn't eliminate any recordings or contemporaneous notes they may have had).

There are two narratives about what took place on that call—one spun by the federal prosecutors and another one that is the truth. Let me outline the outrageous version of events the government sold to the judge. It illustrates their hubris and willingness to violate procedures and serves as a microcosm of the misconduct that we were dealing with throughout this six-plus-year ordeal.

142

On that Friday morning, less than two hours before the Skype call was set to occur, Singer asked Leslie to switch to a FaceTime call instead—something we had never done with Singer before.

While this may seem like a minor detail, it was significant. Skype calls can be automatically recorded and saved for up to thirty days, while FaceTime calls cannot be recorded. I only learned this crucial difference after my arrest when such details became vital to my defense.

Why would the government instruct Singer to switch from Skype to FaceTime? Again, everything Singer did, especially while he was with them for three days in their own offices, was managed by the six government agents. It is unlikely this was a random accident or mere coincidence.

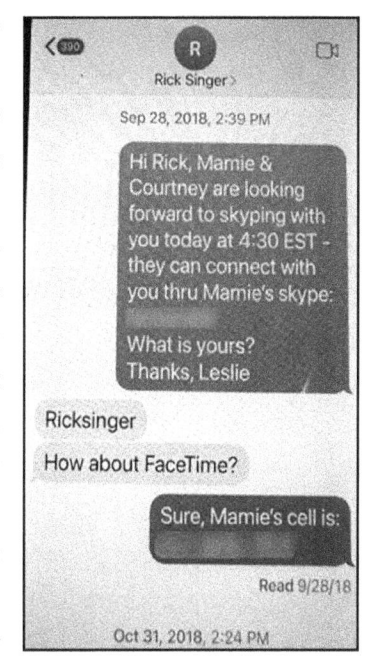

Singer's prior recorded call to me discussed the Harvard president, and his next two meetings with us were canceled at the last minute. Were they still worried that Singer wasn't ready to have the type of call with me that they wanted? Was it a deliberate tactic to ensure that if Singer's first scripted call to us generated exculpatory evidence, there would be no record of it?

The government's narrative strains credulity. They claimed that all six federal officials, including the lead prosecutor who had flown in from Boston, conveniently left Singer alone just moments before the critical 1:30 p.m. PST FaceTime call was to begin (they all purportedly left for an extremely late lunch, a 4:30 p.m. EST lunch for the Boston team).

This was a critical moment in the investigation—Singer's first scripted call to me, the Boston venue hook. Yet none of the six agents or prosecutors stayed to supervise, monitor, or record this call?

Context is essential; this was the introduction to our daughters, meant to compensate for the two previously canceled face-to-face meetings in Boston. The government had Singer cancel those prior meetings, possibly because they weren't confident with what he might say or possibly fearing that I was a "wholesome" account.

Yet somehow just a few days later, the government was so comfortable with Singer that they allowed him to go freestyle—to make unscripted, unsupervised, and unrecorded calls to me and my family. They must have done an extraordinary job of training Singer in those few days.

Think about what the government said under oath. Singer was free to roam the FBI offices for forty minutes, unsupervised. Singer was caught warning other parents on a burner phone, not us. Singer was purportedly left alone in the FBI offices. They supposedly left him all alone to make unsupervised, unrecorded FaceTime calls to anyone he chose. It was a ridiculous mockery of FBI protocols and the truth.

I have spoken with several former senior FBI officials about government policies on handling confidential informants, including a special agent who drafted the FBI's confidential informant policy manual.

According to the government's sworn testimony, six government agents simultaneously left Singer alone in *their* offices just before this crucial call started, and then they all returned *precisely* forty-three minutes after they left, just moments after the FaceTime call ended. What a remarkable coincidence.

This story defies common sense and violates multiple FBI policies.

The first policy violation was leaving a confidential informant alone in the FBI offices, free to roam and make unmonitored, unrecorded FaceTime phone calls to anyone in our family and any other targets. No non-FBI people are ever to be left unattended in FBI offices—period. That's as fundamental as it gets. Yet six senior government officials claim that's exactly what they *all* did. This wasn't just one agent who forgot the rules. This was four FBI agents and two senior federal prosecutors who all simultaneously had crucial mental lapses at a crucial moment in the case.

***

The government tried to downplay the significance of this call at the trial, claiming that only our daughters were on the call. They said neither Leslie nor I were on the call—the call Leslie was arranging for us to introduce our daughters to Singer. Leslie is a very protective mother and would not simply tell our sixteen-year-old daughters to call a fifty-five-year-old man to introduce themselves on FaceTime and talk about college. She would never do that in a million years. The assertion was ludicrous.

Leslie was also an unindicted coconspirator at the time of the call. Under no circumstances is a confidential informant to set up a call to speak with a target or his spouse or their children without agreement and preparation, especially in an unrecorded, unmonitored setting. This was a second major violation of FBI protocols.

The third violation was the failure to record that call, even if it was made to our daughters without us on the call as they alleged. All communications involving a target, including family members, must be recorded. The FBI policies don't allow a confidential informant to pick and choose which calls to record.

The government's version implies that Singer could have called and warned our daughters, "Tell your dad the FBI is listening to my calls." FBI guidelines exist for a reason.

If the government narrative were true, Singer was free to FaceTime call me or Leslie and warn us directly. Additionally, since no agent was in the room, he could have called and warned other parents—right there from the government's own offices! (After all, Singer did call other parents with a burner phone.) These policy violations went beyond incompetence and bordered on misconduct.

After the six government agents returned, there were also no contemporaneous debrief notes that were shared. The only documentation was written weeks later in a vague seven-word memo: "Good first call with the

Wilson daughters." This was how the government summarized this critical thirty-four-minute call with one of their key targets.

This call to me was the longest and most critical call in the entire case, yet it was distilled and sanitized to a mere seven words. They made it sound as ordinary as their deli order for lunch that afternoon.

This was a fourth and fifth violation of FBI policies. Unrecorded and unsupervised calls of such importance should have extensive debriefings. In such situations, FBI policies require detailed notes about the call, its participants, topics covered, the reasons for not recording the call, debrief notes about the call, and so forth. Additionally, those debrief notes should be made immediately, not weeks later as the agent on the stand said they did.

A sixth violation of FBI procedures occurred when the government did not preserve Singer's texts related to the call. They did not keep mirrored copies of his phone or texts related to this call. They allowed him to delete all the relevant messages and did not retrieve any of his deleted texts. The government is compelled to preserve all evidence, yet they allowed Singer to erase his texts about this call (along with thousands of other texts), effectively enabling him to make this critical call disappear.

Setting aside the policy violations, consider this situation through the lens of common sense. Why would six agents, including the lead prosecutor, allow Singer to make a phone call to a key target's family without it being scripted, monitored, or recorded? They could have easily erased the call if it turned out to be a misdial or irrelevant personal conversation. Surely someone could have saved it on a thumb drive or one of their cell phones if they needed storage space.

Additionally, how could Singer, someone they couldn't trust the week before to have an in-person meeting with us (he canceled the two meetings with us the week prior in Boston), suddenly be trusted to have unfettered access to their offices and make unrecorded phone calls to their number one suspect?

***

To add insult to injury, the government threatened me with more charges and prison time for "lying" about being on the call. They used an inference from a recorded conversation the next day, in which I asked Singer how it went with my daughters on the call, as "proof" that I was not on the call.

For years, Singer followed a three-part routine for our meetings and calls. First, he would start with the whole family together. Second, Singer would speak with our son alone. Third, Singer would have a private conversation with us parents alone. This was how the FaceTime call was set up.

The next day, when I asked Singer on a recorded call how the FaceTime call went with our daughters. I wanted to hear how part two of the call went.

At my sentencing hearing, the Boston prosecutors determined to destroy me sought two more years of prison time for what they claimed was my obstruction of justice, all based on a lie of their own making. They claimed I lied under oath about being on this FaceTime call. This is how vindictive and crazy things got. It was a breathtaking level of deceit.

They were the ones hiding the truth, twisting reality to suit their agenda yet I was being accused of lying under oath and obstructing justice. The very call that could have exonerated me was turned into a weapon against me. It was a warped, dystopian nightmare, some kind of *Alice in Wonderland* insanity where up was down and lies became truth simply because they said so.

According to the prosecutors, no one from the government was present with Singer during the call, and there were no recordings of it available. Singer was their sole witness about who was on the call. Yet despite repeated requests, the prosecutors refused to ask Singer for a statement about who was present or make a written statement about who took part in the FaceTime call. Why? Because they knew the truth wasn't on their side. If Singer had been truthful, which they may have worried he might, he would have confirmed that all four of us were on this critical call.

Things got even crazier. To protect myself against the government's charges of perjury and obstruction, my wife and twin daughters signed sworn statements affirming my presence on the call. (Let's be crystal clear: I would never ask them to lie under oath and risk federal felony charges for themselves.) We were all telling the truth. I even volunteered and took additional polygraph tests about being on this call, as polygraph results are admissible in sentencing hearings. Yet none of it mattered.

Despite having four sworn statements and multiple polygraph tests confirming I was on the call, the Boston prosecutors refused to drop the obstruction charge during my sentencing hearing. They dismissed the polygraph evidence as "self-serving." But that wasn't enough. They also refused to ask Singer who was on the call and never made him available to us for questioning. They didn't want the truth—they wanted to punish me with maximum prison time.

And then, with a threat so ruthless it still makes my head spin, we were told that the prosecutors could charge Leslie and our daughters with felonies for lying under oath. The government's logic being if I was lying about being on the call, then my family must be lying too. But we weren't lying and the prosecutors knew that. The prosecutors were the ones being untruthful, bending reality, distorting facts, and weaponizing the legal system against us. Yet my wife and daughters were at risk for alleged perjury. The level of vindictiveness we were dealing with was beyond comprehension.

At my sentencing hearing, the Boston prosecutors—drunk on their own power—demanded two more years in prison for me, all based on their fabricated obstruction charge. This wasn't justice. It was a vendetta. And the scariest part? They didn't care that *they* were the ones lying.

***

During the first few weeks of discovery, I repeatedly asked myself, "Where is the September FaceTime call? Where are the transcripts or recordings?"

I will never forget the call itself—a call that should have proven my innocence. This was the only call in eight years where Singer criticized our children. He said our daughters were smart and had excellent grades. However, he said they should have played on one year-round sport to make them stand out.

Singer explicitly discussed team manager roles on sailing or crew teams for academically qualified children of major donors. He knew about our twin daughters' boating licenses, lifeguard certifications, and years of power boating and sailing experience. Singer said that since anyone could be a team manager, those spots were on a first-come, first-served basis. He said walk-on slots for Division I athletes like Johnny was were a much higher probability since there were far fewer Division I athletes.

Singer's statement that our son was a legitimate Division I water polo player would have shattered the government's case. This alone would have provided a compelling reason for the call to "disappear." That single conversation could have vindicated us.

Another significant reason this call may have "disappeared" was our discussion about Singer's alleged meeting with the president of Harvard, which I naively believed occurred. I remember asking Singer about the meeting and mentioning my connection to the former Harvard president, Drew Faust. (Drew was on the Staples Board of Directors when I was the president of Staples International.)

Singer claimed that his conversation with the current Harvard president revolved around how donations from his foundation were to be distributed within Harvard. Singer said that the president supported donations to specific teams or departments but also wanted to direct a part of his parents' gifts to a general fund to help with other university priorities.

This conversation could have terrified the federal prosecutors; imagine this dialogue presented to a jury. It clearly showed that I believed Singer was engaged in legitimate donations with the president of Harvard. This also could have severely undermined their case against me.

Why would I inquire about Singer's meeting with the Harvard president if I thought that our actions were corrupt? If Singer's donation program was about bribing coaches, why would he tell me about discussing donations with the president of Harvard? It makes no sense for Singer to mention the Harvard president unless I was a "wholesome" account.

If the prosecutors needed me as a venue hook to help keep this case in Boston, then it would be critical for this recording to either never happen or to "disappear." The government recorded every call before and after this FaceTime conversation. Yet this crucial call—the longest call Singer had with me, which was made from their own offices—was somehow missing?

There is an alternative scenario about what happened. Perhaps the six government agents didn't violate multiple FBI policies and leave Singer alone in their offices for the FaceTime call. Maybe at least one person stayed behind and took copious notes or recorded the FaceTime call. Maybe the content of this call hurt their case so badly they needed it to disappear. The government acknowledged that Singer deleted all his texts with Leslie about this call; maybe he deleted this recording too.

I had a clear memory of that September 2018 call; you tend not to forget things like that when they could have prevented your life and your children's lives from being turned upside down. We filed motions to compel the government to produce the transcripts of this call—all to no avail.

An obligation all prosecutors have in criminal cases is to provide defendants with what is called "Brady material"—any exculpatory evidence that prosecutors uncover during their investigation.

Brady material isn't just physical evidence; it's also supposed to cover any exculpatory evidence from investigators' recollections of interviews, setup calls, debriefs, and so on. Every bit of evidence, in agent memory or written form, that could be helpful to a defendant must be shared with defense attorneys. Yet we received nothing about the content of this call.

Critical Evidence Vanishes

There are multiple ways that prosecutors can minimize sharing helpful evidence, ranging from not recording evidence (if it's not written down, it's harder for defendants to get access to it) to misrepresenting evidence (writing things down in misleading ways) to outright destroying evidence.

The standard notes the FBI are supposed to file about witness interviews are called 302 reports. These 302 reports are supposed to be completed contemporaneously where possible and be thorough—typically pages of notes related to call preparation, attendees, the call content itself, and any debrief.

I saw that the other charged parents had pages of 302 notes, so I thought, "Where are all *my* 302 notes?" I had a dozen calls, more calls and text exchanges with Singer over six months than anyone else. Instead of pages and pages of notes, my entire case had a total of seven lines of what some experts described as "sanitized" 302 reports.

There were a dozen calls and more texts over six months and a grand total of just seven lines of 302 notes. Not seven pages, *seven lines* of notes. According to the prosecutor who testified, these notes were often written weeks after an event took place. So the agents relied on their memories to get all the details correct, weeks after the fact, with dozens of parents being monitored.

Their memories were so razor-sharp they were able to distill the critical thirty-four-minute FaceTime call with us, the call that proved my innocence, into, "Good first call with the Wilson daughters." While I was not expecting *War and Peace*, how could their notes covering six months of setup calls and texts with me be captured in just seven lines like this one?

I was the parent who would eventually be charged with more felonies than anyone else in the Varsity Blues case, with more recorded phone calls than anyone else, yet I had the fewest FBI notes.

***

THE SCANDAL WITHIN THE SCANDAL

According to a retired FBI agent from the Boston office, the FBI "runs on paper." In a face to face meeting, he went on to say about this missing FaceTime call,

> "Where is the paperwork to support the trip to California, paperwork that justifies the cost of the trip and value of the objectives to be accomplished documented for a supervisor to approve? Where are the documents created to reflect the work performed, positive or negative? If there are recordings, copies are made as working copies to transcribe—again, more paperwork."

He, too, was flabbergasted that the four FBI agents and two lead prosecutors would leave Singer all alone in *the government's offices* to make unrecorded FaceTime calls to our family and any other family he chose and to have nothing more than seven words—"Good first call with the Wilson daughters"—written about the call.

Perhaps most shocking of all was the statement by the IRS agent who was added to the FBI team on this case. She testified under oath that they didn't write down any exculpatory statements made by Singer in their reports. This was a clear admission of what is called a Brady violation—improperly hiding exculpatory evidence. It was shocking when the judge did nothing. How can that be justice?

It is deeply concerning that this critical FaceTime call, which would have proven my innocence, conveniently "disappeared"—perhaps to save the prosecutors case against me?

Chapter 11

THE FINE ART OF JUDGE SHOPPING

How Prosecutors Achieve Near-Absolute Power

While an unscrupulous prosecutor can deliberately avoid and even destroy evidence helpful to a defendant, their ability to get away with this or to improperly block exculpatory evidence in the record depends upon the judge making the rulings. To handpick the most favorable judge possible to gain a conviction, the prosecutors did something we had never heard of before this case: judge shopping.

***

> Judges in all federal criminal or civil cases are supposed to be randomly assigned. In Boston, the system to assign judges to different cases is known as "the wheel." This approach is critical since the only check on an unscrupulous prosecutor's misuse of power is the judge.
>
> **Lord Acton**
> "Power tends to corrupt and absolute power corrupts absolutely."

THE SCANDAL WITHIN THE SCANDAL

> If a prosecutor can select, or "judge shop" for, a highly supportive judge, then their power becomes near-absolute. Accumulating power is often a dirty business. Unfortunately, there are many frightening truths about power and the abuse of that power that have echoed throughout history. One hundred and fifty years ago, a highly regarded British historian, Lord Acton, wrote one of the most famous axioms about how power affects people when he said, "Power tends to corrupt, and absolute power corrupts absolutely."

***

The reasons that criminal cases are supposed to be randomly assigned are obvious. If a prosecutor could select the judge they prefer, it would not only give them virtually unlimited power, but it would also erode the public's confidence in the fairness and overall integrity of our criminal justice system.

The Boston-based prosecutors knew the judges and the system well. They manipulated the process to ensure that our case landed in the lap of the judge they preferred—the oldest full-time federal judge currently active in the United States, with a long track record of being highly supportive to prosecutors.

To accomplish this judge shopping, the Boston federal prosecutors had some dirty tactics up their sleeves to circumvent the district's random assignment process. They filed separate cases early on against multiple low-profile defendants (test proctors, coaches, Singer staff, and a parent from Canada named David Sidoo). These cases were each randomly assigned via "the wheel."

Once the prosecutors had randomly assigned enough defendants to cover nearly all the federal judges in Boston, including their preferred judge, they stopped the random assignment process. They then announced plans to add a superseding charge against all the parents, alleging a single nationwide conspiracy of parents, and then joined them to the docket of their preferred judge.

This approach was so outrageous that more than two dozen defense lawyers from fifteen nationally prominent law firms immediately wrote the letter below to the chief judge in Boston, which pointed out both the flawed conspiracy theory as well as the judge shopping the prosecutors were trying to do.[31]

April 9, 2019

Honorable Patti B. Saris
Chief Judge, District of Massachusetts
John Joseph Moakley Federal Courthouse
One Courthouse Way
Boston, MA 02210

Re: **"Operation Varsity Blues" Prosecution**

Dear Chief Judge Saris:

    This District uses "the wheel" to randomly assign criminal cases to its district judges. *See* L.R. 40.1(b)(3). The reason that criminal cases are randomly assigned is obvious. If a prosecutor were able to select the district judge that he or she prefers, it would erode the public's confidence in the fairness and integrity of the criminal justice process. We are writing because we are gravely concerned that the United States Attorney's Office is seeking to evade the District's random assignment process—and because we think Your Honor has the ability to deter it from happening.

    We represent parents who were arrested last month as part of "Operation Varsity Blues." Our clients are not among the thirteen parents who have agreed to plead guilty to a pre-indictment criminal information, and we expect that our clients may be indicted as early as this afternoon. The United States Attorney's Office has informed us that it intends to indict our clients together in a single indictment, charging them as disconnected "spokes" in a rimless wheel conspiracy that has Rick Singer as the "hub."

    Joining our clients together in a single conspiracy indictment, based on allegations that each of them participated in admissions-related activities with Singer, would violate well-established Supreme Court precedent. *See, e.g.*, *Kotteakos v. United States*, 328 U.S. 750, 754 (1946). Far more troubling, however, is that the prosecutors apparently plan to charge our clients not through an original indictment that is then randomly assigned to a district judge, but rather by joining them into an indictment that was originally returned on March 5, 2019, against a single individual—a parent named David Sidoo—and assigned to Judge Nathaniel Gorton.[1] None of our clients has any connection to Mr. Sidoo. None of our clients has ever met, spoken with, or done business with Mr. Sidoo. We do not believe that any of our clients had even heard of Mr. Sidoo until a few weeks ago. Simply put, the prosecutors' plan to join our clients into the indictment against Mr. Sidoo is a clear form of judge shopping.

    A severance motion, based on misjoinder under Federal Rule of Criminal Procedure 8(b), is not a solution to any of this. Even after succeeding on motions to sever, our clients' cases would

---

[1] The case is *United States v. David Sidoo*, No. 19-cr-10080-NMG.

---

31   *Full list of lawyers truncated for brevity.*

remain with the district judge who was assigned the *Sidoo* indictment into which the prosecutors plan to improperly join our clients—an outcome that would still reward the prosecutors for subversion of the District's process of randomly assigning criminal cases. Moreover, the notion that all of the indicted "Varsity Blues" parents should be assigned to a single district judge is contrary to Local Rule 40.1(b)(3)'s expressly stated goal of ensuring equal division of cases amongst the District's active judges.

The prosecutors' charging plan, if permitted, would do severe and lasting damage to the District's random assignment system. Prosecutors who seek to evade the District's assignment system by joining more than a dozen new defendants into a previously returned indictment that happened to be assigned to a district judge that the prosecutors prefer should not be rewarded. If such procedural manipulations are permitted to occur without consequence in this high profile case, prosecutors in the District will be encouraged to engage (or threaten to engage) in similar tactics in any future case where doing so might benefit them, to the detriment of all defendants who hope to be treated fairly and equally.

To be sure, we deeply respect Judge Gorton. Several of us have represented criminal defendants before Judge Gorton, including at trials where our clients have been acquitted. Our positive experiences with Judge Gorton, however, are beside the point. The District's process of randomly assigning criminal cases is essential to ensuring the overall integrity and fairness of the criminal process in this District. This is the principle we are seeking to protect. We therefore respectfully ask that Your Honor take action consistent with the spirit of Local Rule 40.1(b)(3), including (i) requesting the United States Attorney's Office to indict our clients in a manner that makes a good-faith effort to comply with Rule 8(b)'s requirements and the Supreme Court's decision in *Kotteakos*, and (ii) taking whatever available steps are necessary to ensure that any indictments returned against our clients are in fact randomly assigned. If, however, the United States Attorney's Office proceeds with its plan to join our clients into the *Sidoo* indictment, we respectfully request that the superseding indictment then be placed back on to the wheel and randomly assigned. This would be the only way to stamp out any perception that the prosecutors have manipulated the charging process in order to select the district judge before whom they prefer to try their case.

Sincerely,

Eoin Beirne (Mintz Levin)
Thomas Bienert (Bienert Katzman)
Walter Brown (Orrick, Herrington & Sutcliffe)
Reuben Cahn (Keller/Anderle)
Colleen Conry (Ropes & Gray)
Melinda Haag (Orrick, Herrington & Sutcliffe)
Laura Hoey (Ropes & Gray)
Aaron Katz (Ropes & Gray)

The reply shown below from the chief judge mentioned a strong commitment to the random assignment process. However, it said that any complaint about all the cases being improperly joined had to be decided by the *presiding* judge—the same judge that the prosecutors had just specifically chosen through judge shopping. What were the chances this judge was now going to decide to have all the cases randomnly assigned to others?

Everyone felt the futility of this circular logic. It was patently obvious to any impartial observer that the prosecutors basically handpicked this judge. A number of lawyers familiar with the Boston federal judges told us what the prosecutors did was the equivalent of having someone from their team sitting on the bench.

That was shocking and frightening. The person who was supposed to be the unbiased umpire, fairly calling balls and strikes, and the only check on an overly aggressive prosecutor's power was now effectively a full supporter on their side.

Within days of this judge assignment decision, half of *all* the remaining defendants changed their pleas from "not guilty" to "guilty." While many of those other parents had bad facts, they did not suddenly discover this and reverse their pleas. It wasn't because their odds of getting a fair trial had suddenly improved either. What did they all know that we didn't to make such an immediate about-face in their legal position?

***

Over the ensuing months and years, it would become clear what a difference a prosecutor-friendly judge can make. This judge would go on to rule against 100 percent of *every* substantive motion we made on *every* pretrial matter. These were not frivolous motions made by novice lawyers. These were highly relevant motions made by some of the top lawyers from across the country. While we didn't expect to win the majority, our pretrial motions were so compelling, we should have won at least several. We got zero.

For example, there was the false conspiracy motion which allowed the prosecutors to combine all the parents into a single nationwide conspiracy. There was a famous Supreme Court precedent which said this was clearly inappropriate and prejudicial.[32] Top legal experts from multiple top law firms in the country raised this issue repeatedly. However, the judge followed the prosecutors and ignored the Supreme Court rulings in this area. (By the time the judge's flawed decision was unanimously reversed by the appeals court years later, the damage was already done.)

During my trial, during our defense witnesses, this judge would go on to rule against my evidence and other motions 98.3 percent of the time. This wasn't just a few isolated bad calls. The judge ruled against our defense motions hundreds and hundreds of times during the core of the three-week trial.

Just one category of critical evidence that our trial judge excluded entirely was devastating to my case. We tried to enter a summary of an enormous amount of work that Mike Kendall and his team had expertly collected over months and months, with over one hundred examples of USC giving admissions preferences to donor families (unrelated to Rick Singer's donors) through athletics. This evidence was critical to my defense as noted in the appeals brief, which said, "The government admits that if USC had condoned side-door donations, there would be no crime—but the court excluded that evidence as *irrelevant*."

This same brief went on to note, "The government admits that a good-faith belief in the donation's legitimacy would have been a defense to all counts—but the court excluded Singer's stock pitch to that effect and even Wilson's own statements indicating that he had fallen for it." As Magistrate Judge Kelley recognized, "all of this evidence was plainly relevant."

---

32   *Kotteakos v. United States*, 328 U.S. 750 (1946).

> Finally, if regaling the jury with days of testimony about *other* misconduct by *other* parents was not bad enough, the court precluded Wilson from presenting evidence at the core of his defense. The Government admits that if USC had condoned side-door donations, there would be no crime—but the court excluded that evidence as *irrelevant*. And the Government admits that a good-faith belief in the donations' legitimacy would have been a defense to all counts—but the court excluded Singer's stock pitch to that effect, and even Wilson's statements indicating he had fallen for it. On all these points, the Government struggles to defend Judge Gorton's rulings and instead throws as many alternative grounds as it can muster against the wall. None sticks. As Magistrate Judge Kelley recognized, all of this evidence was plainly relevant. As Judge Saris illustrated in

The trial judge excluded all the USC and other relevant evidence that proved my innocence. Toward the end of the trial, the judge seemed frustrated that we wanted to continue to try to submit other evidence (as offers of proof for the appeals court record at a minimum). He ruled against all our remaining evidence en masse, sustaining *expected* government objections without even knowing what the evidence was or what the prosecutors' future objections to each piece of evidence were going to be. This is an excerpt from the trial transcripts (Ms. Papenhausen was one of our lawyers, and the judge is labeled "the Court"):

```
17        MS. PAPENHAUSEN: We didn't quite get to the point of
18   introducing all of these, your Honor.
19        THE COURT: If they haven't been so ruled, I will rule
02:22 20  en masse that the objections are sustained. Why don't you read
21   the numbers.
```

THE SCANDAL WITHIN THE SCANDAL

In a criminal trial, where a defendant's liberty is at stake, many judges would give wide latitude to the defense and defense evidence. If my trial were supposed to be an example of how justice was blind, I would hate to see what could happen if justice (or the judge) took their blindfold off.

***

After the trial was over, a former senior member from the Boston US attorney's office said to a colleague at their new law firm, "We were surprised at how supportive the judge was to our case." (They didn't realize that the colleague they confided in was someone who knew me.) Shockingly, this judge was so supportive to the prosecutors that *even they* were surprised.

Once the judge effectively began rubber-stamping their every motion, the prosecutors became emboldened and made even more outrageous objections. At one point in the trial when our lawyers tried to give additional evidence on a topic, the judge asked the prosecutors, "Aren't you going to object to that?" Leslie and I asked ourselves that day, "How was this fair?" How can a judge prompt the prosecutors to object? Of course, we did not understand any of this at the time the judge was "selected," but that is what judge shopping can do for a prosecutor.

A judge is the key check and balance against an overreaching prosecutor. With a highly supportive, handpicked judge, this check-and-balance role no longer functions as intended, and the already-formidable power of a prosecutor becomes as close to absolute as one can get. As Lord Acton noted, the consequences of absolute power can be corrupting.

***

Another small example from the arraignment hearing in Boston gives some insight on the Boston prosecutors' near-absolute power and hubris.

These hearings were a media frenzy as dozens of parents, including Lori Laughlin and Felicity Huffman, came to Boston to enter a plea in this case. The gauntlet of camera crews outside the courthouse doors was painful to experience and difficult to navigate.

After the other defendants entered their pleas, they all left the courthouse to catch their flights back home to California and elsewhere. Leslie and I, as the only locals, didn't have any planes to catch, so our schedules were flexible. We decided to wait inside the courthouse to let the media throngs die down before we drove home. We didn't want to pay our lawyer to wait with us, so we said it was OK for him to leave.

Leslie and I stayed alone in the courthouse until the media throngs subsided. Just before we were going to leave, Leslie went to the restroom. Moments after I was alone in the empty side hallway, one of the senior prosecutors approached me. I was surprised when he came up to speak with me without my lawyer being there.

He told me that if I pleaded guilty, he could get me a deal to have my sentence recommendation reduced. He said that the money we had pledged to Singer but had not yet paid could be excluded from the "sentencing guidelines." He said he would have to get it signed off by the top government attorney, but he was sure that if I took a deal now, he could make that work.

I had no idea what "sentencing guidelines" were, and I kind of winced at him in shock. I said something like, "I'm not going to plead guilty, because I didn't do anything wrong." As Leslie starting to return from the restroom, I remember saying something like, "Besides, isn't it against the rules for you to be talking to me without my lawyer?" For as long as I live, I'll never forget the smirk on his face and his reply as he shook his head.

"Who do you think makes the rules?"

It was a line that epitomized the haughty indifference they held toward the very principles they were supposed to uphold. I was dumbfounded by his brazen cockiness. I immediately told Leslie what he said and called my lawyer that night to relay what had happened. I knew there was nothing we could do since it would be his word against mine, and no judge would do anything without proof.

That's the type of thing that some unscrupulous prosecutors do. The Texas prison experience and bail hearings had already desensitized me to their extremely dirty tactics. But that was over the phone. This brazen act was directly in my face. In that moment, we understood just how warped and extreme our fight for justice had become. This was not a battle for the truth; it was a battle rigged and corrupted by power to defeat me at any cost.

***

Years later, after our appeals case was heard (and I could speak briefly with the media), I was approached outside the courtroom by a *Law360* reporter and shared this experience. The reporter also separately interviewed my lawyer to confirm that I related this incident to them that same night it happened years ago. (He wanted to get the facts about this story before publishing it.) The reporter noted his confirmation in their story.

The reporter also reached out to the former prosecutor, who of course "categorically denied" that he or anyone else ever approached me in the courthouse without my lawyer present.

Why would I make up such a story? Especially if I couldn't share it publicly for several years? More importantly, why would I call my lawyer that night to relate what had happened if it weren't true? This was just a small taste of the abuse of power that was yet to come.

Lord Acton's famous warning, "Power tends to corrupt, and absolute power corrupts absolutely," once an abstract concept, had become our grim reality.

The Fine Art of Judge Shopping

With a highly supportive judge in place, the prosecutors now effectively had absolute power.

Chapter 12

THE PROOF IS IN THE POLYGRAPH

FBI and CIA Leaders Reveal the Truth

Fighting against the absolute power of the prosecutors was daunting. We also worried about the worst worst-case scenario—me passing away from a heart attack or stroke from all the stress before my trial even began. We wanted to document and preserve the truth in an indisputable way to clear our family's name in the event I didn't make it to trial to defend myself against the false allegations.

***

> Allegations, especially those made by federal prosecutors, immediately taint a defendant's motives and any actions to defend themselves. After someone is charged, the presumption of innocence becomes a presumption of guilt. Many people, me included, assume that prosecutors would not charge an innocent person; given their high conviction rates, where there is smoke, there must be fire.
>
> **Mahatma Gandhi**
> "The moment there is suspicion about a person's motives, everything he does becomes tainted."

THE SCANDAL WITHIN THE SCANDAL

> Gandhi said, "The moment there is suspicion about a person's motives, everything he does becomes tainted." Once charged by federal prosecutors, a cloud of suspicion hangs over your head, and your ability to correct the record is impaired by the very fact that you were charged. We understood the general skepticism, but understanding doesn't make the sting and frustration to an innocent person any less painful.

***

We also worried that public suspicions could linger, even if the trial verdict were "not guilty." Not guilty does not mean innocent; cynics could say I got off on a technicality. For us, this wasn't a fight for "not guilty"; we wanted to go further and prove our innocence. We thought about one of the few tools that could reveal the truth and even outlast me if I did have a heart attack: the polygraph.

***

My personal philosophy in every important pursuit, from raising our children to turning around a business to fighting for what's right, is to leave no stone unturned. Growing up under the circumstances I did could have pushed me in one of two vastly different directions—either repeating a cycle of dysfunction and poverty or rising above it and becoming stronger because of it. I chose the latter.

I consciously overinvested in our children's education and development to try to break that vicious cycle. I considered myself fortunate to be able to spend the time I did with our kids during their formative years; a lot of dads don't have that choice. This image below, a four-foot-tall foam-board birthday card that my son created for me in 2009, captures some of the things he enjoyed doing together. He was fourteen then, and I still smile as I read the sentiments and memories this birthday card captured.

My 100 favorite things I love to do with you

Sunset on the widow's walk with you	duck boat with you
Trips to marthards vineyard with you	clam chowder with you
Lobster potting with you	fennial hall with you
Water slide with you	Frisbee with you
Jumpee with you	puzzles with you
You watching me at my water polo games	tire swing with you
You cheering me on at swim meets	freedom trail with you
Treasure hunts with you	squaw island with you
Ice cream with you	sand castles with you
Ghiradeli square with you	camping out with you
Baxters with you	Grammy's beach with you
National sea shore beaches with you	Movies with you
Poker games with you	baxters with you
Movies with you	driving the boat with you
Dive in theatre with you	going to the movies with you
Joke shop with you	dive in theatre with you
Egg Island with you	jumping the raft with you
Ghost tours with you	waterslide with you
Telling scary stories with you	lobster with you
Cookouts with you	lobstering with you
Mini golfing with you	4 seas with you
Sailing with you	chess with you
Whale museum with you	water basketball with you
Fudge store with you	magic tricks with you
Going to Nantucket with you	basketball with you
Bike riding with you	my swim from Alcatraz with you
Beachwitches with you	the black cat with you
Frienifies with you	
Fishing with you	tubing with you
Red sox games with you	murdicks fudge with you
Mad marthas with you	Mikes pastry north end with you
Tubing with you	driving the think with you
Dunkin donuts with you	Going to the beach
Beach club with you	swimming with you
Shopping with you	fishing with you
Walking the jedi with you	Surfing with you
Tennis with you	golfing with you
Riding bikes with you	soccer with you
Skiing with you	road trips with you
Scuba diving with you	deep sea fishing with you
Newport mansions with you	biking with you
Boating with you	snorkeling with you
Planning vacations with you	reading books with you
Sandcastles with you	lightning storms with you
Fireworks with you	4th of july parade with you
Haloween with you	tennis with you
Smores with you	bonfires with you
Kayaking with you	celebrating your birthday
Giants games with you	haunted tours of boston
Treasure hunts with you	Halloween in hillsborough

Leslie and I were actively involved in each of our children's lives, and we tried to do all we could to be good role models and instill the right values. What sickens us most about this case is how the prosecutors intentionally smeared our children's reputations with the immoral acts of others and implied that our children too were unqualified, were test cheaters, and so forth.

It was one thing for social media trolls that make false accusations. The original source for most of the criticism was from federal prosecutors tarring our school-age children in the media. Going after me was one thing; attacking our children in such a high-profile and unethical way was repugnant.

***

To go beyond "not guilty" and prove my innocence, I wanted to take a polygraph test. Several legal experts said that was a bad idea. It wouldn't be admissible at trial (unless the government agreed to let it in), and if I passed, the government would never agree to that. That alone seemed odd. If this was about the truth, and it was done in a credible, high-quality way, why wouldn't the government let the evidence in?

Friends also warned me, "What if you're nervous or stressed when you take the test and fail?" Word could get out, and it would be difficult to keep *that* a secret. A bad result could be leaked and used against me in the media as well. It was a "heads: I lose, and tails: the government wins" type of situation.

Yes, I was concerned the polygraph machine could mistake my nervousness for guilt. However, the benefits outweighed the risks; it could be concrete evidence of my innocence. I had never taken a polygraph before and only knew what I had seen on television. I was told that shady polygraph operators give the industry a bad rap because they can be bought to give you the result you want. To make my polygraph tests credible, I couldn't just hire any examiner.

My brother provided an amazing amount of help throughout this ordeal from the first day in Texas to today. His unwavering support and expertise helped us get through this nearly impossible situation. So when it came time to find the world's best polygraph experts, I asked for his help.

We looked for someone whose credentials and integrity were impeccable. After a few days of research, we found him. His name was Kendall Shull,

The Proof Is in the Polygraph

shown below—the former head of the FBI's worldwide polygraph division and the only holder of a master's degree in polygraph. His experience and integrity were beyond reproach. We hoped he was someone who could help make my truthfulness irrefutable. My brother reached out to his legal connections and hired Mr. Shull.

KENDALL SHULL
FORMER CHIEF
FBI NATIONAL POLYGRAPH PROGRAM

Once Mr. Shull learned about the high-profile nature of my case, he suggested that we have the results independently reviewed by two more experts. The man he recommended as the primary quality control reviewer was a polygraph legend, Don Krapohl, shown below. Don served as deputy director of the polygraph academy and was team leader at the CIA's global polygraph program.

Whether I passed or failed, it would be impossible to argue the integrity and veracity of the results with these two men involved. Mr. Shull suggested we even

DON KRAPOHL
FORMER HEAD OF CIA GLOBAL POLYGRAPH DEPARTMENT
LED FEDERAL GOV'T POLYGRAPH TRAINING SCHOOL

go a step further and have a third independent reviewer, a former supervisor in the FBI's Washington, DC, polygraph unit. He said that this triple review would be unprecedented (he had never done a triple quality review in his career) and that it would be difficult for anyone to argue with the accuracy of the results.

***

THE SCANDAL WITHIN THE SCANDAL

The federal government conducts more than fifty thousand polygraph tests each year across the FBI, CIA, Department of Defense, etc., and Mr. Krapohl's team trained the examiners that performed those tests for over a decade. Even my local post office manager told me that he had to take a government polygraph test when there was a mail theft problem in his region several years back. Clearly the federal government believes in polygraphs—at least when they are administered properly.

Mr. Shull began his examination by applying multiple straps and monitoring devices. He connected me to chest bands to measure my breathing rate, a blood pressure cuff on my arm to measure blood pressure and heart rate, a galvanometer attached to my fingers to monitor sweat gland activity, a pressure-sensitive seat cushion to ascertain if I was squirming in the chair, and so forth.

This screenshot image is me attached to the machine with Mr. Shull behind me administering one of the tests. The electronic data is recorded digitally and printed on the paper chart.

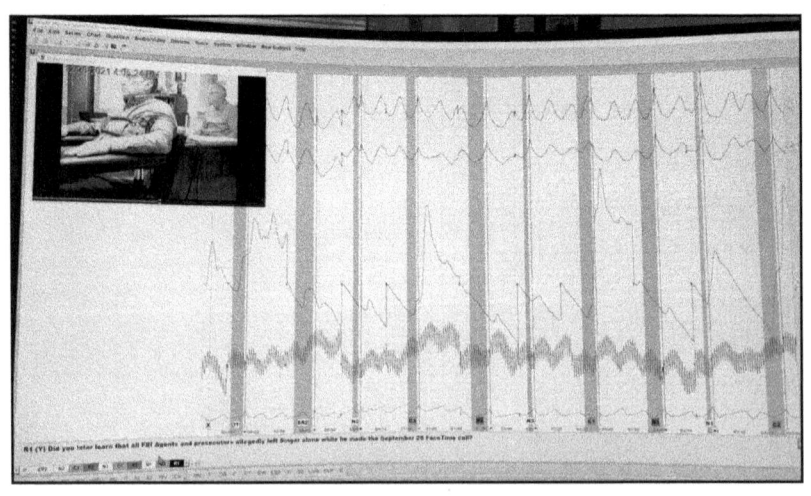

Forget what you may have seen on TV or in the movies—the process of taking a polygraph test, especially from one of the most qualified examiners on the planet, is very intimidating. While I was 100 percent innocent and

170

volunteered to take the test, I was still nervous. What if my nervousness made me fail?

Before the real questions began, Mr. Shull needed to establish a baseline for when I was telling the truth and when I was lying so the machine could be properly calibrated. He asked me to pick a number in my head between three and eight. Then he asked me to reply "no" each time he asked me if that was the number I had selected. He proceeded to go through every number, one at a time, from three to eight, asking me if it was the number I picked.

Five of my answers were obviously the truth, and one answer was a lie. But that simple lie was enough for the sensitive equipment to signal to him, from my body's reactions, that I was lying for that number. I remember being amazed that the measurement equipment could detect a lie about something so innocuous as a meaningless number I had just picked. Yet the equipment was so sensitive, he was able to tell which number I had selected.

All the questions had to be phrased in a yes-or-no format. They could not be open-ended questions like how I felt or why something happened. The process wasn't quick either, because each question was restated and asked in three different ways. For instance, there could be a question like, "Did you approve of Rick Singer putting fraudulent information in your child's college application?" This question could then be restated as "Are you telling me the truth about whether or not Singer put anything false in your child's application?" or "Did you agree to have Singer put anything fraudulent in your child's application?"

He then repeated each set of three restated questions three separate times. So each core question became nine questions in total, all monitored by state-of-the-art technology trained to identify any minor changes in your body's normal breathing or pulse rate or skin sweat, and so forth.

There was a pause in between each of the nine questions to allow my body to return to a baseline level. The entire process (including the admin and equipment hookup) from start to finish for a given core question took about an hour. With some of the waivers signed and calibration done, each subsequent core question took about forty-five minutes.

Mr. Shull told me before we met in person that most participants only got tested on one or two core questions. I came to him with several questions that I wanted to answer to help prove my innocence. I wanted this expert to prove (or disprove) that I was telling the truth about every important aspect of my case.

Mr. Shull asked me questions about my children's test scores, our meetings with the USC coach and a separate athletic development director at USC to verify donating through Singer's organization was fine with USC, my son's merits as a Division I athlete, and so forth.

At the end of the first full day, I wanted to continue and have Mr. Shull ask me more questions about even more topics. Mr. Shull told me that he had never tested someone for two straight days throughout his entire career. I said that it was extremely important for me to prove my innocence on every aspect of this case possible; he agreed to continue into day two.

The tests were more stressful and physically demanding than I had imagined. I never even thought to ask if I passed or failed a test. I was confident that I was telling the truth. Several days later, Mr. Shull told me that it was one of the small clues about the truthfulness of someone who is taking the tests.

If the first thing someone does after taking a test is ask, "Did I pass?" that can be a warning sign. When someone knows they are telling the truth, he said, they don't ask. As Mr. Shull said in a videotaped recording of these sessions, "John never asked."[33]

I kept reminding myself why I was there—I was doing this for my family's honor and our kids' futures. I had done everything possible for two decades to make sure our children were protected and never experienced the abuse and pain that I did as a child.

---

33 A video recording of Mr. Shull is available on the website www.scandalwithinthescandal.com.

But now, because of something I was falsely accused of doing, it seemed like the entire world was falsely denigrating our children. I remember thinking in those moments in between the tests, while I was hooked up to all those devices sitting in the chair, "God, I hope this helps our kids."

I was optimistic that I passed, but it would be weeks before I would see the results. Mr. Shull was stone-faced and the ultimate professional. The monitors that displayed the data interpreting my responses faced him so he could see in real time how I was doing, but he revealed nothing with his expressions—no feedback whatsoever for two full days.

***

It's hard to find a comparison for Mr. Krapohl; he is one of the world leaders in polygraphs. Two lawyers from the JAG Corps (the Judge Advocate General's Corps), a group of military lawyers that represents soldiers and the military, said, "Don Krapohl is the best there is." (Polygraph test results are allowed in military trials.) They said, "Everybody in the polygraph business knows him. He is a legend. If you pass a test that he was a part of, it's a slam dunk. If your case were a military trial, it would have been immediately dismissed."

Two weeks after taking the tests, I received an email with the results. Each test question had a summary page and a multipage report breaking down the details of the data. I had passed everything with no signs of deception. There wasn't a single inconclusive result or score, no gray area. I passed every relevant question. Here is a sample of some of the questions and answers that I passed.

THE SCANDAL WITHIN THE SCANDAL

Former Chief, FBI National Polygraph Program — Plus Attachment

ADDENDUM – POLYGRAPH QUESTIONS AND ANSWERS

Question	Answer
Did you agree with Singer to put any fraudulent materials into any of your children's college application documents?	No.
Prior to 2019, did you ever read the athletic profile that Singer prepared for your son in 2014?	No.
Before college did your son play water polo for top 10-20 nationally ranked teams?	Yes.
At the time you paid money to Singer, did you know Singer's college application process was illegal?	No.
Did Singer tell you that contributions to his charitable organization were totally pass through to the university programs?	Yes.
Did you verify with the USC coach, a separate USC administrator and your tax advisors that making donations through Singer's organization was legitimate?	Yes.
Did a senior USC athletic administrator tell you that your donations through Singer's organizations were appropriate?	Yes.
Did you bribe or direct anyone else to bribe any college official to violate their college admissions policies?	No.
Did you agree for anyone to change the results of any of your children's college entrance exams?	No.
Did one of your daughters get a perfect score on her college entrance exam?	Yes.
Did all of your children score in the top 92-99% on their college entrance exams?	Yes.
Did you verify that each of your children's test scores put them in the middle 50% range or above for their targeted colleges?	Yes.
Is HPC Inc. your wholly owned Sub S corporation where all donations and income are 100% consolidated with your personal tax returns?	Yes.
Does HPC have a multi-year history of making donations to various charities?	Yes.
Did your tax experts tell you the Key Worldwide Foundation was an IRS approved charitable organization?	Yes.

Mr. Shull paid me the ultimate compliment, saying, "John, I have never seen anybody in my career take as many polygraph tests as you have and be as passionate about wanting to prove they are telling the truth as you."

Proving my innocence wasn't just about me; it was about protecting our children and our family's legacy. It was about giving our children the respect and dignity they deserved. I wanted them to know that I would do everything in my power to defend them, to shield them from this nightmare. I would sit through a hundred polygraph tests if that's what it took.

I was humbled by how passionate Mr. Shull was about my truthfulness. He said, "People may think you're lying and that you committed fraud, but I know that you didn't and that you're telling the truth." He wrote this public support letter to Judge Sorokin at my sentencing.

THE SCANDAL WITHIN THE SCANDAL

Honorable Judge Sorokin
U.S. District Court
One Courthouse Way
Boston, Massachusetts, 02210

My name is Kendall Shull, and I am writing this letter in support of John Wilson in advance of his sentencing. As the former Chief and Program Manager of the FBI's entire polygraph program, I fully understand the importance of establishing if someone is telling the truth and have seen firsthand how an individual wrongfully accused of a crime faces irrevocable damage in all aspects of their life — perhaps most deeply within their family.

With no personal knowledge of or connection to this case, I was requested to conduct multiple tests on John Wilson as it related to the accusations against him in the Varsity Blues college admissions scandal. I approached this assignment as I do all cases, with the sole purpose of determining the truth.

The process of testing John Wilson was extensive. I am not sure I've spent as much time or performed as many tests on a single individual in one day in my entire career. He was adamant about his truthfulness; he suggested multiple areas for additional examination that he wanted tested to prove his innocence beyond the primary accusations of fraud, bribery, and conspiracy. I was astonished by his confidence that he would pass every single test. As a test regarding a particularly relevant issue ended and another began, I never shared the results with him. Due to the nature of the tests, the potential for national coverage, and the personal impact on his life and family, I made every effort to conduct each test to the absolute highest standards in order to withstand any future scrutiny.

I have played a significant role in many high profile national and international FBI cases during my career. John Wilson's case reminded me of another case with someone who was wrongfully accused that I handled years ago: Brian Kelley — a CIA agent who was suspected of passing critical secrets to the Russians in the 1990s. No matter how unwavering I was about the results of the polygraph tests I conducted, that Brian Kelley was innocent, everyone working on this counterespionage case thought that Mr. Kelley somehow "beat" my tests. He was sent home on administrative leave and a cloud of doubt and shame surrounded him. He was cleared a few months later when FBI agent Robert Hanson was exposed as the actual Russian spy. By then, Mr. Kelley's professional life had been destroyed and his personal life severely impacted.

Just like in Mr. Kelley's case, I know John Wilson is telling the truth.

I administered, thoroughly reviewed and scored John Wilson's tests myself. In an effort to continue remaining impartial and certify the results beyond a shadow of doubt, I also commissioned two other experts to review my work, Don Krapohl, the former head of the CIA's global polygraph department and one of the world's most recognized leaders in credibility assessment as well as a separate former polygraph supervisor from the FBI's Washington headquarters. They both confirmed what I already knew to be true: John Wilson was telling the truth about each relevant question on every test.

John Wilson was wrongfully charged and convicted. His appeal overturned every one of the fraud, bribery, and conspiracy charges. It's unfortunate that all of the facts related to the remaining tax conviction did not come into evidence during his trial. Although his tax conviction remains, I am confident that John Wilson never knowingly or intentionally broke any laws nor violated any college admission policies.

I sincerely hope that the truth does ultimately prevail and that I may have played some part in clearing John Wilson's name.

Kendall Shull
Kendall Shull,

We wanted to share the polygraph results with the world, but the judge prohibited us from trying our case in public. Prosecutors were supposed to follow the same rules, but they were allowed to go on talk shows and speak about the case, even threatening parents with more charges on TV if they did not plead guilty. It didn't stop there. The former head of the Boston office for the Department of Justice went so far as to create a one-hour podcast bragging about how much media they were able to generate about this case.

These conclusive polygraph results, performed by one of the top examiners in the world and independently quality-reviewed by two other renowned government experts, should have been the golden ticket to get the Boston federal prosecutors to start a dialogue and possibly drop the charges.

The prosecutors did get access to all my polygraph data as part of a public lawsuit I filed against Netflix before my trial even began (more on that in a later chapter). However, the prosecutors didn't even want to meet to discuss the test results. I took that as shocking proof the prosecutors weren't really interested in the truth or justice—at least as it related to my case.

Because I refused to take a plea deal, the prosecutors seemed to be waging a scorched-earth battle to crush me and destroy my children's hard-earned credentials and reputations. In hindsight, to the extent that the government falsely charged and used me as the venue hook to boost their own careers, they needed me to plead guilty or be convicted at trial to cover up these misdeeds.

Dropping the charges could lead the media and the public to question why the prosecutors indicted me in the first place. That investigation could uncover the dark side of why and how an innocent family was being used by the Boston prosecutors to win turf battles for venue and career gains.

Whatever the prosecutors' motivations to not even meet to discuss the polygraph results, I was happy that I had these test results. If the worst worst-case scenario happened and I died before my trial, Leslie and our children would have these polygraph results to help clear their names.

Although I passed multiple polygraph tests, conducted by one of and reviewed by two of the government's top polygraph leaders, the prosecutors smugly dismissed all the results as self-serving.

THE SCANDAL WITHIN THE SCANDAL

Subsequent letter by Kendall Shull with additional context
December 2024

"In life, there are moments when the truth alone is not enough—it needs to be irrefutable. For John, this was one of those moments. When false accusations threatened to destroy his family and everything he had built, he wasn't content with simply convincing people he was "not guilty." John wanted to prove his innocence beyond any doubt. As the former Chief and Program Manager of the FBI's worldwide polygraph program and the only holder of a master's degree in polygraph, I was uniquely qualified to help make John's truthfulness undeniable.

I have administered or supervised thousands of polygraph tests for the FBI over decades. In all that time, I have never seen anyone take as many tests and be so passionate about wanting to prove they were telling the truth across so many areas as John. This was not just about clearing his name; he wanted to protect his children and family from the stigma of false accusations. This case was so high profile, that I had all of John's test results triple quality reviewed by Don Krapohl, the former Deputy Director of the Federal Government's polygraph training school and the former team leader of the CIA's global polygraph program and by a separate former head of the FBI's Washington DC polygraph office.

I know that John is telling the truth about every aspect of this case. I am so confident in this fact that I volunteered to testify at John's sentencing hearing."

Chapter 13

SMEARED BY A STREAMING GIANT

A Netflix "Documentary" Causes Worldwide Defamation

We did find a good use for the polygraph test results several months later in early 2021, when for the second time in two years, I was attacked and falsely smeared by another Goliath: Netflix. This soul-crushing kick to the gut was delivered by the number one streaming service in the world in the form of a purported "documentary" called *Operation Varsity Blues: The College Admissions Scandal.*

***

> A documentary normally refers to a nonfiction film which provides an accurate report about real world events. In recent years, media companies have blurred the lines between fact and fiction in documentaries to create more sensational content and maximize viewership and profits. The example below compares an image we sent to Netflix before their film's release with what they aired.
>
> When Netflix announced plans to release their documentary about Operation Varsity Blues, our lawyers sent them a 550-page letter which included many of the publicly available exculpatory facts in my case as well as the polygraph test results—weeks *before* their release date. Netflix went ahead and released their film anyway. Imagine how our son felt being depicted as a fake athlete by this scrawny boy.

THE SCANDAL WITHIN THE SCANDAL

***

The notice letter was quite clear that our case was different from the other charged parents in the case. In fact, while the charges against me were similar to the other parents, the actual allegations and facts in my case were completely different from all the other parents. The six-page cover letter and single-page addendum with the polygraph results summarized the issues well and is included in its entirety below.

Smeared by a Streaming Giant

Todd & Weld LLP

Howard M. Cooper
Email: hcooper@toddweld.com

March 5, 2021

Via Email

Netflix, Inc.
ATTN: David Hyman, Esq., General Counsel
100 Winchester Circle
Los Gatos, CA 95032
dhyman@netflix.com

Re: **"Operation Varsity Blues: The College Admissions Scandal"**

All:

Please be informed that this office represents the Wilson family, which is comprised of John Wilson, his wife Leslie Wilson, and their three children (together, the "Wilson family").

We write in connection with Netflix's upcoming broadcast of a documentary entitled **"Operation Varsity Blues: The College Admissions Scandal**," which is currently scheduled to begin streaming worldwide to viewers on March 17, 2021. Based upon pre-publication publicity concerning the documentary, we seek both to ensure that the documentary is truthful and accurate of and concerning the Wilson family and to place Netflix on notice that, if it is not, the Wilson family will consider their legal options including a lawsuit seeking damages for defamation.

As you know, Mr. Wilson is a defendant in *United States v. Colburn*, 19-cr-10080, a matter which arises from the so-called "Varsity Blues" investigation currently pending in federal court in Boston. Mr. Wilson is innocent. He was taken advantage of by a highly skilled, confessed con artist and is waiting for his day in court to prove his innocence. The case against Mr. Wilson is made up of out-of-context email fragments and deliberately ambiguous sound bites, neither of which tells the whole story. While there may be no shortage of bad actors caught up in the college admissions scandal, Mr. Wilson and his family are not among them.

While there is little publicly available information concerning the documentary's specific content, it is clear from Netflix's pre-publication promotional material that it will feature what Netflix describes as "an innovative combination of interviews and narrative recreations of the FBI's wiretapped conversations between Singer and his clients."[1] Mr. Wilson was one of those clients whose calls with Singer were recorded by the FBI. As such, we have reason to believe

---

[1] https://www.washingtonpost.com/local/education/netflix-doc-to-examine-man-behind-college-admissions-scandal/2021/02/22/d9bc94c0-7516-11eb-9489-8f7dacd51e75_story.html

---

Todd & Weld LLP • Attorneys at Law • One Federal Street, Boston, MA 02110 • T: 617.720.2626 • F: 617.227.5757 • www.toddweld.com

THE SCANDAL WITHIN THE SCANDAL

Todd & Weld LLP

March 5, 2021
Page 2 of 7

the documentary will make reference to Mr. Wilson and, in so doing, make potentially defamatory suggestions of fact and innuendo of and concerning the entire Wilson family. Accordingly, it is critically important that any reference to the Wilson family and the government's case against Mr. Wilson accurately reflect the government's actual allegations against Mr. Wilson, and not lump him and his family in with the other defendants facing different allegations, many of whom have admitted to wrongdoing. By way of illustration only, neither Mr. Wilson nor his children are accused of participating in any kind of standardized test cheating, "photoshopping" photos for fake athletic profiles, or making a payment to any coach or any other university employee.

On the contrary, Mr. Wilson's son in fact was a star athlete, an invited member of the United States Olympic water polo development program, and his grades and test scores were more than sufficient to gain admission at his chosen school. He was a starter on multiple top 10-20 nationally ranked teams, and was approached by college water polo and swimming teams. The son's high school coach (himself an Olympic-qualifying player) collaborated with the Wilson family and was in contact with the USC coaches in regard to the son's participation in USC water polo. Most telling is the fact that the Wilson's son was a member of the USC water polo team.

Similarly, the Wilson children are all academically gifted, with his daughters achieving legitimate scores in the 99th percentile on their college entrance exams. One of his daughters achieved a perfect score on her exam.

Mr. Wilson did not seek out Singer. Instead, he was referred to Singer by a world-renowned financial advisory firm. This firm told Mr. Wilson that Singer was a highly reputable college admissions counselor used by many of their other clients and that he offered legitimate services. Singer consistently assured Mr. Wilson that the side door program was fully legitimate, and there was no reason for Mr. Wilson to believe otherwise. Nonetheless, the Wilsons have been unfairly branded as cheaters and criminals in the media, without regard to the true facts. We urge Netflix not to contribute to, or amplify, this defamatory portrayal of the Wilson family, which would only result in broader and irreparable reputational harm and emotional distress to the family members, and for which Netflix would bear legal responsibility.

Set forth below are the true and accurate facts, supported by documents, all of which are publicly available to Netflix from readily accessible court filings. Together, we believe they make clear that Mr. Wilson is innocent and has been falsely accused and that any suggestion that his children benefitted from his wrongdoing and were not capable of gaining admission to college on their own is not true.

Netflix is hereby placed on notice of the following:[2]

---

[2] For your convenience, we have attached the cited materials herewith.

Todd & Weld LLP • Attorneys at Law • One Federal Street, Boston, MA 02110 • T: 617.720.2626 • F: 617.227.5777 • www.toddweld.com

Todd & Weld LLP

March 5, 2021
Page 3 of 7

i) Mr. Wilson's son was a highly competitive high school and club water polo player, *and was a member of the water polo team at the University of Southern California* ("USC"). See **Exhibit A**, Dkt. No. 699 at pp. 1-2 and Ex. 3, Ex. 9; **Exhibit B**, Dkt. No. 805 at p. 2; **Exhibit C**, Dkt. No. 995 at Ex. 11 and Ex. 3, p. 5.[3]

ii) Singer wrote in his own notes that Mr. Wilson's payment to USC was a "*donation to USC program for real polo player,*" **Exhibit C**, Dkt. No. 995 at Ex. 14, p. 2, and told the FBI that he had no recollection of Wilson knowing of any "inaccuracies in his son's athletic profile." **Exhibit B**, Dkt No. 805 at p. 2.

iii) Of the $200,000 that Mr. Wilson intended to donate to USC in connection with his son's admission, Singer stole half, and USC itself (not a coach or any other USC employee) received the other half as planned, acknowledging the gift *in an official USC thank you letter.* **Exhibit A**, Dkt. No. 699 at p. 1 and Ex. 2. Indeed, Singer consistently told Mr. Wilson that all monies paid in connection with his "side door" program went to the schools. **Exhibit D**, Dkt. No. 972-45 at p. 9.

Based on the foregoing, it would not be a fair and accurate report of the proceedings against Mr. Wilson to suggest that Mr. Wilson's son was a "fake athlete," that Mr. Wilson knowingly falsified any aspect of his son's USC application, or that Mr. Wilson paid a "bribe" to a USC coach to facilitate his son's admission. Any such suggestion would be defamatory and would be published with a knowing and reckless disregard for the truth.

Further, as the documentary will apparently feature "re-enactments" of recorded calls between Singer and his clients, you are hereby put on notice that any presentation of any recorded calls featuring Mr. Wilson which does not include the following unrebutted facts available in the public record will necessarily be highly misleading to the audience and defamatory of the Wilson family, and not a fair and accurate report of the proceedings against Mr. Wilson:

i) When Singer and Mr. Wilson discussed possible donations to Harvard and Stanford in connection with Wilson's daughters' college admissions, Singer assured Wilson of the propriety of such donations, including by telling Wilson that he was "going to Harvard next Friday, because the president wants to do a deal with me, because he found out that I've already got four already in, without his help, so he's like . . . 'why would you go to somebody else if you could come to me?'" **Exhibit A**, Dkt. No. 699 at p. 2 and Ex. 4, p. 8.

---

[3] Unless otherwise noted, all references herein to "Dkt. No." are to docket entries in *United States v. Colburn*, 19-cr-10080 (D. Mass. 2019).

Todd & Weld LLP • Attorneys at Law • One Federal Street, Boston, MA 02110 • T: 617.720.2626 • F: 617.227.5777 • www.toddweld.com

Todd & Weld LLP

March 5, 2021
Page 4 of 7

ii) Singer promoted the "side door" as a fully legitimate option, including in a presentation to dozens of management employees at Starbucks' offices. **Exhibit E**, Dkt. No. 1533 at p. 4 and Exs. A-D.

iii) In calls which were recorded without Singer's knowledge and prior to his becoming a government cooperator, Singer described payments made as part of his "side door" program as legitimate donations to universities. Then, once he was cooperating, Singer, at the government's direction, began subtly introducing ambiguous language, including in calls with Mr. Wilson. This purposefully ambiguous language allowed the government to insinuate that Mr. Wilson and other defendants understood payments were going to coaches' personal accounts rather than to those coaches' programs. **Exhibit A**, Dkt. No. 699 at p. 9 and Ex. 10, p. 9.

iv) Singer's own notes reflect that, during a "[l]oud and abrasive call with agents" early on in his cooperation, investigators instructed him to "bend the truth" and get "each person to agree to a lie[,]" by "continu[ing] to ask me to tell a fib and not restate what I told my clients as to where there [sic] money was going -to the program not the coach and that it was a donation and they want it to be a payment." and **Exhibit D**, Dkt. No. 972 at Ex. A, p. 1.

The government's manipulation of Singer's post-cooperation recorded calls with Mr. Wilson was particularly egregious, evincing a deliberate effort to create highly misleading "sound bites" which the government could later take out of context to create the false impression that Mr. Wilson agreed to make illicit payments to university officials. On a September 28, 2018 FaceTime call with the Wilson family to discuss the Wilson daughters' college application process, which took place after Singer's cooperation with the government began, Singer made highly exculpatory statements that continued to reassure the Wilson family of the propriety of the side door program. Singer told them that side door donations, like Mr. Wilson's 2014 contribution to USC's water polo program, were a legitimate and prevalent aspect of college admissions that allowed schools to fund their programs. **Exhibit D**, Dkt. No. 972-43 (Affidavit of John Wilson) at 1-2. Singer explained that schools and teams can admit non-athlete applicants with the necessary academic credentials, if those students worked as assistant managers or in other support roles. *Id.* at 2-3. The government made no record of this FaceTime call, even though Singer made the call from an FBI office at a break during an interview conducted by half a dozen agents and the "Varsity Blues" prosecutors. **Exhibit D**, Dkt. No. 972-44 at 1-2. The government has not disputed Mr. Wilson's evidence concerning the FaceTime call, including his own sworn affidavit, or explained its failure to record the call other than to claim their agents were not present with Singer during the call. **Exhibit F**, Dkt. No. 1141 at 6-7. According to a public pleading, the "[g]overnment have taken steps to remove all traces of this call from text messages, reports, and notes[.]" **Exhibit G**, Dkt. No. 1184 at 1.

Todd & Weld LLP • Attorneys at Law • One Federal Street, Boston, MA 02110 • T: 617.720.2626 • F: 617.227.5777 • www.toddweld.com

Todd&Weld LLP

March 5, 2021
Page 5 of 7

As referenced above, beginning September 29, 2018, and continuing for weeks after the government's "loud and abrasive" instructions to Singer to "bend the truth," **Exhibit D**, Dkt. No. 972 at Ex. A, p. 1, Singer began interjecting incriminating phrases during calls that the government *did* record. An October 15, 2018 call with Wilson included this exchange:

> SINGER: So I know when . . . we get the girls in, it's a done deal and you're gonna take care of your part of it, you're gonna make the payments *to the schools* and the -- *to the coaches*. And that's what I need . . . so I'm not worried about that.
>
> WILSON: Uh, uh, help me understand the logistics? I thought I make the payment to you and you made the payment *to the school*.
>
> SINGER: Correct. That's correct.
>
> WILSON: Oh you said that *I* make the payments *to the schools*.

Exhibit D, Dkt. No. 972-17 (10/15/18 Wilson Tr.) at 9. Singer's references to payments going "to the coaches" are misleading and paint a false picture given his earlier statements to Wilson that, as before, his payments would go to the university. That is precisely what the government agents wanted when they told Singer to "bend the truth" and get "each person to agree to a lie." **Exhibit D**, Dkt. No. 972 at Ex. A, p. 1. Of course, the distinction between a payment to a coach and a payment to a university program is critical where the latter is not a crime. Indeed, the court in another of the Varsity Blues' prosecutions observed that a payment which is received by the university, as opposed to a coach individually, is "not a bribe," and the government's prosecution based on payments to universities is "a case in search of a bribe or a kickback." **Exhibit H**, Transcript of Sentencing in *United States v. Bizzack*, 19-cr-10222, at 15-16.

Finally, Netflix is also hereby put on notice that, in order to establish the truth and to protect his children from false claims, Mr. Wilson has taken the extraordinary step of submitting to a two-day polygraph examination which he passed uniformly. Since the trial of his case has already been delayed over two and a half years, Mr. Wilson took this step in order to clear his family's name should anything happen to him before he can be exonerated at trial. The polygraph examination was conducted by Kendall W. Shull, former Chief and Program Manager of the FBI's Investigation Polygraph Unit, and the results were independently reviewed by Donald J. Krapohl, a former polygraph manager and examiner at the CIA.[4] The results indicate that Mr. Wilson was being truthful in response to all questions asked. The complete set of the results is attached hereto as **Exhibit I**. A complete list of the questions and answers is included in an Addendum to this letter. Those questions and answers included the following:

---

[4] Curriculum vitae for Mr. Shull and Mr. Krapohl are attached hereto as **Exhibits J & K**.

Todd & Weld LLP • Attorneys at Law • One Federal Street, Boston, MA 02110 • T: 617.720.2626 • F: 617.227.5757 • www.toddweld.com

Todd & Weld LLP

March 5, 2021
Page 6 of 7

Question	Answer
At the time you paid money to Singer, did you know Singer's college application process was illegal?	No.
Did you agree with Singer to put any fraudulent materials into any of your children's college application documents?	No.
Did you bribe or direct anyone else to bribe any college official to violate their college admissions policies?	No.
Did you verify with the USC coach, a separate USC administrator and your tax advisors that making donations through Singer's organization was legitimate?	Yes.
Prior to 2019, did you ever read the athletic profile that Singer prepared for your son in 2014?	No.

  At stake in your broadcast is nothing short of the future of the Wilson family from a reputational and emotional health perspective. Mr. Wilson's reputation, and the reputations of his wife and children, have already been tarnished by the media's desire to paint with an unfairly broad brush that lumps all of the "Varsity Blues" defendants together and presumes their guilt. Mr. Wilson is a hardworking, generous person with no prior criminal record who is extremely supportive of his family and his children. Mr. Wilson and the Wilson family have a long record of community service, including Mr. Wilson's fifteen-plus years of service as a board member of Cure Autism Now and Autism Speaks, and charitable contributions which over the past twenty (20) years have been noteworthy and considerable.

  We ask to hear from you in response to this letter as soon as possible, but in any event no later than Friday, March 12, given the March 17 scheduled release date of the documentary. Please forward this letter to counsel for Jon Karmen and Chris Smith, and anyone else who should receive it.

Very truly yours,

Howard M. Cooper

HMC/lmm

cc: The Wilson Family

Todd & Weld LLP • Attorneys at Law • One Federal Street, Boston, MA 02110 • T: 617.720.2626 • F: 617.227.5777 • www.toddweld.com

Netflix not only dismissed the uncontroverted facts in our 550-plus-page letter but also released their movie (on March 17, 2021) *one day* after responding to us (telling us effectively to go pound sand) and saying that their film was not defamatory on March 16, 2021. They released their extremely defamatory film about our family to their then more than 230 million global subscribers and more than 500 million viewers—just a few months before my trial began.

The false portrayal of our son and me, as well as our daughters, was so outrageous and defamatory that we implored our friends and their children not to share what they had seen. The film triggered another round of horrific emotions for us and our children. The overall impact of the film was much worse for our family than all the earlier media we had encountered in many significant ways.

First was how different the content of the film was versus all the prior media coverage. The prior news coverage focused on the Hollywood celebrities. The only good news was that it seemed like my name was only mentioned about 5 percent of the time in the news stories about Varsity Blues.

When I was mentioned, it was usually a minor passing reference with a list of other lesser known parents. In stark contrast, I was depicted as one of the primary characters in the Netflix film. The actor playing me, Roger Rignack, got second billing, right after Matthew Modine, who played Singer. The film intertwined my image and name over and over again with depictions of other parents who had pleaded guilty to unethical acts, thereby creating a misleading narrative that implicated me in the other parents' wrongdoing.

The film selected a dozen other parents who were recorded explicitly acknowledging their guilt and mixed me in to create a toxic swamp of immoral acts. I was front and center in a drama depicting parents who were openly agreeing to cheat on tests, bribe college officials, and fake athletic profiles for kids who didn't even play the sport.

Then the film repeatedly smeared both my children and me. The film showed the actor portraying me—or his voice and captioning showing my name interlaced with depictions of the corrupt acts of others—two dozen times during the film's first twenty-five minutes.

I wasn't just an afterthought or minor mention in a news article. I was one of the most featured parents in the film. Again, the actor portraying me received second billing in the credits only to Matthew Modine (I mention this twice because I still can't believe their drama focused on my son and me so much).

It's bad enough to take my words out of context. Netflix went even further by splicing different conversations from different days to fabricate composite quotes that sounded more incriminating—all while showing on the screen a single date to give the fake quote a sense of legitimacy.

Additionally, the film intentionally truncated my conversations or used portions of a second repeated conversation to deliberately change the meaning of what I actually said.

For example, when I was trying to clarify where to wire the money for my donations, I said to Singer, "So I send the money to you, not to the schools…" The film shows this quote out of context and then cuts to a different parent. This editing clearly misleads a viewer to infer that I never intended to give money to the school.

However, the actual conversation continues, and I say, "…then *you* give the money to the schools." Clearly, I said that Singer would give the money (which I sent him) to the schools. Leaving out this part of the taped conversations deliberately misled the audience. I was simply trying to clarify whether I would send the money directly to the schools or through Singer's IRS-certified charity.

This editing trick was used repeatedly until a typical viewer got the false impression that I was the worst parent in the entire case.

***

The medium itself also amplified the damage. Watching a full-length film leaves a vastly different impression than seeing my name listed as part of a 2,000-word article or mentioned briefly in a newscast focused on Felicity Huffman and other celebrities. I have been told by media experts that the impression and retention of a message embedded as a key part of a film is orders of magnitude greater than the same mention in a traditional news format.

The third and fourth factors which made the Netflix film more harmful were the scale and scope of their streaming network. While many newspapers had audiences in the tens to hundreds of thousands, Netflix had audiences in the tens to hundreds of millions. That is a thousand times difference!

Additionally, international news coverage had largely excluded me; overseas, it was all about the Hollywood stars. Netflix has an international subscriber audience which currently covers 190-plus countries, and their international subscriber base is larger than the US. For an international business executive like me, that also made an enormous difference and had profound implications.

A fifth factor was the constant availability of the movie, unlike the transient news articles or TV broadcasts. An article or news show would hit, then be replaced and buried by other hot stories. The news coverage was painful, but it went away fairly quickly.

The Netflix film remains available for hundreds of millions of viewers to stream twenty-four hours a day, 365 days of the year in over 190 countries. Netflix public statistics showed that millions of viewers were still downloading and watching the film even years after its initial release.

A sixth factor, which became more painful over time, was the permanence, lack of updates, and the legacy that this would create for me and my children. Unlike the news media, which reported on my appeal victory and the prosecutors dropping the overturned charges, Netflix *never* updated their film to correct the record. Our family must endure a permanent legacy of false innuendos and smears, broadcast to a global audience in the hundreds of millions.

The final and most devastating blow was the fact that Netflix rushed the release of their film and ignored the facts in our warning letter (versus incorporating some of our facts into the film) to ride the wave of public interest. They promoted the film heavily and released it to more than 100 million US viewers just a few months *before* my trial began. They clearly poisoned the jury pool about me and my family.

Many people had seen the Netflix film, and the extent of the damage was shocking. I overheard one random parent say before my trial that the parents in the Varsity Blues scandal were "worse than Hitler … because they had murdered every child in America's dreams for college." Since I was depicted as the worst parent in the Netflix film, it felt like a dagger straight to my heart.

It was painful beyond words to describe my shock when I heard how strongly some people felt. The film fueled a resentment and hate toward me and my children that was devastatingly palpable. The false narrative of my son being depicted as a "fake athlete" was the most painful thing to endure.

This "documentary" from a highly trusted source like Netflix portrayed our son as a fraud and fake athlete. In those moments, thousands of hours of his hard work, training and competing at the national level for years, were suddenly wiped out and replaced with fake images of a scrawny kid standing in the shallow end of the pool with a ball in his hand.

Netflix's actions obliterated any chance of a fair trial for me and derailed our son's career before either had the opportunity to begin.

Chapter 14

NO TURNING BACK

Preparing for Trial

The false Netflix "documentary" created an oppressive backdrop of deep public resentment as we fought against every obstacle the government threw against us. The government was doing everything possible to prevent us from obtaining exculpatory evidence in pretrial motions. As we prepared for trial, we had the truth on our side, but would that be enough? We knew we needed a powerful trial strategy.

***

> Whenever you chart a course in any major endeavor, there are usually multiple points where you can take an off-ramp or turn around. However, when fighting against the federal prosecutors in this case, there were no good off-ramps. Anything other than going to trial required me to confess to a crime that I didn't commit, destroy my integrity, impugn my children's reputations, and serve time in prison.
>
> **Franz Kafka**
> "From a certain point onward, there is no longer turning back."

> There are critical junctures in life where you reach a point of no return. As Franz Kafka said nearly one hundred years ago in his novel *The Trial*, "From a certain point onward, there is no longer turning back." We reached that point in the summer of 2021. We never second-guessed our decision to go to trial because we were still (naively) optimistic that the truth would prevail and that we would be given a fair trial.

***

We were more prepared for this battle than any other confrontation I had ever experienced. We had prepared our witnesses, our cross-examination materials for the government's witnesses, and so forth. The lawyers had multiple giant binders of documents with tabs and indexes to use throughout the trial. We were ready to go, and there was no turning back. My overall trial strategy had five key elements.

The first element was to emphasize the uncontroverted public record that my facts were fundamentally different from those of all the other charged parents and that our children were all qualified for admissions on their own hard-earned merits.

The second element was to emphasize the uncontroverted public record that our donations to USC did affect admissions chances and that this was a widespread practice at the school for VIPs, walk-on athletes, and non-player team-support positions.

The third element was to emphasize the uncontroverted public record that Singer told many parents and corporations that both side-door and back-door donations were legitimate and accepted practices at many universities; they were not corrupt or illegal.

The fourth element was to emphasize the uncontroverted public record that showed the context for each email sent and the full transcripts of the recorded calls between Singer and me and my family.

Finally, we wanted to show the jury how the FBI and Boston federal prosecutors had treated me entirely differently during Singer's scripted setup calls versus the calls with all the other parents.

Mike Kendall had assembled an experienced team of highly skilled attorneys and support staff who knew the rules of evidence and had battled the federal government in this very courthouse many times before with a great track record of winning. Our lawyers knew the facts we had were extremely compelling. Good facts translate into a strong defense that should end in a favorable outcome—*if* we were allowed to present our facts to the jury.

***

By the time my trial began on September 8, 2021, it had been exactly 910 days, two and a half years since the two FBI agents greeted me at the Houston airport with handcuffs, placed me under arrest for a felony charge they'd never heard of, and gave me an armed escort into a federal prison.

We knew I was in one hell of a deep public relations hole too. The media barrage and the Netflix "documentary" viewed by tens of millions had done what you'd imagine it would—the public resented *all* the parents in the Varsity Blues scandal with little distinction between any of the parents.

Leslie helped me pick out my suit and tie for each day of the trial. On that first day, I wore a dark-blue suit with a light-blue collared shirt and a dark patterned tie as I sat with my lawyers in the courtroom. Leslie sat one row directly behind me as the jury selection process began. Her presence was a wellspring of strength. Her unwavering support fortified my resolve to face the daunting proceedings ahead.

***

Jury selection, known as voir dire, is a process that allows both sides to question potential jurors to determine the final twelve who will serve. The questions all need to be approved by the judge.

Each side is allowed to dismiss a small number of potential jurors "without cause." Others can be dismissed for cause or a good reason—such as obvious bias or a personal hardship. Given all the negative pretrial publicity, our jury selection felt more like crisis management and finding the least bad choices.

The prosecutors instantly rejected people they perceived as a threat to their outcome. For example, one woman in the candidate pool worked in the admissions office for a local college. She said during the voir dire questioning that giving admissions help to donors was common at the university she worked at—which got her instantly canceled by the prosecutors.

That was a bad blow, because she had intimate knowledge of the inner workings of the admissions process and could have educated the other jurors about the truth of this process.

Another potential juror the prosecutors blocked was a young man who was a high-functioning person on the autism spectrum. The government sent him packing; they knew I had served for nearly fifteen years on the boards of Autism Speaks and Cure Autism Now.

The government argued that this potential juror would be unable to handle this case. We objected. The judge overruled our objections, and this potential juror too was dismissed.

There is no way to describe the feelings you have at the start of a federal trial when it's literally your freedom on the line, especially knowing in your heart that you never knowingly broke any laws. But having seen firsthand how aggressively the prosecutors were willing to play for two and a half years (despite my evidence and polygraph results), guilt or innocence didn't seem to matter to them. It was frightening.

There was at least one juror who admitted that she had seen the Netflix film, and we asked the judge to dismiss her for cause (bias). Both the prosecutor and judge objected, and she was allowed to stay on the jury. It was a huge disappointment.

We weren't delusional; given all the media spin and market research, we knew I was starting in a deep hole with the jury. Everyone knew about this case, and everyone had seen dozens of people plead guilty. Throughout the jury selection process, I kept reflecting on that horrifying quote I overheard from one random father: I was worse than Hitler and had "murdered every child in America's dreams for college."

The selected jurors in my case seemed like honest, decent people. But like anyone, they were susceptible to the constant negative media barrage and the false narratives being spun by the prosecutor, the media, and Netflix.

Plus, a juror's natural inclination would be to think (as I would), "If there's smoke, there must be fire." With thirty other charged parents who had already confessed to felonies, why would Wilson be any different? He must be guilty too. If they, or anyone they knew, had seen the Netflix documentary, they had to believe I was the worst parent by far.

I remember thinking to myself that if I were in a juror's shoes: "Why would the government charge Wilson with nine felonies, far more than Singer or any other parent, if he were innocent? Why would an innocent person get charged by federal prosecutors? At a minimum, Wilson must be guilty of at least something."

The jury selection was complete, and each juror seemed to resent me; not a single juror would look me in the eye. At that point, I was still hopeful that my facts could win them over—so long as we were permitted to share my facts.

***

One small but significant point before the trial began was also very disheartening. I didn't realize it at the time, but it clearly foreshadowed what was yet to come. We asked the judge to exclude the conversation I had in one recorded call with Singer where I mentioned a birthday party I was planning to have at the palace of Versailles—or as Big Sam would say, "Ver-sighhhhh."

When I was living and working in Europe with my family, I learned that Versailles, like many museums, rents out rooms for events. I planned to rent out one of the rooms in the chateau for my birthday to bring my childhood dream to life.

These birthday plans were totally irrelevant to anything in the case. It was simply wealth evidence that could only add fuel to the class warfare fires that the prosecutors were trying to stoke. It could make the jury hate me even more and reinforce the extreme damage that the Netflix film and other media had done.

The judge simply said my lawyers could make the argument that I was only renting out a room in the palace to the jury but that the prosecutors could share this irrelevant and highly inflammatory wealth evidence during the trial.

My plans to fulfill a childhood dream were now being weaponized against me.

**

It was hard to see the process as fair. We weren't allowed to bring in clearly exculpatory evidence about USC practices, yet the prosecutors were permitted to bring in irrelevant and highly prejudicial evidence against me. Our faith in an impartial process was fading even before the trial began.

This was demoralizing. After all, this was a federal courtroom, and the legal system that our founding fathers carefully crafted was intended to be impartial. If only the system lived up to the impartiality standards that the quote etched into the wall of the Boston courthouse said was essential:

"It is essential to the preservation of the rights of every individual, his life, liberty, property, and character, that there be an impartial interpretation of the laws, and administration of justice. It is the right of every citizen to be tried by judges as free, impartial, and independent as the lot of humanity will admit."

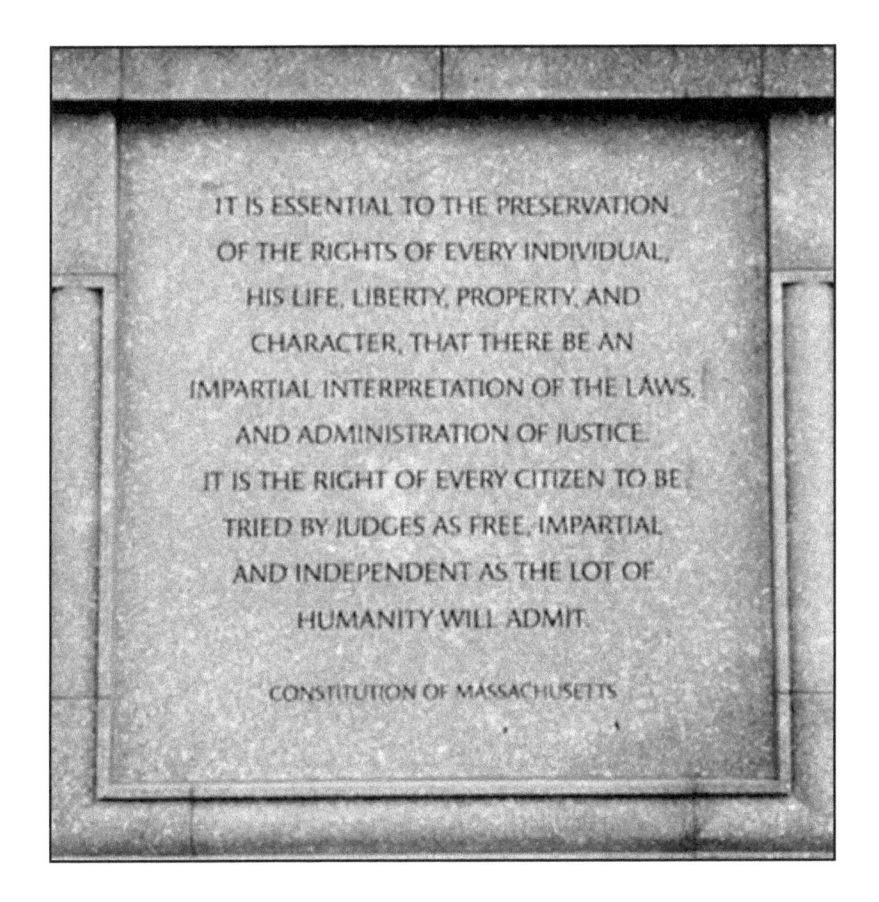

***

THE SCANDAL WITHIN THE SCANDAL

Although the trial was off to a completely unfair start, the support from our group of friends and family was incredible. I can never thank them enough for taking time off from work, in many cases flying to Boston, to support me and our family.

One friend was an amazing standout, Fred Lukens. He has been a friend since early childhood. (He picked tobacco with me when we were children and would tease me about mother's ten-word scream to call me in at night.) He was a constant source of support throughout the process and beyond. The daily contingent of friendly faces really boosted our spirits.

Leslie's late aunt, Anna Loughlin, a former magistrate judge with the state of Massachusetts, was also a great inspiration. She knew our facts and some of the prosecutors and judges in the courthouse. She said she had encountered many corrupt prosecutors and biased judges over the years. She said we should never give them the satisfaction of letting them intimidate us. She said never look down in shame; we had done nothing wrong. She said always, "Hold your heads high."

We took Aunt Anna's advice to heart, walking in and out of that courthouse each day with our heads held high, refusing to let an unjust system break our spirit.

Chapter 15

OUR JUDICIAL NIGHTMARE

Were We in the Wrong Courtroom?

After jury selection, the real trial began. Sitting in the courtroom, not allowed to speak, you're essentially a spectator while your entire life and freedom are in other people's hands. It felt like being tied to the railroad tracks while a freight train was coming right at me—forced to keep my composure, even as the prosecutor repeatedly stabbed his finger in the air at my face, shouting, "You crossed the line."

***

> There is an interesting expression used in legal circles that my appellate lawyer shared. It aptly captured what was done by the prosecutors in my case. He said, "When the law is on your side, you argue the law. If the law isn't on your side, you argue the facts. If the facts aren't on your side, you argue someone else's facts." The third scenario is what happened in my case.
>
> **John Adams**
> "Facts are stubborn things"
> - *Defending the British soldiers on trial for the "Boston Massacre"*

> As John Adams said more than two centuries ago, "Facts are stubborn things." We had the best facts, and if we were allowed to show them to the jury, we would win. The prosecutors knew this all too well. So rather than argue against *my* facts, the prosecutors shared other parents' facts over and over again. They inundated the jury with the corrupt acts of other parents, smearing us through guilt by association.

***

The opening statement by the prosecutors set the stage for their entire strategy. Trial transcripts show that the prosecutors only mentioned my name or referred to the allegations against me 12.2 percent of the time. (In other words, 87.8 percent of the names they referred to in their opening were other parents.) It was shocking how the prosecutors were allowed to poison the jury up front with the corrupt acts of other people.

The government had a list of thirteen witnesses that it was planning to call, and our list had seven names. We remained optimistic about our chances based on the strength of our evidence. Throughout the trial, there was one giant elephant in the room—which was actually a snake who *wasn't* in the room—Rick Singer himself, who was conspicuously absent. The government's key witness, the ringleader of this whole scheme, was not going to testify at any time during the entire trial.

Compounding this challenge, the government blocked our access to Singer for interviews before the trial. This prevented us from uncovering critical details on how each of his setup calls were scripted, what they asked him about each parent's knowledge and culpability, how he may have replied and pushed back, and who was really in the room during that critical yet "missing" FaceTime call.

It seemed to us to be a direct violation of our constitutional right not to be able to confront my accusers. The judge allowed the government to use Singer's recorded tapes without having him take the stand, leaving us unable to challenge or cross-examine the very person at the heart of the allegations against us.

***

The prosecutors began their case with a Bay Area parent unknown to me. He and his wife had both been caught red-handed on taped calls with Singer discussing bribing, cheating on tests, and falsifying applications for their children. They both agreed to testify for the prosecution in exchange for neither having to serve any prison time, plus other benefits.

His testimony went on for two days, and his basic message to the jury was, "If you were smart, you knew Singer was corrupt and committing fraud and bribing coaches." He implied it was common knowledge that Singer was bribing the coaches and faking athletic profiles for kids who didn't even play the sport and that there were people who could cheat on tests for your kids too. *He* did those things, not me.

This parent suggested that I must have known what Singer was doing was illegal since I had a degree from Harvard. He said that anyone who was smart had to be a corrupt coconspirator with him and Singer.

When my lawyers cross-examined him, he said that he had never spoken with me at any time about anything, including Singer. However, each time he was questioned by us or redirected by the prosecutors, he would repeat what seemed like a pre-rehearsed script. Like a wind-up doll, he would say, "Everyone who was smart knew that what Singer was doing was illegal."

This baseless refrain was devastating. It was difficult, if not impossible, to un-ring that bell with the jury. He planted the seeds, right up front, that everyone working with Singer knew he was corrupt, and therefore, they were corrupt. Those seeds took root in the jury's minds and seemed impossible to remove.

Adding to our frustration, we had a complete list of Singer's 1,794 client children (total parent clients were likely over 3,000), and yet we couldn't

THE SCANDAL WITHIN THE SCANDAL

THE KEY
Customer List
all years in QB

Customer	
	1765
	29
	1794

mention the names or even the number of Singer's other, uncharged clients. This is the last page on the spreadsheet of Singer's clients from his company (called the Key) with the names blurred to protect their privacy.

As mentioned previously, the Palo Alto newspaper had published the fact that Singer's clients included many Silicon Valley icons. It would have been helpful to ask the parent on the stand, "Steve Jobs, John Doerr, and Joe Montana were clients of Mr. Singer. They are smart, honest men. Are you saying that since the CEO and cofounder of Apple was smart, he must have known that Singer was corrupt?" Was he really saying that Steve Jobs was knowingly working with a criminal mastermind?

The harm went beyond being able to refer to Singer's other smart and highly respected clients who were not charged with any crimes. It limited our ability to put the entire case into proper context. If the jury and public knew that Singer had 1,750-plus student clients (and over 3,000 parent clients) and that fewer than 2 percent of his clients were charged, it would change the perception about the very nature of the overwhelming majority of Singer's clients and the case.

Instead, we were blocked from sharing this, and the public and trial narrative was that Singer only dealt with corrupt clients. Therefore, anyone who worked with Singer was in on his fraud. We were not allowed to show Singer's client list or tell the jury that more than 98 percent of Singer's clients were never charged. Singer had over three thousand parent clients who trusted him and were victims of his long con scheme—like we were.

For two grueling days, this other California parent went on and on about the corrupt things he did, bribing and cheating and committing fraud, while the prosecution positioned him as the "poster person" for the entire case. During cross-examination, this parent had the audacity to confess that he lied readily to help get his daughter into college but that he would never, ever lie to keep his wife and himself out of prison. The hypocrisy was galling. If he were Pinocchio, he could have poked the judge's eye out.

The Varsity Blues scandal had a face and a voice sitting just feet away from the jury…but the guilty, confessed felon speaking of a nationwide conspiracy, of fraud, of cheating on tests and other criminal behavior who had been caught red-handed committing crimes on the FBI's recorded calls was not me—it was the parent on the stand testifying for the government in exchange for staying out of prison.

While the judge gave the prosecutors wide latitude on the evidence they could introduce about other unrelated parents' immoral acts, he simultaneously blocked our motions to enter evidence that would prove that what the government's witnesses were saying was false. This imbalance in evidentiary rulings was disheartening, alarming, and devastating to my case. It started before the trial began and grew worse as things went on.

For example, there is a category of evidence called impeachment evidence—material that goes to the credibility and truthfulness of what a witness is testifying about. This impeachment evidence is critical when government witnesses make misleading statements or actually lie under oath. In any normal courtroom, impeachment evidence is an exception to the hearsay rule, meaning that you could show the jury other emails from the witness on the stand (emails that the prosecutors didn't offer as evidence) which contradicted the witness's own testimony.

It was shocking that even when we had compelling impeachment evidence proving that a witness wasn't telling the truth, the government and judge blocked it from being used. This destroyed our ability to effectively cross-examine any government witness making false statements to the jury. This happened repeatedly. One small example was a government witness who provided testimony completely inconsistent with the facts, the assistant water polo coach, Casey Moon for USC.

Moon was a key witness for the prosecution. He tried to corroborate their false narrative that our son was not a Division I–level athlete. This assistant coach told the jury under oath that he "never saw [our son] after the first day of practice."[34]

This was not true, and there were multiple pieces of evidence to show that. One piece of hard evidence that this wasn't true was the USC team photo that I had shown before. Here stood Moon—just four feet in front of our son—weeks after the first day, posing together for the team photo.

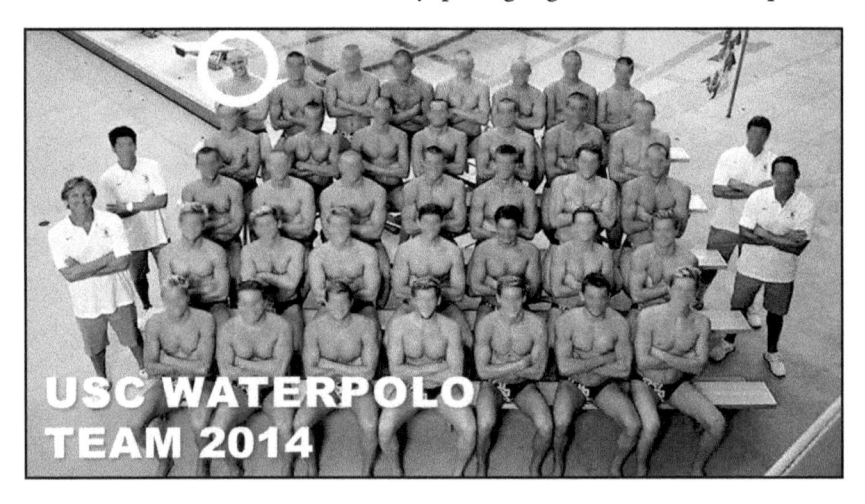

Photo of 2014 USC water polo team, including our son

Moon communicated with Johnny and Leslie about team assignments, schedules, practice times, and team functions months after the first practice. Moon also acknowledged, under oath, that he worked with Coach Jovan to add misleading statements to Johnny's profile (which he did unbeknownst to us) and submitted these statements to USC's Athletic Subcommittee for

---

34   United States v. John Wilson Trial transcripts, day 13, September 28, 2021 page 116.

admissions ("SUBCO")[35], Moon is the only USC employee we are aware of who admitted adding misleading information to a student's application who was not charged with a crime by the prosecutors nor fired by USC. In fact, after throwing our son under the bus with false statements, Moon was promoted and is currently the head coach of USC's women's water polo team.

It seemed very odd to us how someone could brazenly lie on the stand with impunity. We learned the hard way, that as long as a witnessed lied to help the government's case, the prosecutors weren't very motivated to pursue perjury charges against that witness.

***

The former USC team captain and another USC teammate testified that our son was at all the team practices and worked all the weekend tournaments with the other redshirts. It was shocking that Moon said that Johnny wasn't there at the USC weekend tournaments and that the emails showing the redshirt work schedules mistakenly included Johnny with the other redshirts to video tape games.

These tournament video assignments were always done with two redshirts per video camera so that taping the live games could keep rolling even if one team member needed to take a restroom break or grab a snack during the all day tournaments. Leslie and I both attended games and could only meet Johnny briefly during breaks because he had to get back to the video camera. If Moon's testimony were true, then all the redshirt partners that Johnny was assigned to video tape tournament games throughout the season would be single handed and unable to take breaks.

One teammate also testified under oath that Johnny was a much faster swimmer. The prosecutor challenged him and asked how he could know that with certainly. His teammate's reply was that Johnny would often close

---

35 United States v. John Wilson Trial transcripts, day 13, September 28, 2021, page 108.

the distance set up between players in the swim drills and bump into his feet and pass him. How could this happen if Johnny were there for just the first day?

A critical fact that also proved Johnny was training with the USC team relates to when he was taken from the pool to the USC hospital during practice early in the season when he vomited during practice due to a concussion. The former USC team captain told the prosecutors that he let the team goalie borrow his car to drive Johnny to the USC hospital. (It was that serious.) Moon had no recollection of a team member vomiting during practice and losing his starting goalie during practice as the goalie drove Johnny to the USC hospital. Really?

The prosecutors seemed incredulous that the former team captain would remember such a minor detail about whose car was used (seven years before his trial testimony) and who drove our son to the hospital. The team captain said he remembered this detail because Johnny had vomited in his car, and he remembered having to clean it up, and that the team goalie didn't help him do that. Pretty graphic evidence that Johnny wasn't just there for the first day of practice.

The prosecutors also objected to the admission of evidence for the jury about Johnny's USC medical records and emails between the medical staff and the team trainer asking when Johnny would be cleared from his concussion protocols to go back into the pool to train. (While our son was injured, he followed concussion protocols for six weeks and helped above deck during practices, filmed tournaments on weekends with the other redshirt players and trained in the weight room.)

The email from the team trainer to the USC medical staff asking when he could go back into the pool also proved Moon was not truthful about our son not being there after the first day. It was frustrating that the judge sustained the prosecutor's objections to this impeachment evidence being shown to the jury.

Leslie also had multiple emails with this coach about registering Johnny with the NCAA. Johnny's registration had issues at first because he used "Johnny" instead of his legal name, "John," on the official forms. Leslie eventually cleared the name confusion up with the coach and the NCAA. Unfortunately, none of these emails were seen by the jury.

Leslie and I had also traveled multiple times to California from Europe to watch our son practice and cheer the team on at games. The below photo is me and our son at the national championship tournament in San Diego, which took place in early December 2014. Why would I fly out eleven hours each way from Europe to San Diego to attend games over three days and cheer the team on if our son wasn't on the team?

Photo of Johnny and me at the national championship tournament

***

Another category of critical evidence that was improperly blocked from the jury related to USC admissions. The prosecutors argued that USC was the "victim," and we shouldn't be allowed to tarnish the "victim" or share data which showed that they had a regular practice of giving donor families admissions support. The trial judge blocked all this evidence.

The magnitude of the USC admissions evidence was amazing and critical to our case. As a separate judge, Magistrate Judge Kelley noted *pretrial*, "The evidence that Athletics regularly traded walk-on slots for donations would suggest USC's acquiescence." Unfortunately, but not surprisingly, the trial judge selected by the prosecutors for our trial didn't agree with Magistrate Judge Kelley, who ruled before my trial (or the unanimous decision of the appeals judges after my trial).

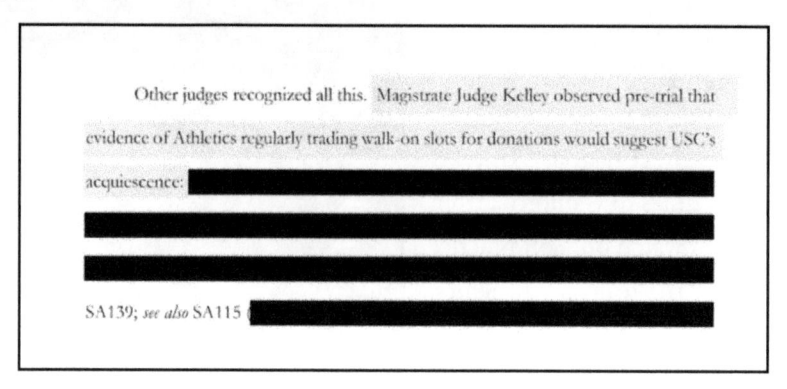

> Other judges recognized all this. Magistrate Judge Kelley observed pre-trial that evidence of Athletics regularly trading walk-on slots for donations would suggest USC's acquiescence: ▮▮▮▮▮▮▮▮▮▮▮▮
> ▮▮▮▮▮▮▮▮▮▮▮▮
> ▮▮▮▮▮▮▮▮▮▮▮▮
> SA139; *see also* SA115 ▮▮▮▮▮▮

The prosecution had a lower-level USC employee testify instead of the head of admissions. This government witness effectively told the jury that USC did not give admissions help to the children of large donors for any sports programs.

Our lawyers verbally cited several shocking examples of children of donors being admitted into the school (through the athletic process) onto tennis, golf, and other teams. Many of these students had little to no athletic qualifications and never showed up for a single team practice. Over a five-year period, there were more than one hundred cases (unrelated to Rick Singer) of donor families who got preferential admissions treatment as part of sports programs at USC.

As noted in the *Courthouse News* article,[36] USC giving admissions boosts on athletic teams to donor families was a common practice at the school: "USC had a 'culture' of accepting students with dubious athletic credentials in return for large donations."

---

36 "Touchdown in reach for 'Varsity Blues' parents at 1st Circuit", *Courthouse News Service*, November 7, 2022

Mike Kendall did submit the records we had access to as "offers of proof" so it could be shown to the appellate judges, even though it was blocked from the jury. This evidence told a completely different story from what the USC witnesses said under oath in front of the jury. This material was clearly impeachment evidence and went to the heart of the case. Yet the prosecution objected, and the judge excluded it all.

This blocking of USC witnesses and evidence was so wrong, and the testimony and evidence so crucial to our defense that the appeals court would later specifically call the government out on this issue during my appeal. As shown in this excerpt from a *Courthouse News* article, First Circuit Court of Appeals Senior Judge Kermit Lipez asked the government prosecutors during the appeal oral arguments, "How can you argue that that [excluded USC] evidence was not relevant?"

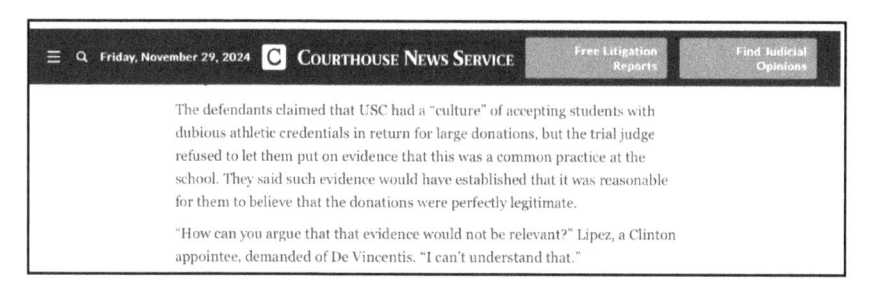

> ☰ Q Friday, November 29, 2024 C COURTHOUSE NEWS SERVICE   Free Litigation Reports   Find Judicial Opinions
>
> The defendants claimed that USC had a "culture" of accepting students with dubious athletic credentials in return for large donations, but the trial judge refused to let them put on evidence that this was a common practice at the school. They said such evidence would have established that it was reasonable for them to believe that the donations were perfectly legitimate.
>
> "How can you argue that that evidence would not be relevant?" Lipez, a Clinton appointee, demanded of De Vincentis. "I can't understand that."

Additionally, in the fall of 2024, two Pulitzer Prize–winning investigative reporters for the *LA Times* wrote a series of independent articles which shared many detailed examples of donor families at USC getting admissions help related to sports programs. These articles went far beyond the Varsity Blues cases and offered far more details and examples than I had ever seen or heard about.

It clearly supported the arguments we tried to make during my trial that "[i]n pursuit of donations, USC admitted affluent kids as walk-on athletes." These donor families had acceptance rates of 85 to 90 percent compared to the 15 percent school average.

THE SCANDAL WITHIN THE SCANDAL

Beyond Varsity Blues: In pursuit of donations, USC admitted affluent kids as walk-on athletes

BY HARRIET RYAN, MATT HAMILTON

OCT 22, 2024 | 06:00

FOR SUBSCRIBERS

- A Times investigation found that USC quietly offered wealthy and well-connected families an alternative path to admission with much lower academic expectations and an acceptance rate of 85% to 90%.
- Internal records show USC fundraisers anticipated significant donations from families of those admitted and, in some cases, became enraged when money failed to materialize.
- When the Varsity Blues scandal threatened to expose the secret system, the university and some employees involved took steps to keep the details hidden, an effort that continued through at least 2022.

Energy and telecom mogul Sarath Ratanavadi, one of the richest men in Thailand, wanted his son to attend the University of Southern California a decade ago. The admissions officer who reviewed his file, however, termed him a "mediocre student at best" with grades at a Bangkok private school that USC equated to four Ds and two Fs.

***

The prosecutors also blocked our access to key government witnesses. For example, we tried to call Singer's CFO to the stand to clear up the facts surrounding my donations. He was allowed to plead the Fifth—even though he had a cooperation agreement with the government that included an obligation to testify. He said he was worried about California prosecuting him, and the judge allowed him not to testify.

My lawyers protested, as this was effectively a made-up excuse to block our access and ability to question him, since state charges are extremely rare and are something that the federal government could address, if they chose. He was *their witness*, but *we* couldn't question him.

The prosecutors played similar tricks with two USC witnesses as well. One was the head of all the athletic programs at USC. We had some powerful emails to and from this witness and FBI 302 notes that could have helped my case and shed light on USC's practices. However, the judge blocked us, *in advance* of calling this witness, from using any USC emails in a cross-examination of this witness. This ruling made calling this person to testify meaningless, and our lawyers didn't bother to call them to the stand.

The prosecutors knew about all the impeachment evidence against their witnesses since they also actively blocked this evidence piece by piece during the trial. Given all the damning evidence we had, I asked, Why can't *we* charge those witnesses with perjury?

Then I realized, what were the odds the government would pursue criminal perjury charges against one of their witnesses for lying under oath when that testimony was helping their case? This ability for government witnesses to lie under oath, with little risk of ever being prosecuted, was another example of how the unlevel playing field was tilted in the government's favor.

The prosecutors flooded the jury with audio tapes of some of the most egregious statements of *other* parents. The conversations on some of the tapes were so horrific that if I put myself in the jury's shoes, I would loathe every parent in this case. What the *other* parents agreed to do and what they said was that bad; their behaviors were truly reprehensible.

For over two weeks, the prosecutors laid out their case, and we absorbed one body blow after another from the egregious acts of *other* parents. We objected to this guilt-by-association approach dozens of times, because unfairly painting someone with the illegal acts of others was disallowed by well-established law in a landmark US Supreme Court decision in a case with a defendant named Kotteakos.[37]

It was little consolation that the First Circuit Court of Appeals would later unanimously overturn this tragic injustice and the flawed trial court decisions. (We would have to lose at trial and only then go to the appeals court to get a sound legal ruling.)

As our appellate attorney Noel Francisco, the former solicitor general of the United States, told the appeals court, "Wilson was convicted not for what he did but for what others did."

"[Wilson] was convicted not for what he did," Francisco charged, "but for what others did."

---

[37] *Kotteakos v. United States*, 328 U.S. 750 (1946).

The lead Boston prosecutor graduated from Harvard Law School, and he knew the Kotteakos precedent well enough to fight it each of the dozens of times we raised it before and during the trial. Unsurprisingly, their highly supportive judge ruled in their favor on each of these Kotteakos motions 100 percent of the time.

What was surprising was when one of the senior former prosecutors from the Boston office told a colleague at his new firm that even they (the prosecutors) were surprised at how almost reflexively "the judge supported virtually every motion they made."

These mistaken judicial rulings emboldened the prosecutors, and they got even more aggressive as the trial went on. The prosecutors would go on to use the guilt-by-association strategy right through to the closing arguments when they referenced *other parents' names and facts* a total of thirty-one times in their one-hour summary of their case against *me*.

As outrageous as the prosecutors' guilt-by-association strategy was, we still believed we could win—*if* we were allowed to share our evidence with the jury.

While facts may be stubborn things, we worried that even the best facts in the world wouldn't matter if they couldn't be shared with the jury.

Chapter 16

OVERRULED AND OVERWHELMED

Prosecutors Blocked 98.3 Percent of our Evidence

The judge's rulings against us during the prosecution's case were shocking. Many lawyers who watched the trial said they had never experienced judicial rulings as one-sided in their careers. The court's decisions violated any sense of fairness as well as the normal rules of evidence. Many friends also watched the trial as it was streamed live and told me that they couldn't believe how biased the rulings were.

***

> The famous opening paragraph from Charles Dickens's *A Tale of Two Cities* is an apt description of the extreme emotions that we felt during the trial: "It was the best of times; it was the worst of times…"
>
> **Charles Dickens**
> "It was the best of times; it was the worst of times…"
> -From a Tale of Two Cities

THE SCANDAL WITHIN THE SCANDAL

> For us, however, the emotions always started in reverse order—it was the worst of times as each judicial ruling had a devastating effect on our case. We could see it daily in the faces and eyes of the jury.
>
> The positive aspect of each painful ruling was captured in a phrase repeated far too often during my trial: "This was reversible error." It was bizarre; during the trial, we were openly discussing the need to go to the appeals court for a fair hearing. It was perverse logic; the judge's rulings were so bad; they gave us extremely compelling grounds for appeal—the current worst of times created a future best of times.

***

The critical part of the trial was our defense; this was our opportunity to finally get my evidence before the jury. I didn't think it was possible, but the prosecutors got even more aggressive during my defense. They moved beyond blocking all the impeachment evidence against their witnesses to blocking all my critical defense evidence through objections.

***

Things went from bad to worse as the trial progressed. Trial transcripts show that during the twelve active days of the trial, the prosecutors made a massive 660 objections to our defense motions and evidence—an average of fifty-five objections per day. (This was more than 400 percent of our objections, and the prosecutors were the ones violating the rules of evidence—as the appeals court unanimously agreed.)

If this trial was about truth and justice, why did the prosecutors block our defense motions 660 times?

As shocking as the sheer number of prosecutor objections was, the percentages of each side's motions that were sustained or overruled by the judge were even more astonishing. We had assembled some of the best criminal lawyers in the world (and the legal bills to prove it); they were not novices. The evidence we tried to introduce was highly relevant and complied with all the normal rules of evidence.

However, the judge ruled against us at every turn. In criminal trials, when defendants are fighting for their freedom, many judges give wide latitude to defense evidence. The judge is supposed to be like an umpire in a baseball game, calling balls and strikes fairly and ruling on close calls fifty-fifty.

Having seen what had already happened earlier in the trial, we were expecting some bias in favor of the government—maybe instead of giving us a fifty-fifty split, the judge would give us a sixty-forty split in close call rulings against us. After all, both sides had top lawyers, and they would each make compelling arguments.

It is hard to describe our shock when the judge ruled against our motions 98.3 percent of the time during the defense part of the trial. How could I have a fair trial when only 1.7 percent of my evidence was allowed to be shown to the jury? At the same time, the trial judge only overruled the government's objections twice during my defense. Yes, just two times. By comparison, the judge sustained our 24 total objections just 37.5 percent of the time.

It felt like the scales of justice had the prosecutor's finger as well as a sledge hammer tilting all the trial decisions in their favor.

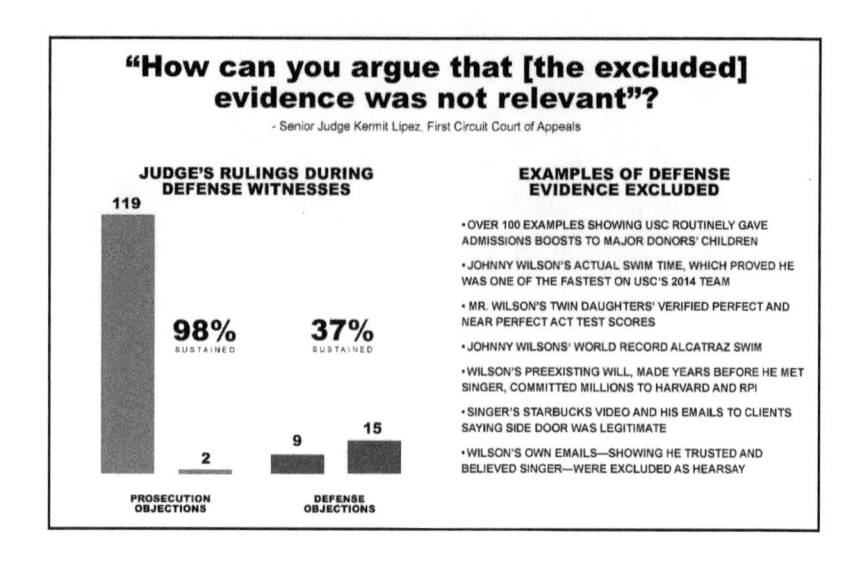

"How can you argue that [the excluded] evidence was not relevant"?

- Senior Judge Kermit Lipez, First Circuit Court of Appeals

JUDGE'S RULINGS DURING DEFENSE WITNESSES

- Prosecution Objections: 119 / 98% SUSTAINED / 2
- Defense Objections: 9 / 37% SUSTAINED / 15

EXAMPLES OF DEFENSE EVIDENCE EXCLUDED

- OVER 100 EXAMPLES SHOWING USC ROUTINELY GAVE ADMISSIONS BOOSTS TO MAJOR DONORS' CHILDREN
- JOHNNY WILSON'S ACTUAL SWIM TIME, WHICH PROVED HE WAS ONE OF THE FASTEST ON USC'S 2014 TEAM
- MR. WILSON'S TWIN DAUGHTERS' VERIFIED PERFECT AND NEAR PERFECT ACT TEST SCORES
- JOHNNY WILSONS' WORLD RECORD ALCATRAZ SWIM
- WILSON'S PREEXISTING WILL, MADE YEARS BEFORE HE MET SINGER, COMMITTED MILLIONS TO HARVARD AND RPI
- SINGER'S STARBUCKS VIDEO AND HIS EMAILS TO CLIENTS SAYING SIDE DOOR WAS LEGITIMATE
- WILSON'S OWN EMAILS—SHOWING HE TRUSTED AND BELIEVED SINGER—WERE EXCLUDED AS HEARSAY

This overwhelming bias during the defense portion of the trial, shown in the above chart, reminded us of what the other law firms said to us years prior when the prosecutors judge shopped up front. The total impact of any one objection could be massive.

For example, just one of the prosecutors' objections was a binder our lawyers had prepared with many examples of how USC gave admissions help to major donors' children through the athletic process. These examples were all cases that had nothing to do with Rick Singer. This evidence alone was a critical part of the case. The fact that USC was regularly giving donor families preferential boosts in admissions was the very heart of this trial.

This was not improper or illegal; it appeared to be a frequent practice at USC that the *LA Times* would later disclose to the public. As noted in an earlier chapter, First Circuit Court of Appeals Senior Judge Kermit Lipez challenged the government's outrageous position which excluded all the USC evidence during the appeals hearing. He asked the government lawyers, "How can you argue that the [excluded USC] evidence was not relevant?"

The excluded evidence went way beyond the detailed USC history that was improperly blocked. The list of items the judge excluded during the trial shocked us to our core. This blocked evidence was extremely important to my case.

It included things like our son's certified swim times, which proved he was one of the fastest players on the USC team. Even our daughters' perfect and near-perfect ACT scores were ruled inadmissible—in a criminal case about college admissions. Think about how bizarre this was.

A three-minute videotape of our son's world-record swim and going on the Oprah show was also excluded. It showed how our son had a lifelong history of excelling in the water and giving back—gone with the simple pounding of a gavel.

My written will, which showed our decades-long commitment to giving to colleges many years before we even met Rick Singer was excluded. The jury was allowed to hear the Goldman Sachs advisor who had helped draft the will discuss it, but they weren't allowed to see a written copy of the will.

Videos and emails of Singer telling people side-door donations were legitimate—excluded.

Each piece of excluded evidence we offered was critical to my defense.

As noted in the appeals court, the government admitted that if "Wilson believed Singer's side door was legitimate, he would not be guilty of any crime."

The prosecutors couldn't let that happen. It was all blocked from the jury's eyes with another rap of the gavel. Even my own emails were excluded from my own trial as hearsay. As noted in our appeals court filings, "The district court reflexively excluded it all."

> **B. The Jury Should Have Seen Wilson's Good-Faith Evidence.**
>
> The Government admits that if Wilson genuinely believed Singer's side-door was legitimate, he would not be guilty of any crime. Opp.66. At trial, the Government tried to defeat that defense based on how Singer pitched his scheme to *other* parents, and how *those* parents understood the side-door as unlawful. *Supra* III. In response, Wilson proffered parallel evidence cutting the other way—where Singer sold the side-door to parents as a wholly above-board enterprise. Wilson also tried to admit evidence of *his own* statements and behavior showing he fell for that pitch. The district court reflexively excluded it all. That too was egregious error. And the Government's defense of this "all goose, no gander" approach is without merit.

***

Additionally, as it related to the tax charge, the jury never got to see a critical email exchange (shown below) with my assistant Debbie Rogers from 2014 where I say, "I have never looked at a return in twenty years."

While it sounds flippant, my returns were over two hundred pages long, and I assumed that my assistant and the tax experts I paid from Goldman Sachs and Price Waterhouse had prepared my taxes correctly.

This exchange was critical since a tax charge requires (a) knowledge of the tax law and (b) the specific false statements being made in a return. I knew I donated to USC through Singer's organization and that I had gotten a receipt from USC. However, I was working and living in Europe at the time while my assistant and tax files were in California.

My 2014 tax return didn't include the receipt I got from USC. Instead, my assistant used the placeholder invoice from Singer's company. Given that I went through the effort to request and obtain a receipt from USC, why would I deliberately not use the USC receipt in my tax return?

From:	John Wilson [john@hyannisportcapital.com]
Sent:	Friday, October 10, 2014 07:10:01 PM
To:	Debbie Rogers
Subject:	Re: 2013

Why can't mass be done w power of attorney and file docusign ?

Sent from my iPad

On Oct 10, 2014, at 21:04, "Debbie Rogers" <debbie@hyannisportcapital.com> wrote:

> Ok, then I will forgo emailing the returns and you and Leslie can file the E-file authorizsations.
>
> <image001.jpg>
> Deborah Rogers
> Phone: 650-347-5757
> Fax: 650-343-6757
>
> **From:** John Wilson
> **Sent:** Friday, October 10, 2014 12:04 PM
> **To:** Debbie Rogers
> **Subject:** Re: 2013
>
> Oh. I have never looked at a return in 20 years
>
> Sent from my iPad
> On Oct 10, 2014, at 21:00, "Debbie Rogers" <debbie@hyannisportcapital.com> wrote:
>
>> I figured you would want to look over prior to signing the efile authorizations
>>
>> <image001.jpg>
>> Deborah Rogers
>> Phone: 650-347-5757
>> Fax: 650-343-6757
>>
>> **From:** John Wilson
>> **Sent:** Friday, October 10, 2014 11:59 AM
>> **To:** Debbie Rogers
>> **Subject:** Re: 2013
>>
>> What am I supposed to do with these?
>>
>> Sent from my iPad
>> On Oct 10, 2014, at 20:48, "Debbie Rogers" <debbie@hyannisportcapital.com> wrote:
>>
>>> Here are the statements for the Federal Return. Next I will be emailing CA return followed by e-file authorizations via docusign.

Perhaps the most critical piece of evidence that the prosecutors raised during the trial—the key to their entire fraud allegation—were some inaccuracies in a one-page profile that *Singer* had created while I was working and living with our family in Europe. (I later took a polygraph test to prove that I never saw this profile before the charges were brought against me.) I would never condone making fraudulent statements.

My lawyers created a profile with verified statistics to compare with the profile Singer edited. This chart was crucial to my defense. We offered it as evidence with all the facts verified by his high school coach and other sources. Shockingly, the prosecutors and judge didn't allow it to be shown to the jury.

The comparison would have shown the jury that there were many things in Singer's profile that actually hurt our son's credentials. For example, the incorrect profile omitted one of our son's highly regarded water polo teams. His world swim record was missing. It had the wrong coach's name for his Stanford Club team. Even our home address was incorrect. Why would I do any of those things?

Most damning of all, it excluded our son's best ACT test score, one in the ninety-third percentile. Singer used our son's worst SAT score, the one in the eighty-second percentile, instead. The difference between the ninety-third and eighty-second percentiles is huge when applying to highly competitive schools.

If we were conspiring with Singer to falsely inflate our son's profile, why would we include inaccuracies which *hurt* our son's credentials?

Overruled and Overwhelmed

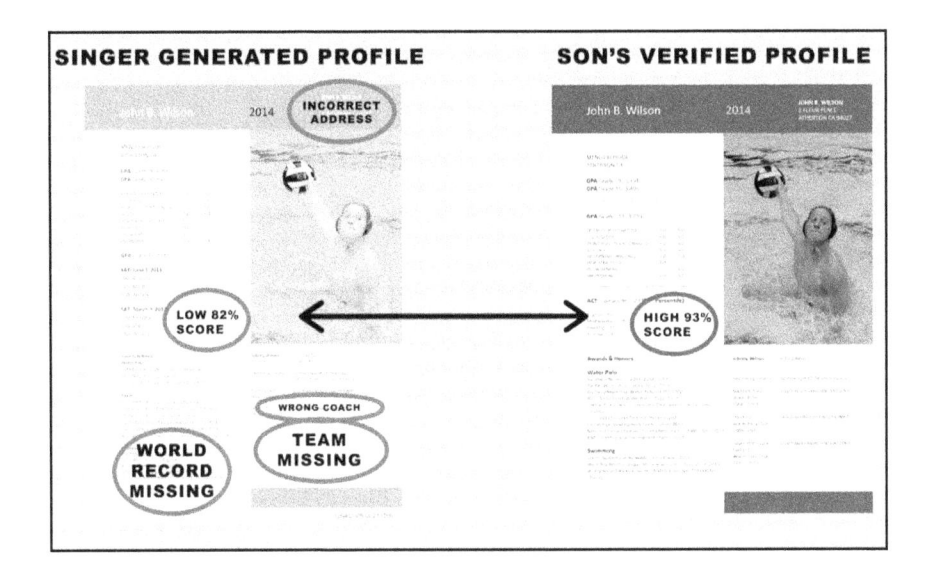

SINGER GENERATED PROFILE	SON'S VERIFIED PROFILE

- INCORRECT ADDRESS
- LOW 82% SCORE
- WORLD RECORD MISSING
- WRONG COACH
- TEAM MISSING
- HIGH 93% SCORE

The judge did not allow us to share any of this verified profile or to ask our son's high school water polo coach about many of the things that were critically important to my case which were on this verified profile.

Coach Bowen was nationally recognized and had trained our son for six years from middle school through high school. He testified that he called the USC coaching staff to recommend our son to the team.

As shown in the trial transcripts excerpted here, he testified that our son was an A-plus player for speed by USC standards, which is one of the most important attributes for a field player, and an A-plus by USC standards for his work ethic.

```
13   Q.   Mr. Bowen, I think when you were under examination you
14        said he had A plus speed?
15   A.   Yes.
16   Q.   Did you also say he had an A or A plus work ethic as a
17        grinder?
18   A.   Yes.
```

223

Coach Bowen also testified that he was confident that our son could be a contributor to the USC team by his junior or senior year.

```
1  phone must have influenced the coach. Like, I said, "That call
2  must have done it."
3  Q.  Okay. And that's because you thought Johnny had speed for
4  the high level of college play?
5  A.  It's a combination of his speed, which you can't teach.
6  So the speed and the water polo IQ just by virtue of starting
7  for a team, a national caliber team for three years, that is
8  enough to confidently say by your junior year, maybe senior
9  year, you could contribute to a high-level program like USC.
```

But Coach Bowen was not allowed to share our son's certified swim time with the jury. This was insanity; this critical fact, which proved beyond any reasonable doubt that our son was qualified for a walk-on spot on the USC team, was blocked. It also proved there was no need to lie in the profile about Johnny's swim times.

The swim time Singer put on the profile didn't matter. Our son's actual swim time proved he was qualified for a walk-on role on the USC team. By blocking our son's actual swim time, the prosecutors were able to spin their false narrative that this was fraud and that our son wasn't qualified.

The prosecutors knew that Johnny was one of the fastest players in the country and on the USC team. Yet they continued to label him as an "alleged athlete." I watched Johnny beat other players during swim drills with the USC team. The team captain, another teammate, and his high school coach all testified that Johnny was a solid member of the team and one of the team's fastest players. It was insane.

If truth and justice were the goal, why not err on the side of caution and fairness and allow me to bring in my evidence? What were the prosecutors so afraid of?

I recall the exact moment when Coach Bowen wasn't allowed to mention Johnny's actual swim times to the jury. It was like a dagger straight into my heart and the heart of the case.

It was *the moment* when I knew I had lost the trial.

***

Near the end of the trial, at 1:56 a.m. on October 1, 2021, I held my iPad and hit send on what I felt was one of the most important emails of my remaining life. In a few hours, Leslie, my lawyers, and I would have one final opportunity to inform the court of who our final witnesses would be.

I had been arguing for weeks that I wanted to testify. I felt strongly there was one critical person the jury *had* to hear from if I had any chance of winning the case, the only person on the planet who could clear up the many things which the jury had been misled and misinformed about. That person was me.

The email to a close friend who was following the trial each day on the live video stream captured what was racing through my mind all night long: "The thought that I now have a high chance of losing and I wouldn't even get the chance to clear my son's name for another two to three years during an appeal process is an unacceptable course of action. I would rather go to prison in order to clear my son's name. I prefer to go down fighting than sheepishly walk out of the courtroom not having testified. I can't bear the thought of watching my kids suffer while I remain muzzled in a three-year appeals process."

> The thought that I now have a high chance of losing and I wouldn't even get the chance to clear my son's name for another 2-3 years during an appeal process is an unacceptable course of action. I would rather go to prison in order to clear my son's name. I prefer to go down fighting than to sheepishly walk out of the court room not having testified. I cant bear the thought of watching my kids suffer while I remain in a muzzled 3 year appeals process.

Was this an email from a corrupt parent who had conspired with Singer to bribe and cheat and fake his kids' way into top colleges? The decision not to testify weighed heavily on me, but it was driven by the harsh realities of our legal system. The nonstop insinuations the government kept making about me—and more importantly, about our children—through other people's evidence stung like a betrayal as they twisted reality into something grotesque and unrecognizable. It was maddening to see my intentions warped into a narrative I couldn't control, but the stakes were too high to let my indignation dictate my actions.

The hard truth was that we were likely to lose this trial; a staggering 98.3 percent of our evidence was blocked, and the jury instructions the judge planned to give would almost certainly lead to a guilty verdict. All those trial errors were reversible, and the odds of winning on appeal were extremely high. However, if I testified and lost, the odds of winning at appeal could go down by 80 percent, because a defendant who testifies and loses would imply to the appeals court judges that the jury concluded that I was a liar.

The jury instructions the judge was going to give, saying a donation to the schools could be considered a bribe to the coach, would effectively lead the jury to render a guilty verdict. While I desperately wanted to share my side of the story, testifying and still getting a guilty verdict could destroy my chances of winning an appeal.

If I lost at **both** the trial and the appeal, my family's name would be forever smeared, something I couldn't bear to risk. As agonizing as it was to remain silent, the best chance of clearing my name and protecting my family's reputation in the long term was to endure a conviction at trial and fight to win on appeal.

Talk about being stuck between a rock and a hard place. It was the hardest decision of my life—and one I still wrestle with to this day.

***

The prosecutors' closing arguments were extreme and harsh. Three things stood out. First was his yelling and jabbing his finger toward my face from just a few feet away as he shouted repeatedly, "You crossed the line. You lied," etc. Second, was how the prosecutor moved the goalpost about our son's qualifications. Johnny's high school coach and USC teammate testimony (even without the hard facts of Johnny's actual swim times) proved that Johnny was a Division 1 level athlete and highly qualified for a walk-on role on the USC team.

This had to cause some concern for the prosecution. It forced them to change their narrative about Johnny. In their closing arguments, the prosecutor told the jury it didn't matter if our son "was the Tom Brady of water polo."

```
14              But, again, it's all beside the point.  It doesn't
15   matter whether he showed up for practice or whether he didn't
16   show up for practice.  Frankly, it doesn't matter if he was the
17   Tom Brady of water polo or whatever the equivalent is in water
18   polo.  Or the Lebron James of water polo.  It doesn't matter.
```

The prosecutor told the jury that if there was one fact in the profile (the one Singer wrote and submitted, not me) which was deliberately overstated, even by a small percent, it was fraud. When the prosecutors and trial judge improperly blocked the jury from seeing Johnny's actual swim times (which showed this mistake was not material) the jurors were misled to believe this Singer swim time error was enormous. He even went on to say it didn't matter if I ever read the profile.

He ended his closing comments about the tax charge by telling the jury that my donations to USC were bribes and that everyone knows that bribes are not tax deductible.

It was unbearably painful to be forced to sit there throughout the trial and listen to these egregious and knowingly false statements. I wanted to scream out multiple times and state that they were lying. But I couldn't.

***

The judge instructed the jury that "a payment to a school could also be a bribe to a coach." He told the jury that the "victim" of the bribe, USC in this case, could be the one who got the money. How could this be? This was a world upside down. As noted in my appeals case, "'The government has not identified a single case in all of American history' that says that paying money to an institution in return for a benefit is a bribe."

> A key argument is that it's not a "bribe" if the beneficiary of the payment — in this case, USC — is also the alleged victim of the scheme.
>
> "The government has not identified a single case in all of American history" that says that paying money to an institution in return for a benefit is a bribe, argued Wilson's lawyer, Noel Francisco of Jones Day in Washington, who served as U.S.

The judge's erroneous instructions to the jury were an example of what's called "directing a guilty verdict." I had heard about Russian show trials in school and how innocent people could be railroaded, but I thought those things were all in the past. I didn't think things like that could happen in twenty-first-century America.

***

Yet as we left the courtroom and the jury began their deliberations, it felt as though this entire trial was a colossal waste of time and money. It was as if I had poured gasoline onto a giant pile of money and set it on fire. Years of preparation, research, and discovery were vaporized as I had been railroaded.

My trial was so unfair that eleven former US attorneys from across the country (including two from Massachusetts), appointed by both Republican and Democratic presidents and unpaid by me or my team, took the extraordinary step of publicly criticizing their former colleagues in a brief stating, "John Wilson did not receive a fair trial."

> Jackson, *supra*, at 6.
>
> I. **JOHN WILSON DID NOT RECEIVE A FAIR TRIAL.**
>
> There are two general forms of hub-and-spoke conspiracies: rimmed conspiracies (where the defendant-spokes are interconnected in some way)

Criminal trials don't need to be perfect, but they <u>do</u> need to be fair.

Chapter 17

APPEALS COURT REVERSAL OF FORTUNE

All My Core Convictions Were Overturned

As the jury deliberated, we had to stay near the courthouse to wait for the announcement of a verdict. Leslie and I waited in a small room in the back of the courthouse or walked to the church just 200 yards away or around the courthouse grounds. We stayed within a fifteen-minute walk, so we could be back when the jurors had finished their deliberations. We had already begun discussing our plans for appeal.

***

> There are a lot of important life lessons that Big Sam taught me. At this moment, perhaps the one piece of advice that I had to draw upon most was getting back up no matter how many times life knocked me down. The value of never giving up, especially when fighting for something important, can't be overstated. As baseball legend Babe Ruth said, "It's hard to beat a person who never gives up."
>
> **Babe Ruth**
> "It's hard to beat a person who never gives up."

> If there is one theme that has resonated throughout my life, it was that one. I had faced, and beaten, long odds over and over again, and perseverance and resilience were the keys to my ultimate success. In many ways, the grit I had developed from an early age prepared me well to take on difficult challenges. While I felt I was about to become another notch in the government's 99.6 percent conviction rate belt, I wasn't giving up.

***

On Friday, October 8, 2021, the jury had reached its verdicts, and we made our way back to the courtroom. Once settled, we all stood up as the judge and then the jury entered the room. We knew it was bad, since not a single person on the jury looked our way. The jury foreman read the verdict, and it was a bloodbath.

The other defendant, Gamal Abdelaziz, learned his fate first: guilty on all charges. It was my turn next. Each charge was read, one at a time—guilty on every single count. I glanced at the prosecutors and noticed how they stayed in character all the way to the end, giving smug looks of celebration with each announcement of the word "guilty," even giving small, victorious fist clenches with each guilty verdict.

The prosecutors seemed joyous, as if they had just stopped a serial killer dead in his tracks. It was possible that the judge could have had me handcuffed and taken away right then, but he agreed to a sentencing date that fit into the two sides' schedules—and that was it.

Then, when I walked out of the room, I was a newly minted member of a very exclusive group—a group that you should say a prayer tonight (if you are at all religious) that neither you nor anyone you love is ever forced to join: someone convicted of multiple federal felonies but who had committed no crimes.

***

Mike Kendall and his trial team did an amazing job under impossible circumstances. Given the extreme nature of the prosecutors' approach and the judge's decisions, no legal team, strategy, or defense could have stopped the injustice that had been done to us.

While we expected the result (given the lopsided nature of the trial), there was still the harsh reality of knowing I was now a convicted felon in the eyes of the world. I would have to wear that label and stigma potentially forever. And we now had to wait two more years for the appeals process.

We had so many fantastic grounds for appeal that Mike and Andy had preserved for us, and we knew we had an extremely good chance at the appellate level with a panel of more qualified and more balanced judges. Many observers agreed that systemic failures of this sort should never happen, as our constitution and judicial process is supposed to be geared to let nine guilty parties go free to avoid one innocent party being wrongly convicted. At that point, in our minds, evil had prevailed at the Boston federal courthouse.

However, we still had hope because we had so many strong grounds for appeal. Many suggested that we hire new lawyers who specialized in appeal (versus trial lawyers). Mike was incredibly supportive and said that his firm would do all they could to help us in the appeals process.

Leslie was as defiant and indignant as I was, maybe more so. As unfair as the trial was, we were determined to take the fight to the government in this next stage. We were going to appeal my case and prove that what had happened over the last three years and during the trial was a total miscarriage of injustice.

I had heard the expression, "There is a fine line between optimism and delusion." I didn't know if we were walking that fine line or about to cross it, but the fight instinct inside me was triggered. This instinct had been key to my survival from early childhood. When things look as bleak as they can possibly get, it's not time to give up; it's time to redouble your efforts.

Now, we just had to find the right appellate lawyers.

233

THE SCANDAL WITHIN THE SCANDAL

***

By this point, our financial resources had been totally depleted—we were in serious debt, and with no source of income, we would need to pay any further legal fees over time. Our facts were so strong that multiple appeals firms wanted to take our case. Mike and Andy strongly recommended Noel J. Francisco, the partner in charge of the appeals practice at the powerhouse Jones Day law firm, and we quickly zeroed in on this team.

He had sterling credentials and had just finished a three-year stint as the forty-seventh solicitor general of the United States. His professional accomplishments listed on the Jones Day website were beyond impressive. Noel was responsible for all the Supreme Court cases for the entire US government during his tenure as solicitor general and was now the head of the Jones Day appeals practice.

After speaking with him on the phone, we were even more convinced. He was the person we needed, but two serious obstacles lingered. As we researched Jones Day, we stumbled upon a piece of information that was almost impossible to believe. We didn't know at the time if it would be valuable or a potential roadblock; all we knew was that it was darn near unfathomable coincidence.

The *Boston Business Journal* published a story on March 11, 2021, about the former US attorney who had led the overall Varsity Blues case but had resigned before my trial took place and had taken a new position as a partner in the white-collar defense practice of Jones Day.

Incredibly and ironically, this former lead prosecutor was a partner of Noel's, the man we hoped to entrust our critical, one-time appeal. It turned out that this was a blessing in disguise. The firm could take my case and partition the new partner from any involvement. More importantly, if I were to hire Jones Day, they said that would prohibit the former prosecutor from making any further public statements about the case.

Our ability to pay was extremely limited. Gratefully, Noel and Jones Day were flexible and accommodating. Important to us was the fact that Noel was also willing to take on my case personally, a huge vote of confidence as he had his choice of all the firm's major appeals cases and Jones Day would set up solid "information walls" and rules between his team and the former Boston prosecutor to allay any perceived conflicts of interest.

Leslie and I traveled to Washington to meet with Noel in person. He hosted a dinner for us on an outdoor patio at the Jones Day office in DC. The view was directly overlooking the Capitol building; it was a clear spring night, and the view overlooking the Capitol was spectacular. The scene exuded the power and influence represented at this meal with Noel and his go-to person, Yaakov Roth.

Yaakov was a down-to-earth guy but also a legal genius—and definitely the smartest person I've ever met in my life. Noel referred to him as a "once-in-a-lifetime legal mind" and "probably the smartest guy in the entire firm." Yaakov's genius would come through in his writing of legal briefs and explaining strategy. He could transform complex legal issues into undeniably persuasive, simple, and compelling arguments that would resonate with any honest reader, judges, and the public alike.

***

At a time when we needed good news, their confidence in the strength of our appeal was comforting. We had so many appealable issues to address that it took the first couple of months for us to decide which appeal issues we should focus on. Because the trial had been such a wall-to-wall betrayal of legal principles and errors, we had seventeen separate grounds for "reversible error" with the appeals court.

Mike Kendall and the trial team did an excellent job of preserving our appeals case and cataloging the egregious, reversible errors to provide the appellate court a clear record from which to read and refer to in our appeal. He was extremely helpful and professional in working with Jones Day. After being bludgeoned by the legal system for two and a half years, we could now go on offense.

At first, I thought, Why not use all seventeen grounds of appeal? We ultimately decided upon a more focused approach zeroing in on three or four key trial issues.

For example, in obtaining a search warrant against me, we could prove that the government had made misrepresentations to the court and that when the agents executed the search warrant, they clearly exceeded the approved scope of the warrant—they obtained all my emails and all my texts from the past ten years, not just the Singer-related materials which they were approved to obtain. Prosecutors even used some of this improperly obtained material to try to smear me at trial.

Upon careful reflection, I realized that even if we had the government dead to rights on the search warrant, that is not how you want to win an appeal. The public perception would be that I was guilty but got off on a technicality.

Another example we needed to address was the prosecution's false claim that Varsity Blues was one giant nationwide conspiracy of parents. A conspiracy requires a shared objective among the coconspirators, not a common objective.

Sound confusing? It was to me at first as well. Let me try to explain.

Just because you have a common objective doesn't mean you have a shared objective. For example, the Boston Red Sox and the New York Yankees have a common objective: they both want to win the World Series. However, it is not a shared objective; they both want to win, but to achieve that, they each need to beat the other team.

Similarly, all the parents in the Varsity Blues case wanted to help get their kids into top universities; they had a common objective. However, it was not a shared objective, because the parents were, in effect, competing for the same admissions spots and would even try to displace other parents in the process. Additionally, unlike in a true conspiracy, none of the parents had any interest in Singer's business success.

Despite being a convicted felon, it felt great hearing Noel and Yaakov saying publicly, "You didn't bribe anybody; your money went to the schools; that's not bribery." At my sentencing hearing, Noel gave the following statement to the media: "Making a donation to improve a qualified applicant's chances of admission is a well-established process at colleges and universities across the country and is still in use today. It is not a crime." If only the prosecutors and trial judge had been so reasonable.

Wilson Sentencing Statement: Noel Francisco, attorney for John Wilson

"We will appeal this conviction. John Wilson's case is fundamentally different from others in Varsity Blues. First, his children were well qualified for admissions on their own. His son was a strong student and a nationally competitive water polo player who actually participated on USC's water polo team during his freshman year. His daughters had perfect and near-perfect ACT scores. Second, none of John's money went to personally enrich anyone at the school; instead, his payments were for the schools and their athletic programs. Making a donation to improve a qualified applicant's chances of admission is a well-established process at colleges and universities across the country, and is still in use today. It is not a crime. We look forward to presenting a powerful appeal to the First Circuit Court of Appeals."

***

The first two sentences in my appellate brief, shown below, were simple yet profound:

> **"The first fundamental problem in the government's case is that even accepting its *factual* narrative, Wilson committed no crimes."**

Here was the voice of reason. Even if every accusation the government alleged were true, I committed no crimes. The government's theory that a donation to a USC foundation—for which I got a receipt and which the school was allowed to keep—was somehow a bribe was absolutely flawed and wrong. Full stop. Secondly, inaccuracies in a swim time and awards on an athletic profile for a genuine Division I athlete who joined and took part on the team for the entire season was not a federal felony.

The second sentence of my appeal filing goes on to address the blatant unfairness of the trial:

> **"The second is that even accepting the government's unprecedented *legal* theories, Wilson's trial was skewed by erroneous admission of grossly prejudicial evidence and exclusion of critical exculpatory evidence, both in enormous volumes."**

These were our core grounds for appeal in two sentences that also essentially said I should never have been charged with a crime.

> Case: 22-1138   Document: 00117924659   Page: 8   Date Filed: 09/23/2022   Entry ID: 6521769
>
> ### INTRODUCTION
>
> The first fundamental problem in the Government's case is that even accepting its *factual* narrative, Wilson committed no crimes. The second is that even accepting the Government's unprecedented *legal* theories, Wilson's trial was skewed by erroneous admission of grossly prejudicial evidence and exclusion of critical exculpatory evidence, both in enormous volumes. The Government's response ("Opp.") manages to make things worse—grasping for ineffectual limiting principles that appeared nowhere in the jury instructions and only underscore the centrality of the excluded evidence.
>
> Start with the substance. The Government says Wilson agreed to donate to the universities and, in exchange, coaches would promote his children for admission. But that is not bribery, not at all and certainly not with the clarity the Supreme Court has demanded. The Government admits it has not found a single case—in any court, at any time—that treats a <u>benefit to a *principal*</u> as a "<u>bribe</u>" to an *agent*. Nor does it dispute

As Noel's team worked on the appeal, our trial attorneys prepared for my sentencing hearing. (I still had to be sentenced for my convictions while we waited for the appeals process.) I asked a dozen or so friends and family members to write character letters on my behalf. So we reached out to a few friends and were surprised by the response—not surprised that we had great friends who were supportive but that everyone we asked was comfortable attaching their names to mine under these circumstances. They were now vouching for a convicted felon.

People volunteered, and we ended up receiving over a hundred letters of support. Seventy-seven of them were sent to the judge. (About thirty were excluded because the letters were critical of the trial process or the judge himself.)

I was able to read the letters after they were sent to the judge, and it was an incredibly emotional experience to feel the support of so many people. Letters came in from people I had served with on charity boards, company CEOs, work colleagues, neighbors, former college classmates, and friends from all occupations, all walks of life, from countries around the globe.

Teddy Bogosian, an award-winning documentarian, and filmmaker who teaches at Brown University who was helping to document my experience, read all of them. He said to me, "You know, there are very few people in the entire world who could have so many people write such amazing and supportive letters."

***

Dr. Dick O'Keefe is a close family friend who followed my case and all our filings intensely. He knows our kids firsthand as our children spent every summer together for twenty-five years. Dick shared an op-ed he sent to the local Boston and Cape Cod newspapers. The papers didn't publish it (I guess it didn't fit their preferred narrative), but it is a great example of the type of support we received.

Appeals Court Reversal of Fortune

The John Wilson I Know
By: Dr. Richard O'Keeffe

When I received an unexpected diagnosis of cancer in 2014, I found myself in an unusual position as a physician -- my insurance wouldn't cover the cost of the out-of-state travel that I needed to make for my life saving regimen of cancer treatments. Without the funds to cover those expenses, I was in a very bad spot. John Wilson voluntarily stepped in without me asking, and helped me with the financial burden. He is one of the reasons I am able to write these words today. His critical help during my medical emergency is typical of the upstanding person I know him to be.

I have been Cape Cod neighbors with, and known John and his family well, for over 20 years. His name has been in the headlines for the past few years as part of the Varsity Blues investigation and I've been dismayed to see how the media has portrayed John. John was painted with the guilty actions of other parents at his trial and is currently appealing his conviction. Unlike the other cases, none of John's children cheated on tests, nor did John submit fraudulent athletic photos, nor did he give any money to any coaches.

I have seen how hard John's children worked and studied over the years. His children all earned top ACT test scores. His son was an elite swimmer and water polo athlete, even breaking a world record while swimming from Alcatraz to the San Francisco shore at the age of 9. Echoing the generosity of his father, he even made this swim into a Red Cross fundraiser for Hurricane Katrina victims. I have spent time with John and his son every summer and heard directly how his son trained for hundreds of hours, year-round, on multiple teams, and how he competed each summer in national Junior Olympic tournaments.

John hired Rick Singer eight years before Singer became the infamous con man of the Varsity Blues investigation. Over those years, Singer lulled John with his long con scheme by providing real tutoring services and legitimate charity activities for his children. John trusted Singer to help with his son's college applications when John relocated to Europe with the rest of his family for his job, while his son stayed back in California to finish his last year of high school. The government acknowledged that all of John's donations went to college programs or was intended to go to college programs, but was instead taken by Singer.

The John Wilson portrayed by the media and the prosecution is not the John Wilson I know. The John Wilson I know is honest, has consistently demonstrated high integrity, and has generously contributed to our community in multiple ways. For example, when the Hyannis Harbor Master was in need of a new patrol boat, John and several other community members donated the money. Here again, he donated privately and inauspiciously, as he often did when giving back to his community. He also recently contributed funds toward the repair and restoration of the steeple at Union Chapel, a longstanding symbol of our neighborhood's close-knit fabric. In addition, for many years, John quietly supported the youth programs at the West Beach Club and Hyannis Port Yacht Club.

> John's generosity, performed largely behind the scenes, has helped to make our community the special place that it is — especially for families. In fact, some of my fondest summer memories are the July 4th evening barbecues when John would host over 100 families from our village to watch the town's fireworks. Beyond our immediate community, John has donated his time and expertise to help make a global impact as well. For example, he served on the national boards of Cure Autism Now and Autism Speaks for more than 15 years – despite having no affected members in his family.
>
> When it comes to the good of our small Cape Cod village, John has contributed more than his fair share. John has overcome many obstacles since his humble beginnings, believes strongly in giving back, and has instilled that same spirit in his children. I am extremely proud to call John Wilson my good friend.

At my sentencing hearing, the government argued I should start my prison sentence right away. However, we were successful in getting a bond pending appeal motion granted.

After the legal briefs for the appeal were completed by both sides, the next big event was the oral argument hearing. The oral arguments took place on November 7, 2022.

We felt confident, because unlike the trial court, most of our facts *were allowed* into evidence for the appeals court to see (that was why Mike Kendall and the trial team submitted our evidence as "offers of proof" for the appellate record even though the trial judge blocked it all from the jury).

We had three knowledgeable and impartial judges overseeing the proceedings. It was a stark contrast to all that had happened in my criminal trial. The mood and tone inside the courtroom was more solemn and professional. There was no jury, three judges, me, the other defendant from my trial (who was also appealing), our legal teams, and a few reporters and supporters.

Within seconds, it was so obvious how well-prepared and knowledgeable these judges were. It was like a whole different world. I kept saying to myself, Why couldn't we have had a smart and fair-minded judge like any one of these three judges?

These three judges were strong legal experts, the best of the best. The personalities in this hearing felt elite—in a good sense, not in an arrogant kind of way. The judges had read everything, allowing their questions to be laser-focused, which did not bode well for the prosecution team.

The appeal was not about the facts of the case but about the law and how the law was applied to the facts. The government appeals attorney spent most of the hearing on defense; their aggressive but fundamentally flawed trial strategy was being exposed, and that seemed to rattle them.

Since March 2019, when Operation Varsity Blues went public, the prosecution had been over the top at every stage. It was not a proud moment for the Boston prosecutors, especially the assistant US attorney who was tasked with heading up the appeal for the government. She was an attorney who specialized in handling appeals cases for the government. She was in a precarious position, because she inherited horrible facts from the prosecutors.

***

The hearing was supposed to last forty-five minutes but wound up taking two hours. One of the most shocking moments occurred when the government lawyer was asked a pointed question by one of the judges along the lines of, "What *specific* actions did these two defendants take that was criminal?" Having recently convicted me of eight felonies, common sense would dictate that she should be able to lay out mountains of incriminating evidence.

Of course, since I didn't actually commit any specific criminal acts, she had to do a "rope-a-dope." Her first response was, "All the parents in this case were cheating and bribing and committing fraud." (She did not specifically refer to me or the other defendant in any way.) The trio of judges looked shocked by this reply. The judge followed up, "No, no, no. That is not what *these* defendants did. I asked you what *these* defendants did?"

Her second reply was, "The evidence we have against these two defendants is overwhelming!"

The judge was frustrated at this point and asked the government attorney for specifics for a third time: "What *is* that overwhelming evidence?"

The government lawyer replied (which reporters captured), "They were sending in photos of their kids. They were editing their children's essays."

Even this reply was slippery; it was phrased to sound like I was sending in fake photos or writing false things in the essays. The photos I sent were all real and the essays I helped edit were truthful, and the appeals court judges knew that—they had the records.

Yes, college applications are supposed to be completed by the student alone, and it was a technical violation to get help from tutors, teachers, or parents on editing essays in the applications.

Judge Lipez then shot an incredulous look and almost scoffed at the government's lawyer asserting these were crimes, saying, "That's the kind of thing that parents do all the time."

Assistant U.S. Attorney Alexia De Vincentis replied that there was "overwhelming evidence" that the parents knew what they were doing was wrong. "They were sending in photos of their kids. They were editing their children's essays," she noted.

But "that's the kind of thing that parents do all the time," U.S. Circuit Judge Kermit Lipez observed.

Things went so badly for the government that the judges spent much of the two-hour argument debating whether, if they found for the defendants, they should order a new trial or throw the case out altogether.

Most of the prominent parents caught up in the scandal pleaded guilty, including actresses Lori Loughlin and Felicity Huffman. But John Wilson and Gamal Abdelaziz went to trial and were convicted of bribery and fraud. Wilson runs a hedge fund and is a former president of Staples; Abdelaziz is a top casino executive.

Altogether dozens of parents were accused of paying more than $25 million to ringleader Rick Singer to gain college admissions between 2011 and 2018. More than half the tainted admissions were to USC.

Wilson and Abdelaziz claimed that Singer told them that making donations in return for admissions preferences was legal and above-board, and they had no reason to doubt him. They said they had no idea that Singer was altering their children's applications to make them sound more impressive.

A key argument is that it's not a "bribe" if the beneficiary of the payment — in this case, USC — is also the alleged victim of the scheme.

"The government has not identified a single case in all of American history" that says that paying money to an institution in return for a benefit is a bribe, argued Wilson's lawyer, Noel Francisco of Jones Day in Washington, who served as U.S. solicitor general under President Trump.

Saying that the government "jumped the shark," he added that, "if Congress wanted to overturn the entire history of bribery jurisprudence, it had to say so."

Barron, an Obama appointee, agreed that "there needs to be proof of private gain" to establish a bribe. "Otherwise it's not a bribe, it's a gratuity."

After three years, someone was finally holding the Boston federal prosecutors' feet to the fire about what real evidence they had against me. Their answer: I edited our son's essay, and I sent in real photos of him playing water polo—instead of our son doing that on his own.

That was the "overwhelming evidence" of the crimes that I had committed? I am still dumbfounded every time I read that quote and relive that moment in the oral arguments.

* * *

Another important interaction was related to the government's false conspiracy angle. A Reuters article quoted US Circuit Judge David Barron, "*Maybe* there's evidence of a nationwide conspiracy. You still have to prove evidence that *these* defendants agreed to be in it." Then he said, "You have to pile inference on top of inference" to believe that the parents knew they were participating in a nationwide fraud conspiracy.

Touchdown in reach for 'Varsity Blues' parents at 1st Circuit

Two families made six-figure payments to get their kids into USC, but the appeals court looks unlikely to label those checks as bribes.

THOMAS F. HARRISON / November 7, 2022

This March 12, 2019, file photo shows the University Village area at the University of Southern California in Los Angeles. (Reed Saxon/AP)

BOSTON (CN) — The First Circuit gave a sympathetic hearing Monday to two wealthy executives convicted in the "Varsity Blues" college admissions scandal who insisted that they acted completely innocently in making more than $500,000 in donations to the University of Southern California's athletic department in return for getting their children admitted with puffed-up athletic profiles.

"You have to pile inference on top of inference" to believe that the parents knew they were participating a nationwide fraud conspiracy, Chief U.S. Circuit Judge David Barron said at oral arguments this afternoon in Boston.

The *Boston Globe*'s coverage also printed powerful quotes from the hearing. One centered on the trial judge denying our request to subpoena USC witnesses who could testify about the admissions culture and process at USC and whether applicants were routinely given a boost if their families made large donations.

THE SCANDAL WITHIN THE SCANDAL

Judge Kermit V. Lipez said, "The notion that, 'We were not doing anything wrong; this was just the way business was done'—how can you argue that that evidence would not be relevant? I don't understand that." Judge Lipez asked what everyone who knows about this case (at least everyone that didn't have an agenda) was asking themselves.

It was a powerful rebuke of the government's entire theory of the case as well as their bad acts during the trial.

It felt like the government was having their lunch handed to them. On the subject of bribery, there was quite a bit of discussion about whether the beneficiary of the payment—USC—could also be the alleged victim of the scheme.

A separate group of law professors wrote an unpaid support brief saying, "The government has not identified a single case in all of American history that says that paying money to an institution in return for a benefit is a bribe."

In oral argument, Noel Francisco told the appellate judges that the government "jumped the shark" and added, "If Congress wanted to overturn the entire history of bribery jurisprudence, it had to say so." It was one of many mic drop moments Noel had. He went on to say, "Donating to a university is not bribing its employees; the school cannot be both the victim of the scheme and its beneficiary. No bribery case in history merges those two incompatible roles, for good reason."

> A key argument is that it's not a "bribe" if the beneficiary of the payment — in this case, USC — is also the alleged victim of the scheme.
>
> "The government has not identified a single case in all of American history" that says that paying money to an institution in return for a benefit is a bribe, argued Wilson's lawyer, Noel Francisco of Jones Day in Washington, who served as U.S.

Judge Baron seemed to agree with Noel, saying that "there needs to be proof of private gain" to establish a bribe.

A story published for a website called *Courthouse News* reported that things went so badly for the government that "the judges spent much of the two-hour agreement debating whether, if they found for the defendants, they should order a new trial or throw the case out altogether."

I remember sitting there during the oral arguments thinking, Finally, someone is holding the government accountable. What a difference this was from a judge who the prosecutors had hand-selected. These were three strong judges who knew what they were doing.

For me, it felt as if I had been living in an alternate universe or a never-ending episode *The Twilight Zone* for nearly four years. Suddenly, it felt like a shade had been lifted, and sunshine and sanity had finally crept into the building.

It was an incredibly good day in court; however, it wasn't time for high fives. I was still branded a felon, our children and our reputations were still in tatters, we'd been drained of our entire life's savings, and until and unless they overturned my convictions, I still faced fifteen months in prison.

***

On May 10, 2023, the appeals court released their decision reversing *all* the core charges against me and the other dad who went to trial. It was fantastic news! However, the court left a residual felony tax conviction for filing a false tax return with a $1,425 difference related to deducting our donation to USC on the wrong line (something many lawyers said was the equivalent of throwing a bone to the prosecutors and judge).

It didn't matter that I overpaid my taxes that year, or that I had email proof that I DocuSigned the return without reading it (unfortunately, the tax emails I included in the book weren't shown during the trial—so they couldn't be shared with the appeals court), or that all my bribery and fraud convictions were overturned, the vindictive prosecutors pressed to stick me with this tax conviction.

THE SCANDAL WITHIN THE SCANDAL

A federal appeals court tossed Varsity Blues convictions of two parents in nationwide college admissions scandal

By **Shelley Murphy** Globe Staff.
Updated May 11, 2023, 10:04 a.m.

John B. Wilson of Lynnfield and his wife, Leslie, left Moakley Federal Courthouse in 2021. ERIN CLARK/GLOBE STAFF

A federal appeals court Wednesday overturned the convictions of two parents accused of paying hundreds of thousands of dollars in bribes to get their children accepted to elite colleges, rejecting one of the legal theories used by the government to prosecute Hollywood celebrities, titans of industry, corrupt coaches, and administrators in the sprawling Varsity Blues college admissions scandal.

In a 156-page decision, the US First Circuit Court of Appeals vacated all of the conspiracy, bribery, and fraud convictions against Gamal Abdelaziz, 65, a former casino executive who lives in Las Vegas, and John B. Wilson, 63, a real estate private equity investor from Lynnfield and Hyannis Port. The only count the court let stand was one conviction against Wilson for filing a false tax return.

It's impossible to describe how we felt having all my core convictions overturned. This was such an unprecedented turn of events that even the media started to pay attention. From day one, the media had convicted me through guilt by association. The verdicts at my trial further reinforced their negative views.

Now, with three objective judges' ruling unanimously in my favor, the media began to look at my case differently.

For someone who never gives up, the momentum was finally beginning to turn—proof that with unrelenting determination, the truth could prevail, even against very long odds.

Chapter 18

PROSECUTORIAL MALICE

Vindictive Lawfare and Double Standards

The appellate decision, released at 5:30 p.m. on Wednesday, May 10, 2023—exactly 1,521 days after I was arrested in Houston back in 2019—reversed *all* my core convictions. The stress clock had been ticking the entire time. Those years felt more like dog years. Friends congratulated us, and legal colleagues said that the odds of getting every substantive charge overturned in a high-profile case were ten thousand to one!

***

> Injustice can rear its ugly face in many places and in many different forms. Critically, injustice left unchecked can embolden the perpetrators and enable it to spread and affect still more people. Dr. Martin Luther King Jr. said it well: "Injustice anywhere is a threat to justice everywhere." His cause of speaking truth to power and his commitment to confronting injustice is an inspiring call to action for everyone.
>
> **Martin Luther King Jr.**
> "Injustice anywhere is a threat to justice everywhere."

THE SCANDAL WITHIN THE SCANDAL

> What the Boston federal prosecutors did was so wrong and so disproportionate to the allegations against me that it still shocks us. Did they really believe that charging me with nine felonies, 180 years of potential prison, and six years of ruinous legal battles—for donating to a college foundation and getting admissions help for a Division I athlete who played on the USC team because his swim time was misstated (by someone else) by 8 to 12 percent—was truly justice?

***

The appellate court's decision to unanimously overturn all my core convictions underscores the importance of judicial oversight in preventing prosecutorial overreach. It was a true vindication. To boot, the prosecutors dropped all the overturned charges.

The appellate court recognized that the government's novel interpretations of the law and the prosecutors' extreme overreach throughout the trial were excessive. As *Sportico* wrote on May 11, 2023, in the article shown below, "It's hard to defeat the government in court; the odds are almost always in the government's favor. But occasionally private citizens—including dads—show the government went too far."

Sportico
The Business of Sport

BUSINESS LEAGUES FINANCE LAW MEDIA VALUATIONS TECH PERSONALITIES EVENTS

HOME / LAW / ANALYSIS

HARVARD, USC DADS CLEARED IN VARSITY BLUES DOJ REBUKE

BY MICHAEL MCCANN   May 11, 2023 9:18am

Gamal Abdelaziz, second from left, and John Wilson, second from right, had been convicted of defrauding universities in the course of paying for admissions help.

It's hard to defeat the government in court; the odds are almost always in the government's favor. But occasionally private citizens—including dads—show the government went too far.

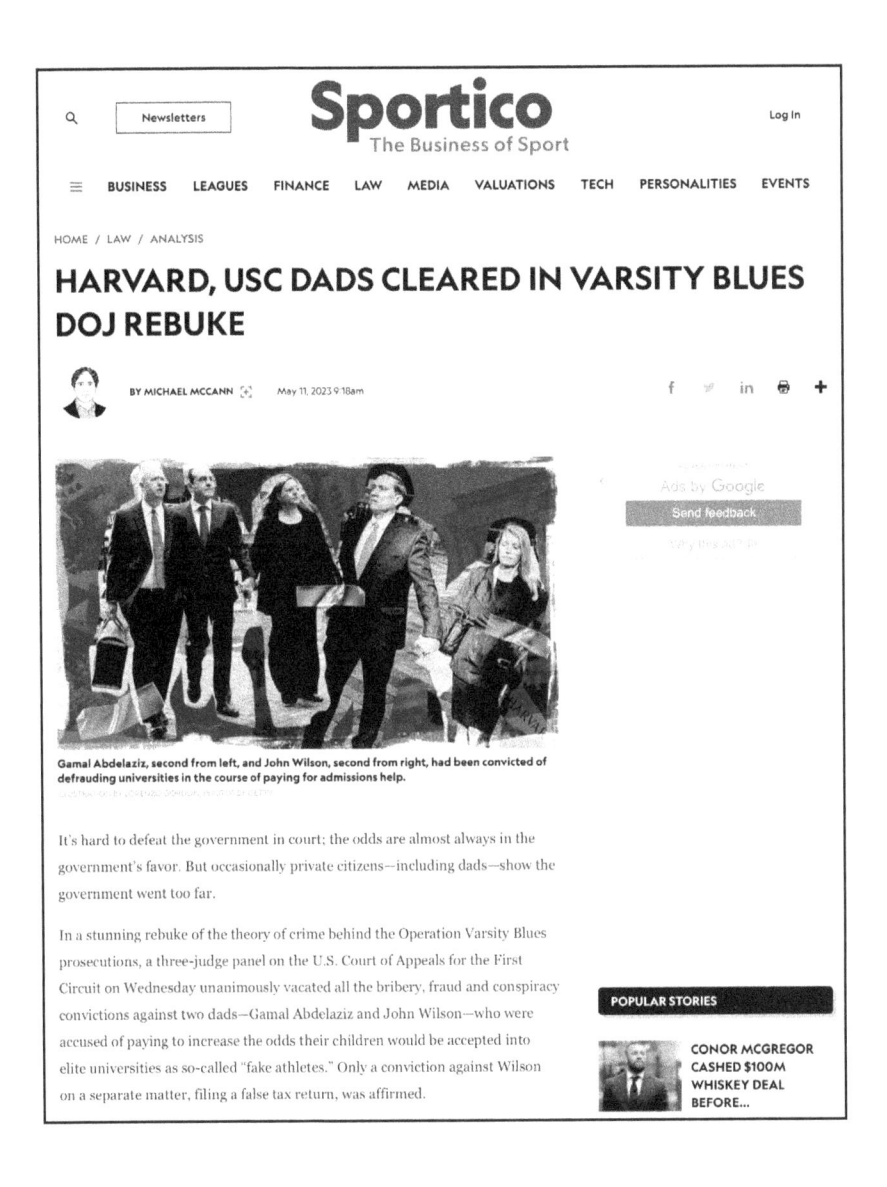

In a stunning rebuke of the theory of crime behind the Operation Varsity Blues prosecutions, a three-judge panel on the U.S. Court of Appeals for the First Circuit on Wednesday unanimously vacated all the bribery, fraud and conspiracy convictions against two dads—Gamal Abdelaziz and John Wilson—who were accused of paying to increase the odds their children would be accepted into elite universities as so-called "fake athletes." Only a conviction against Wilson on a separate matter, filing a false tax return, was affirmed.

POPULAR STORIES

CONOR MCGREGOR CASHED $100M WHISKEY DEAL BEFORE...

The relief we felt that day was monumental, but it was far from the end of our ordeal. Many career Boston lawyers congratulated me and told us that they had never seen or heard of a case where so many felony convictions were all overturned. This exoneration was gratifying to be sure.

Yet our fight was not over. Our reputations were tarnished by the government and Netflix, our finances were depleted, and we still faced a new sentencing on the $1,425 tax-related conviction for the (false) charge of making a false statement in a tax return for the year 2014, when the government acknowledged that I overpaid my taxes by more than $100,000.

The tax conviction was not tax fraud or tax evasion. This tax conviction was related to taking the tax deduction for my donation to USC on the wrong line on my tax return—using the invoice from Singer's organization on my tax return instead of the receipt I got from USC. (Again, this was a donation for which we received an official receipt from the school; USC has kept our money to this day.)

However, losing the appeal appeared to increase the Boston prosecutors' anger. It felt like their sentencing memo to the judge was dripping with rage and vicious attacks against me. It was written like they won the appeal, despite having lost on every major aspect of the case.

In their sentencing memo on the single tax charge, the prosecutors argued that I should get the same prison sentence that the prior judge had assessed for eight felony convictions.

We had commissioned a nationwide review of sentences over the past five years for first-time offenders facing a single charge for filing of a false return. The median sentence was zero months.

Yet the prosecutors recommended that I should get fifteen months in federal prison.

***

Now we had a hearing with a new, fair-minded judge for the sentencing oral arguments. We had so many friends show up to support us for that sentencing hearing that the courtroom was literally overflowing and standing room only.

Prosecutorial Malice

I remember seeing the prosecutors constantly turning around in amazement at the size of the crowd in the courtroom for the sentencing hearing. In fact, one of our friends wrote us a text below about their experience as they went through the security station at the courthouse entrance to attend the hearing.

> Let me add to this: As I entered the quiet Moakley Courthouse lobby and turned in my cell phone, the polite guard asked me first: are you here for the Wilson Case. Yes. He then said: I don't know who he is but he must be famous…and then he said this with a kind smile and a gentle voice: whoever he is …he sure has a lot of friends who care about him. Yes, I said. And then I gave up my water bottle and went through security, up to the 5th floor and joined the battalion of …those very friends.

The prosecutors brought four lawyers—yes, *four* lawyers to my sentencing hearing for a minor tax charge. They argued passionately for forty-five minutes that my case was far worse than the average tax case. They went on to argue that since I was wealthy, the judge should make an example of me.

Thankfully, the judge saw through this, assessed a fine, and sentenced me to six months of home confinement, six months of probation, and 250 hours of community service, the same as all the other people across the US who had similar convictions over the past five years.

The prosecutors' never relented, even after I had completed my community service. This time, it involved the forfeiture of my 2018 donations through Singer's organization. Since all the charges related to my donations were dropped, I was entitled to a refund of the $1 million the government had confiscated as part of their setup calls with me.

The government fought this across three different judges and forced me to spend hundreds of thousands of dollars in additional legal costs to get these funds returned. While I ultimately prevailed, it was a Pyrrhic victory—I netted only a fraction of the total proceeds as most went to legal expenses.

THE SCANDAL WITHIN THE SCANDAL

A final example of vindictiveness continues even as I write this chapter. I filed an amended tax return in April of 2024 for the years 2022 and 2023 which had a meaningful refund due. We were told the normal processing times were somewhat longer than usual, but I could expect a refund by the summer of 2024. We called multiple times and were repeatedly delayed.

After several months, our tax preparer called the IRS again for an update. The IRS agent told them that someone had been assigned to review my return last summer. However, they also said someone within the government told them not to start processing my file. The IRS agent said they could not tell us from whom that instruction came.

Even now in 2025, we are *still* waiting for our tax refund.

***

The double standards in the Boston office were also shocking. Before my appeals case was over, the lead US attorney for the District of Massachusetts was forced to resign in disgrace.

She had been under investigation for some time by the Office of Special Counsel (OSC) for multiple violations of the Hatch act, which prohibits government employees from engaging in partisan political activity while on duty, as well as for committing perjury, or lying under oath.

Prosecutor Rachael Rollins Resigns in Disgrace

May 22, 2023 · 7 min read

Commentary By

Charles "Cully" Stimson
@cullystimson
Senior Legal Fellow and Deputy Director, Meese Center

Zack Smith
@tzsmith
Senior Legal Fellow, Meese Center for Legal Studies

George Soros-backed rogue U.S. Attorney Rachael Rollins is seen in Boston on Jan. 13, 2022.
Barry Chin / The Boston Globe / Getty Images

KEY TAKEAWAYS

1. Rollins resigned right before the Department of Justice's Office of the Inspector General and the Office of Special Counsel released devastating reports.

2. She fallaciously claimed that not prosecuting crimes resulted in lower crime rates, repeating ad nauseum that "data and science" backed up this nutty approach.

This was not a minor set of infractions—especially for someone who is supposed to uphold the law. In their letter to the president of the United States, the investigators from the Office of the Special Counsel (OSC) in the Department of Justice said that her conduct had been "among the most egregious transgressions that the OSC has ever investigated."

The report went on to state that "her conduct was an extraordinary abuse of her authority..." This was the very same US attorney who was leading the aggressive fight against me during my appeal process.

I have never met or interacted with the former leader, and I don't have any ill will toward her. I would just like to be treated the same way.

It was shocking when the Justice Department announced that it would not be pursuing charges against her. Not only were no charges filed, but this former US attorney for the District of Massachusetts also got to keep her law license after a six-month period and was hired for a part-time, *state-funded* job paying $96,000 a year.

This sure seemed like double standards to me. Recalling the award the prosecution team all received for the Varsity Blues case, I zoomed in on the first two sentences below to refresh the message about the college admissions trials.

> accountable dozens of individuals who sought to cheat the college admissions process. From the outset, this case has stood for the principle that we do not have a two-tiered system of justice in this country and that everyone - regardless of wealth, power or fame - must operate under the same set of rules. This case reaffirmed that principle," said Acting United States Attorney Joshua S. Levy. "This case resulted in concrete changes to make the college

Joshua S. Levy, the acting United States attorney, said, "From the outset, this case has stood for the principle that we do not have a two-tiered system of justice in this country and that everyone—regardless of wealth, power, or fame—must operate under the same set of rules. This case reaffirmed that principle."

What type of message does that send when the former head of the office gets off this easily? It seems to me that it just reinforces the ability for federal prosecutors to violate ethical and legal standards with impunity, especially when you consider how aggressively and viciously the prosecutors pursued me for over six years for making donations to colleges—where those colleges gave us a receipt and were allowed to keep our donations.

I may be naive, but I still do believe most people working in the Justice Department and law enforcement are honest, hardworking individuals doing difficult jobs. But as in any large organization, there can be a few bad apples. We just happened to get more than our fair share of rotten apples.

We pray that someday, someone from either the FBI or the Boston prosecutors will follow their conscience, listen to their better angels, and step forward to tell the truth about what was done in my case.

The notion that someone or some group working in the government may have been willing to destroy an innocent family to help keep the Varsity Blues case (and the career-enhancing media spotlights) in Boston is as despicable as it is frightening.

Vindictiveness and double standards should have no place in any "Department of Justice."

Chapter 19

THE TRUTH BEGINS TO PREVAIL

The Media Slowly Turns in Our Favor

Overcoming years of disinformation splashed across media headlines and a wildly popular Netflix "documentary" is not a small challenge. We know it will take many years to correct the false narrative and get the truth out, especially since we must simultaneously fight against three Goliaths—each seemingly determined to bend or hide the truth for their own gains. But we had to start somewhere.

***

> The phrase "The truth will ultimately prevail" almost makes it sound like it will just happen naturally. However, as George Washington wrote, this is not the natural course of events—"The truth will ultimately prevail where pains are taken to bring it to light."[38]
>
> **George Washington**
> "Truth will ultimately prevail when there is pains to bring it to light."

---

38 *In a letter to Charles M. Thruston on August 10, 1794, about a potential insurrection in Kentucky fueled by false stories.*

> Disseminating truth requires "pains"—especially if the falsehoods are spread by strong foes with dark secrets and strong motivations to hide the truth.
>
> "The truth *could* prevail" might have been a better choice of words. It is a conditional statement that better reflects reality. Without effort, or "pains," the truth could end up in the trash heap of history's many forgotten stories. Fighting for the truth is a noble cause, but to be victorious requires resources, strength, and determination equal to or greater than those with a vested interest in blocking the truth.

***

Had we accepted my trial verdict or taken a plea deal for crimes I didn't commit, I would have become nothing more than a forgotten footnote in the Varsity Blues scandal—a faceless name doing time in a federal penitentiary. Most of my life savings would have been preserved, but the truth about our facts and our family's honor would have been buried beneath the rubble of falsehoods and history's indifference.

While the Boston prosecutors may have preferred that I did just that—confess to crimes I didn't commit and slink away into the night—that was never in my nature. I was not afraid to fight against long odds and I have never shied away from following a difficult path, especially where my integrity and reputation were at stake.

This fight wasn't just about clearing my name; it was about protecting our family's dignity, our legacy, and everything Leslie and I had built together. We were willing to fight for the truth and, as George Washington said, take whatever pains necessary to bring the truth to light.

***

The Truth Begins to Prevail

One of the first opportunities to share our story publicly came shortly after my sentencing hearing. A former classmate at Harvard invited me to speak at a reunion. He paid me a modest stipend to share my story with a group of three hundred HBS alumni, and I got permission from my probation officer.

Photo of me giving speech to Harvard Business School alumni

It was an emotional speech, especially at the end when I received a standing ovation. That standing ovation was a truly joyous moment. It was confirmation that the truth would resonate and prevail—if only we could get the message out there more broadly.

***

I then worked hard to get an op-ed into a major national newspaper. Finally, on Christmas Day 2023, the *Boston Globe* published this op-ed.

THE SCANDAL WITHIN THE SCANDAL

GLOBE STAFF

I was unjustly targeted in the college admissions scandal. This is my story.

JOHN WILSON
December 25 at 03:00 AM ET

My life has been bookended by extreme circumstances. I grew up in poverty in the projects of Hartford, Conn., with three half siblings and an abusive single mother. After I was adopted, education and hard work transformed my life and enabled me to achieve financial success as my wife and I pursued our version of the American dream for over 30 years.

On March 12, 2019, my American dream came crashing down. That's the day I was swept up in the Varsity Blues college admissions scandal. There were many bad actors in this scandal, parents who paid people to cheat on tests, bribe coaches, and create fake athletic photos of their children to get their unqualified kids accepted into top universities. I wasn't one of them.

Still, I was wrongly charged with multiple counts of bribery, conspiracy, and fraud, based on donations that I made to the University of Southern California for my son and Harvard and Stanford universities for my twin daughters. Years later, the First Circuit Court of Appeals unanimously overturned my convictions on all those counts and the prosecutors dropped the charges.

While my donations were meant to boost their prospects of admission, my three children were all qualified academically and athletically on their own merits. One of my daughters got a perfect 36 on the ACT; the other scored near perfect. They were to be team managers on sailing or crew programs given their Red Cross lifeguard certifications and years of boating experience.

My son scored in the 93d percentile on his ACT and was an elite athlete who broke a world record at 9 by being the youngest person to swim from Alcatraz to San Francisco — landing him on "The Oprah Winfrey Show" in 2006.

His high school coach confirmed that he was being recruited by other Division I water polo teams and that he personally called and recommended my son to the USC water polo coaching staff. My son joined the USC team as a non-scholarship recruit and his certified swim times proved he was one of the fastest players on the 2014 team.

My donations went to college foundations and IRS-approved charities, not to any individuals. USC gave me a receipt and kept my donations.

I also passed multiple polygraph tests, administered by the former chief of the FBI's polygraph program and quality controlled by the former head of the CIA's polygraph program.

Prosecutors for the US attorney for Massachusetts knew all of this, yet they charged me anyway. As former Boston assistant US attorney David G.

Lazarus said about this case in a July 2022 Law360 article, "Boston positions itself to get those big cases and win any turf battles to keep them."

As the sole initial defendant in Massachusetts, I was the venue "hook" prosecutors needed to help bring the trials (and media spotlight) for all the Hollywood celebrities and wealthy West Coast parents to Boston.

My lawyers warned me that fighting these charges could take years and cost millions; they said the odds of winning, even though I was innocent, were very uncertain since the government had seemingly endless resources.

My family was faced with the simple yet difficult decision: Do I take the easy path and plead guilty to a felony or stand up for truth and justice? We thought long and hard and decided to fight. I couldn't live with myself confessing to a crime I didn't commit. More important, pleading guilty would reinforce the false narrative that my children were unqualified. What happened to me was wrong and should never happen to anyone.

I was shocked at how tilted the playing field was. As court filings showed, the trial court excluded virtually all of my exculpatory evidence. For example, the jury was not allowed to see my daughters' ACT scores or my son's world record and certified swim times. They also weren't allowed to see my will where I committed, a decade before my son entered high school, millions to fund college scholarships at Harvard University (where I got my MBA) and Rensselaer Polytechnic Institute (where I received my bachelor of science) for low-income, first-generation students like me.

My trial was so unfair that 11 former US attorneys (including two from Massachusetts) took the extraordinary step of publicly criticizing their former colleagues in an amicus brief, stating, "John Wilson did not receive a fair trial." While all of my core convictions were overturned, I was left with a residual tax conviction for deducting my donations to USC, even though it was verified that I substantially overpaid my taxes that year. My sentence included a fine and probation.

Being falsely accused and wrongly convicted is a devastating experience for anyone. Imagine how my college-age son felt having his entire athletic record destroyed, not by a schoolyard bully but by federal prosecutors who repeatedly told the media that he was an "alleged" athlete.

My twin daughters were only 16 when this happened. Unfortunately, the internet makes sure that all my children's scars are both deep and permanent.

The legal costs to fight this injustice were over $10 million — my entire life savings — plus I lost five years of my peak career earnings, and all of my credit cards, bank accounts, and insurance coverages were canceled.

In the end, was the fight worth it? Absolutely. I believe my family's reputation is worth far more than money. Confessing to a crime I didn't commit would have left a permanent stain on our honor. I'll continue to fight to defend my children's reputations. I'd rather leave them with a legacy of fighting for what's right than money.

While the road ahead will be difficult, we can all hold our heads high. And I'm thankful that I still have the skills and energy to start rebuilding — hopefully with the help of friends, colleagues, and classmates.

John Wilson is the former president of Staples International.

This has to be my all-time favorite Christmas present—from *The Boston Globe* to my family.

The following summer, a separate op-ed came out in the *Wall Street Journal*. It was written by Harvey Silverglate, a well-known legal scholar and author in the Boston area. He had been following my case and had written a supportive op-ed in *The Globe* a couple of years prior. His piece in July 2024 was particularly powerful because it spoke to the business community.

How 'Varsity Blues' Swept Up an Innocent Father

Aggressive Boston prosecutors targeted John Wilson, whose children were legitimately accomplished athletes.

John Wilson. (Photo: JOSH REYNOLDS/Associated Press)

By Harvey Silverglate
Jul 29, 2024 17:39 ET

Listen to this article
4 minutes

I've practiced criminal law for more than half a century, but I'm still capable of shock at how easy it is for an innocent person to be falsely charged and convicted. Practicing in the Boston area, I followed the federal college-admissions prosecutions known as Operation Varsity Blues. These cases centered on several Hollywood celebrities and dozens of wealthy parents who confessed to scheming with admitted con man Rick Singer to get their unqualified children into top colleges by cheating on tests and bribing coaches to label the applicants as athletic recruits.

THE SCANDAL WITHIN THE SCANDAL

Most pleaded guilty because they had committed the crimes and to avoid the pernicious prosecutorial practice of recommending higher sentences for those who choose to fight rather than take a plea bargain—a practice that itself should qualify as the crime of extortion. But the only defendant who lived near Boston chose to fight.

John Wilson's facts were different from the others'. His children were highly qualified on their athletic and academic merits. His twin daughters got top scores on the ACT. His son scored in the top 93% and played on multiple nationally ranked water polo teams. His son's nationally recognized high-school coach testified that he called the University of Southern California to recommend the boy. Unlike any other Varsity Blues family, his son played on the USC team.

Mr. Wilson's donations went to USC's Trojan Athletic Fund and Mr. Singer's IRS-certified foundation, not to individuals. USC gave Mr. Wilson a receipt and kept his money. Giving donor families, legacies, political VIPs, faculty children and others preference in admissions is a longstanding practice that may seem unfair but has never been illegal.

Less than 2% of Mr. Singer's 1,750 clients were charged; most were innocent victims of his con. Mr. Wilson was innocent, yet prosecutors charged him and smeared his children. Former Boston prosecutor David G. Lazarus wrote in a Law360 article titled "Life After 'Varsity Blues' " that the Boston U.S. attorney's office "positions itself to get those cases and win any turf battles to keep them."

The prosecutors used high-pressure tactics, pushing Mr. Singer to cooperate and move beyond "singing" to "composing," as criminal lawyers say. To maximize media attention, they alleged a conspiracy across unrelated parents and charged everyone with "honest services fraud"—actions that the First U.S. Circuit Court of Appeals later deemed improper. They shared misleading sound bites and email fragments with the media to fuel sensational headlines.

ADVERTISEMENT

7 Ways To Help Generate Income Once Your Portfolio Reaches $500,000
Fisher Investments

The trial judge overruled more than 600 defense motions. He held that the Wilsons' perfect and near-perfect ACT scores were inadmissible. He also excluded the son's world-record and certified swim times that proved he was one of the fastest players on USC's team.

The right to a fair trial is the bedrock of our legal system. The judge excluded almost all of the defendant's proffered evidence. The prosecutors were improperly

THE SCANDAL WITHIN THE SCANDAL

allowed to inundate the jury with the unethical acts of other, unrelated parents. Eleven former U.S. attorneys from across the country, appointed by Democratic and Republican presidents, wrote a supporting appeals brief stating "John Wilson did not receive a fair trial." A three-judge panel of the First Circuit agreed and unanimously reversed almost all of Mr. Wilson's convictions. Prosecutors dropped those charges rather than retry the case.

Mr. Wilson was left with a single conviction—for making a false statement on a tax return. This false statement was for deducting his donations to USC using the invoice from Mr. Singer's company instead of the receipt he had received from USC. The difference in taxes owed was $1,425. Mr. Wilson overpaid his taxes that year by far more than that.

The Wilsons went through five years of hell. Mr. Wilson spent his life savings on legal costs and lost his job and reputation. He remains radioactive to employers. Ensnaring someone with a felony conviction for a $1,425 error on a tax return is the type of abuse that should cease.

Mr. Silverglate is a criminal defense and civil liberties lawyer and author of "Three Felonies a Day: How the Feds Target the Innocent."

After his op-ed came out, I drove to his office in Cambridge, Massachusetts, to meet him in person. I had to thank this man who was a sort of knight in shining armor defending me. He is a wonderful gentleman who is passionate about fighting against government overreach. Mr. Silverglate has authored several books about prosecutor and FBI overreach and corruption.

His most famous book, <u>Three Felonies A Day: How the Feds Target the Innocent</u>, was now a metaphor for my life.

Chapter 20

STRIKING BACK AT THE STREAMER

Netflix Blurred Fact and Fiction to Maximize Profits

The progress we were making getting the truth out was important, but it was small steps in a marathon. The fight was far from over. The next big battle was to take on a second Goliath—the streaming giant Netflix, who defamed us in a falsely labeled "documentary" which deliberately blurred fact and fiction and poisoned the jury pool by rushing the release of their film just months before my trial began.

***

During the discovery phase of the case, the producer and the director of the Netflix film acknowledged that they took Johnny's real image and photoshopped it into their movie. This contradicted their previous public statements that their film was "not of and concerning Johnny." How could a movie not concerning Johnny include his profile and image?

Johnny's high school photo *Screenshot from Netflix movie- Operation Varsity Blues*

> The voiceover (included in the closed captioning in the screen) while Johnny's image is shown says, "There was a water polo player who didn't play water polo in high school." This manipulation of the truth and blatantly false statement about our son took their film from the realm of documentary to pure fiction. To knowingly smear Johnny in this way is beyond despicable.
>
> Perhaps the most vicious part of this manipulation is the fact that Netflix blurred our son's real photo to deliberately make him look like a fake athlete. The irony is impossible to overstate: this case was about other parents photoshopping kids who didn't even play the sport to look like star athletes. In *our* case, Netflix photoshopped our son's photo playing water polo (on a nationally ranked team) and made it look fake in order to fit their false narrative.

***

The reach of streaming media has grown exponentially over the past two decades, with trusted sources like Netflix garnering the lion's share of that market. Netflix's true crime and corruption series have captivated many audiences. It is a bit ironic that Netflix's series *Trial by Media* examines a critical issue *they* created in our case: "Trials are examined with a focus on how the media may have impacted the verdicts in trials."

The global impact of a streaming service which currently has over 280 million subscribers and more than 500 million viewers across 190 countries is hard to overstate. Combining that reach with a brand as trusted as Netflix and a film described as a "documentary" makes the power of their message unstoppable. Whether the narrative depicted is true or false, audiences will believe that it is a fair and accurate representation of the facts.

Their film prominently highlighted me and essentially portrayed me and my family as the worst of the worst families involved in the scandal. Every other family featured in the film had confessed to outrageous criminal acts; they explicitly discussed committing their crimes with Singer cheating on tests, bribing school officials and coaches, or photoshopping photos of their nonathlete children as sports stars in sports they didn't even play.

There was no need to include a parent like me, one of the few who not only never discussed fraud in any call or email or text with Singer (including his scripted setup calls while under federal supervision) but also never committed any crimes, to make all the points in their film. Including me seemed almost gratuitous and vicious. I believe a part of why I was included in the film was the fact that during one of the recorded calls, I had invited Singer to a once-in-a-lifetime birthday party I was planning to have at Versailles. Yes, I was going to rent out a room at Versailles. (I learned when I was working in Europe that you could rent a large room there for private events.)

Again, this planned event had nothing to do with the criminal charges against me. It was simply wealth evidence designed to fan the flames of the underlying class warfare that this film was trying to sensationalize. What was Netflix's motive to knowingly demonize and destroy a family? It appears they were willing to treat me and our children as collateral damage to drive viewership and profits.

So, my lifelong dream since I was five years old, sitting by the crackling campfires with Big Sam by the projects in Hartford, now came back to make me the personification of evil. The irony was extreme. The prosecutors and film used my birthday plan to portray me as an out-of-touch elitist, born with a silver spoon in his mouth, bribing people because his kids were totally unqualified. Although nothing could be further from the truth, that didn't seem to matter.

More concerning to us was how their film poisoned the jury pool in my case. In fact, the ability for media to affect a trial is well documented by Netflix's own series, *Trial by Media*, released in May of 2020. A search on ChatGPT summarizes this Netflix series: Netflix's Trial by Media dissects how high-profile legal cases are shaped—sometimes even driven—by media influence. The documentary series exposes how sensationalized coverage, bias, and public spectacle can distort facts, sway opinions, and pressure the justice system. It questions the balance between a free press and a fair trial, revealing how courtroom battles can be turned into entertainment rather than a true pursuit of justice.

The irony here, too, is staggering. This Netflix series serves as a stark warning against the power of the media and its potential to distort facts and manipulate public opinion. Yet the very same streaming giant ignored its own warning message when they produced and released their 2021 Varsity Blues film before a single trial in the case had occurred. Instead of adhering to the truth, they chose to blend fact and fiction in a shameless attempt to sensationalize a story to maximize viewership and profits, betraying the integrity of documentary filmmaking in the process.

As Candice Patrick noted below, in addition to several other film critics in other critical reviews, this so-called documentary brazenly "defies documentary conventions" and "blurs fact and fiction." It wasn't an exposé of truth—it was a cinematic hit job, designed to sensationalize and sell a distorted narrative at the expense of our innocent family. Netflix's hypocrisy in producing this purported "documentary" speaks volumes about their priorities and their callous disregard for the very principles they claimed to champion.

'Operation Varsity Blues: The College Admissions Scandal' defies documentary conventions

The story of how one man single-handedly ruptured the American higher education system. "Operation Varsity Blues: The College Admissions Scandal" is now available to stream on Netflix.

Candace Patrick, Staff Writer
April 30, 2021

A WSN Review

"Operation Varsity Blues: The College Admissions Scandal" on Netflix tells the story about one man's impact on higher education. Actors play out reenactments of events in the dramatic documentary. (Illustration by Renee Shohet)

Just over two years ago, the college admissions scandal — later coined "Operation Varsity Blues" — sparked an uproar throughout the public, especially amongst students and parents recently involved in the college application process.

The recent Netflix documentary, "Operation Varsity Blues: The College Admissions Scandal," depicts reenactments of actual wiretapped phone conversations between Rick Singer, the infamous mastermind behind the entire scandal, and his clients, while revealing the reprehensible actions that were taken in order to guarantee students' admission into America's elite colleges such as Stanford, Yale, USC, UCLA and more.

The film defies the conventions of a typical crime documentary by using actors to play out the events tackled, a decision that casts the film in a haze of fiction. By depicting the chronological events with actors and realistic reenactments, it becomes quite easy to forget that nearly everything featured is accurate and verbatim, as its highly dramatized adaptation is executed similarly to a scripted movie.

Over the course of only seven years, Singer accumulated approximately $25 million from some of America's wealthiest families in order to get their children into the country's most prestigious schools. Their exorbitant wealth is largely conveyed in the film through mansion settings, expensive cars and references to luxurious international trips, demonstrating the wealth that allows them to afford Singer's exclusive services.

Families paid Singer anywhere from $300,000 to $500,000 for assurance that their child would be attending the school of their choice. Despite a strong focus on his fraudulent dealings, not once does the film lessen its condemnation of the admissions process as a whole. Throughout the entire documentary, there remains a clear focus on how the system values wealth

THE SCANDAL WITHIN THE SCANDAL

The best way to describe our case against Netflix is to share the executive summary of the brief, which was filed in Massachusetts Superior Court in March 2024.

COMMONWEALTH OF MASSACHUSETTS

BARNSTABLE ss.   SUPERIOR COURT DEPARTMENT
                                                     OF THE TRIAL COURT

JOHN B. WILSON and JOHN B. WILSON, JR.,

    Plaintiffs,

v.   Civil Action No. 2472CV00092

NETFLIX, INC., NETFLIX WORLDWIDE
ENTERTAINMENT, LLC, 241C FILMS, LLC,
LIBRARY FILMS LLC, JON KARMEN,
and CHRIS SMITH,

    Defendants.

SUPERIOR COURT
BARNSTABLE, SS
MAR 04 2024
FILED
Scott W. Nickerson, Clerk

COMPLAINT AND JURY DEMAND

I. SUMMARY OF THE CASE

1. John B. Wilson ("Mr. Wilson") has now been exonerated of all the core charges against him arising out of the so-called "Varsity Blues" case. It is time to hold accountable Defendants Netflix, Inc. ("Netflix") and the other Defendants named herein who defamed both his son, Johnny Wilson, and him before Mr. Wilson's case was even tried. Defendants depicted false narratives about the Wilsons while consciously disregarding the substantial evidence given to them and that was publicly available prior to publishing their film. Defendants' highly unfair, inaccurate, and defamatory "documentary" entitled, *Operation Varsity Blues: The College Admission Scandal* (the "Purported Documentary" or the "Film") has destroyed the Wilsons' reputations in the eyes of Netflix's, on information and belief, more than 260 million global subscribers and 720 million global viewers.

2. The action herein is for defamation. From 2019 to 2023, Mr. Wilson was subjected to an unfair and legally invalid prosecution in the "Varsity Blues" case brought in federal court in Boston. Mr. Wilson was the sole initial defendant in Massachusetts, and the presumptive "venue hook" to justify bringing the trials for all the Hollywood celebrities and dozens of other West Coast defendants in this high-profile case to Boston. In 2023, the First Circuit Court of Appeals unanimously overturned all of the core convictions against Mr. Wilson, rejecting, among other things, the novel and unprecedented theories of bribery, conspiracy, and honest services fraud upon which the government's charges against Mr. Wilson relied. The prosecutors subsequently dismissed all the overturned charges against Mr. Wilson.

3. No individual, including a defendant in a criminal case, is required to sit by to permit the unlawful and unfair destruction of his family's hard-earned reputation by a global media giant. Accordingly, prior to the Film's scheduled release on March 17, 2021, the Wilson family emphatically warned Defendants, in a detailed letter with voluminous attachments from their counsel, that Mr. Wilson and his children could not simply be grouped into a narrative with other individuals who, unlike him, had pleaded guilty (because *they* were guilty) to their roles in the college admissions scandal. The Wilsons' 450+-page letter to Netflix implored Defendants to avoid guilt-by-association and pointed to the specific, publicly available record of the allegations and evidence underlying the charges against Mr. Wilson before publication of the Film.

4. Among other things, the Wilsons highlighted documents in the record which showed that their children were all qualified on their own merits (his twin daughters achieved perfect and near perfect ACT scores and Johnny Wilson earned a 93rd percentile score); and that Mr.

THE SCANDAL WITHIN THE SCANDAL

Wilson's donations went to college foundations and IRS certified charities, (not to individuals) including a copy of the receipt from USC for his donations.

5. Critically, the letter also detailed Johnny Wilson's *bona fides* as an elite swimmer and water polo player. Johnny Wilson was an extraordinary athlete from an early age, including being honored on *The Oprah Show* for breaking a world record as the youngest person to swim from Alcatraz Island to San Francisco while raising over fifty-three thousand dollars for Hurricane Katrina victims. Johnny Wilson was twice selected for the U.S. Olympic water polo team Development Program, was pursued by other NCAA Division I colleges (e.g. the Air Force Academy), joined and participated on USC's 2014 water polo team, the then-reigning national champions. Johnny Wilson's verified swim times proved he was one of the fastest players on USC's 2014 team. Additionally, his high school coach (an NCAA two-time MVP and US Olympic team alternate water polo player) called USC's coaching staff to recommend him to the team.

6. The warning letter to the Defendants also included the complete reports of Mr. Wilson's extensive polygraph testing, conducted by the former Chief of the FBI's worldwide polygraph division and independently quality reviewed by the former head of the CIA's global polygraph program, where he passed all the questions truthfully (e.g. "Did you agree with Singer to put any fraudulent materials into any of your children's college application documents?" Reply: No.)

7. Mr. Wilson has fought against the false charges against him in the "Varsity Blues" case for five years because he is innocent. Notably, although viewers are notified at the end of the near 90+-minute Film that Mr. Wilson had pleaded not guilty, the Film has not been updated to indicate that Mr. Wilson has been exonerated of all the core charges against him.

- 3 -

8. In fact, the Wilsons were never even alleged to have participated in any of the three types of nefarious actions depicted throughout Defendants' Purported Documentary, namely test cheating, staging and photoshopping fake photos of non-athlete children and making bribe payments to line the pockets of individual college coaches or employees. To the extent that Defendants wanted to include the Wilson family in their Film, they had an obligation to depict the actual allegations underlying Mr. Wilson's charges fairly and accurately.

9. Instead, Defendants vilified the Wilsons through multiple pernicious filmmaking techniques which lead a reasonable viewer to falsely conclude, among others, that the allegations against Mr. Wilson were the same as the unrelated bad characters portrayed in the Film.

10. Defendants accomplished their cinematic sleight of hand by repeatedly immersing the Wilson family into a toxic swamp of despicable acts committed by the unrelated "worst of the worst" parents who the Defendants cherry-picked to illustrate the three schemes. Through their robust understanding of how the film medium can be uniquely manipulated, Defendants blurred the lines between the wrongdoer parents and Mr. Wilson by interspersing Mr. Wilson's edited words and images at least twenty-six times before and after depicting other parents brazenly committing illegal acts.

11. Defendants even went so far as to superimpose Mr. Wilson's name and voice over a scene depicting other actors photoshopping fake photos of a non-athlete child. However, Defendants knew or should have known that connecting Mr. Wilson's voice and name to the photoshopping scene is indefensible — as they were given actual photos of Johnny Wilson and were aware that Mr. Wilson was never alleged to have engaged in any such photoshopping conduct since his son, unlike any parents' child depicted in the Film or indicted under the Fake Athlete Scheme, was a Division I level athlete.

THE SCANDAL WITHIN THE SCANDAL

12. The composite image below compares the actual practice photo of Johnny Wilson which was shared with Defendants before the airing of their Purported Documentary (on the left) with screenshots of scenes from the Film staging fake photos and photoshopping over which Defendants played Mr. Wilson's voice (on the right.)

[Composite image with labels: "2013 practice photo sent to Netflix *before* film's release" | "Close up of Johnny Wilson from 2013 practice" | "Netflix's false portrayal of the Wilsons staging fake photos" / "Johnny Wilson - 1st Place 2013 League Championships" | "Netflix's portrayal of Photoshopping"]

13. The Defendants went further in their conscious disregard for the truth when they deliberately excluded critical portions of several of Mr. Wilson's conversations that are played throughout the Film. For example, Defendants cut Mr. Wilson's dialogue right after he says *"you don't have to play the sport"* leading viewers to falsely believe that Mr. Wilson was therefore going to portray his children as fake athletes. However, seconds later in the same conversation, Mr. Wilson confirms that his daughters could be "scorekeepers" or team "managers," assuming they have the requisite academic credentials for admission to their schools of choice. Taking edited sound bites out of context can have a devastating effect, as

- 5 -

Cardinal Richelieu observed in the 17th century, "If you give me six lines written by the hand of the most honest of men, I will find something in them which will hang him."

14. Market research conducted by Lightbeam Communications on January 22, 2024, confirmed just how devastating the effect of these repeated innuendos actually are on a group of the Film's viewers. After watching the Film, a majority of participants (who were Netflix subscribers selected randomly from all backgrounds and parts of the country) concluded that the Wilsons had cheated on the ACT tests; that Johnny Wilson was a fake athlete; that Mr. Wilson created fake photos of his son and that Mr. Wilson made bribe payments to individual coaches and administrators. None of the conclusions drawn by the viewers was true or even alleged to be true by the government against the Wilsons.

15. Defendants mislabeled their work a "documentary," a designation that signals to viewers that what is to be presented is truthful. Defendant Chris Smith's long history of blurring truth and fiction was noted by the *Washington Post's* chief film critic, Ann Hornaday, who interviewed Smith, who directed the Film, about his directorial approach to the Film in March 2021 writing, "Blurring the lines between fact and fiction is nothing new for Smith." She went on to quote Smith himself saying, "Now with *Operation Varsity Blues*, Smith says, 'It finally made sense to put [fact and fiction] together.'"

16. Defendants blurred the lines between the other parents who had all confessed to egregious crimes and Mr. Wilson. Further, by deliberately ignoring publicly available information on the docket in Mr. Wilson's criminal proceeding to which Defendants were specifically directed and with which they were provided in a detailed letter, and through repeated suggestions of fact and innuendo, through carefully crafted filmmaking techniques, of and concerning Mr. Wilson and Johnny Wilson, the Defendants gave and continue to give their

global audience the false and defamatory impression, among others, that Mr. Wilson and Johnny Wilson engaged in substantially similar conduct as the other parents and children included in the publication. The Wilson family members named herein seek monetary damages and other legal redress for the malicious and reckless destruction of their reputations caused by Defendants.

II. PARTIES

17. Mr. Wilson is an individual and a resident of Barnstable County, Massachusetts.

18. Plaintiff Johnny Wilson is an individual and a resident of Los Angeles, California. He is the son of Mr. Wilson. Although Johnny currently resides in California, he was born in Massachusetts where his family and he have spent significant time in Massachusetts every year since 1999 and where Johnny has developed numerous decades-long friendships. Johnny Wilson has consequently suffered his most substantial injury from Defendants' defamation of him in Massachusetts, where his father and the rest of his family still reside, where most of his lifelong and closest relationships exist, and which was the epicenter of the "Varsity Blues" cases.

19. Defendant Netflix is a media-services provider and company that streams media content worldwide to its subscribers, including the Purported Documentary. Upon information and belief, it is a Delaware corporation with a principal place of business in the State of California.

20. Defendant Netflix Worldwide Entertainment, LLC ("Netflix WE") is, upon information and belief, a wholly owned subsidiary of Netflix. Upon further information and belief, Netflix WE owns the trademarks and copyrights for the Purported Documentary at issue here. Upon

A media executive I know told me that media companies win 95 percent of their cases at the outset by filing a motion to dismiss, especially in cases where they are purportedly relying on government records and the "Fair Report Privilege."

What Netflix did in their film was so egregious and so defamatory, Massachusetts Superior Court Judge Michael K. Callan denied Netflix's motion to dismiss in September 2024. As noted in the *Sportico* article below, he said, "The film mistakenly gave the 'clear impression' that Wilson Jr. was a fake athlete or that he cheated on his ACT exam."

Judge Callan went on to say, "A viewer of the film could wrongly draw inferences on Wilson Jr. on account of 'truncated' conversations as well as contemporaneous images strongly implying that John Jr. was a fake athlete and that his own father staged photos of him as a fake. The son, in reality, was a 'highly accomplished' water polo player in high school who scored in the ninety-third percentile on his ACT and made the Trojans' water polo team."

Defeating Netflix's motion to dismiss our case was a *major* victory. We are now in the discovery phase of the legal process where we can collect more facts in preparation for trial.

THE SCANDAL WITHIN THE SCANDAL

VARSITY BLUES DAD SCORES WIN VS. NETFLIX, CLAIMS FILM DISTORTS REALITY

BY MICHAEL MCCANN August 27, 2024 9:00am

John B. Wilson (center) says Netflix inaccurately portrays him and his son, John B. Wilson Jr., in a film about the Varsity Blues admission scandal.
PHOTO BY JESSICA RINALDI/THE BOSTON GLOBE VIA GETTY IMAGES

John B. Wilson, whose conviction in the Operation Varsity Blues case was overturned last year on appeal, scored another legal win Aug. 13 when a Cape Cod judge denied Netflix's motion to dismiss Wilson's defamation case over the film *Operation Varsity Blues: The College Admissions Scandal* (2021).

Barnstable County (Mass.) Superior Court Judge Michael K. Callan ruled Wilson has plausibly alleged Netflix defamed him and his son, John B. Wilson Jr., when the film mistakenly gave the "clear impression" that Wilson Jr. was a fake athlete or that he cheated on his ACT exam to gain admission into the University of Southern California.

A viewer of the film, Callan wrote, could wrongly draw inferences about Wilson Jr. on account of "truncated" conversations as well as "contemporaneous images strongly implying that John Jr. was a fake athlete, and that his own father staged him as fake." The son, in reality, was a "highly accomplished water polo" player in high school who scored in the 93rd percentile on his ACT and made the Trojans' water polo team.

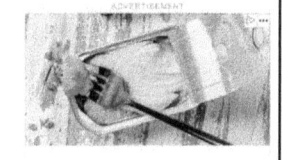

POPULAR STORIES

WHY NORTHWESTERN WANTS BIG-TIME FOOTBALL'S...

MICHAEL JORDAN AND NASCAR REACH DEAL AS LAWSUIT...

TOP 50 HIGHEST-PAID ATHLETES OF ALL TIME

290

Defeating the Netflix motion to dismiss was another massive win—one that we also hope will cause media companies to be more careful when they develop future documentaries.

When media companies get a documentary right, it can be great entertainment. When they get it wrong, it can create unimaginable devastation.

We look forward to presenting the truth in court and holding Netflix accountable for their defamatory portrayal of our family.

Chapter 21

TAKING ON THE TROJANS

USC Defrauded Us to Protect Their Dark Secrets

Taking on a third Goliath—USC—was not a decision we made lightly. However, certain actions by the USC administration caused our family profound harm. To ensure the truth prevailed, we knew we had to confront the falsehoods at their source. These battles weren't of our choosing, but we are committed to seeing them through to the end. A friend of mine teased me about fighting three Goliaths, "They picked on the wrong guy. You've got them outnumbered."

***

> Darkness creates the opportunity for illicit behaviors. Underhanded practices, or shady deals, are euphemisms for doing improper things which others cannot see. The best way to prevent corruption, or to root it out where it exists, is to shine a light on those bad practices. Over a century ago, US Supreme Court Justice Louis Brandeis said, "Sunlight is the best disinfectant…"
>
> **Louis Brandeis**
> "Sunlight is the best disinfectant…"
> -U.S. Supreme Court Justice 1856-1941

THE SCANDAL WITHIN THE SCANDAL

> In his 1913 article in *Harper's Weekly*, "What Publicity Can Do," he made the case for combating "the wickedness of people shielding wrongdoers and passing them off (or at least allowing them to pass themselves off) as honest men." His proposed remedy was to make illicit actions visible and widely available for all to see; his sunlight quote is the precursor to today's mantra of "full transparency."

***

The USC lawsuit goes to the root cause of what happened to our family in this case. When Leslie and I visited USC in 2013 to personally meet with two senior representatives of the school, head Coach Jovan Vavic and assistant athletic development director, Alex Garfio. They both independently confirmed that donating through Singer's organization was consistent with school policies and could help our son's chances of admissions.

It's important to note that we didn't pre-arrange to meet with the athletic development person, Alex Garfio. We asked for that meeting after we met with head coach Vavic. This spontaneous confirmation with two separate people was something I had been taught at work to prove the validity of a policy or contract. Why would we do this if we were knowingly involved in fraud?

Leslie, Johnny and I also watched the team practice and met with head coach Vavic. Johnny shared his water polo credentials and discussed the various coaches he had at Menlo school and Stanford club over the years with coach Vavic. Coach Vavic confirmed that Johnny's experiences made him a strong fit for the team as a walk-on redshirt player.

Every interaction with the school during Johnny's time on the team, as well as the facts we made public throughout my litigation that we painstakingly gathered, confirmed that this was the case. Johnny was a solid member of the team, and the school had confirmed to us personally and repeatedly that they had a longstanding practice of providing donor families with admissions support through both the VIP and athletics programs.

Yet it was only at my trial in 2021 that USC's narrative inexplicably shifted. USC, in a dramatic departure from all prior communications and evidence, claimed that Johnny was essentially not a member of the team. The USC witnesses at the trial outright denied any history of helping donor families through admissions processes. If we take USC's trial testimony at its word, then we were lied to by numerous USC representatives throughout 2013, 2014, and 2015.

It felt like an outright betrayal, not just of our family, but of the truth itself. This glaring contradiction became a focal point in a case that had already drawn relentless media attention. Headlines buzzed with sensationalized stories, while the school's false claims added fuel to an already raging fire and cast a dark cloud over Johnny's hard-earned athletic abilities and achievements and our family's integrity.

In addition to the USC team photo shown earlier, Johnny was officially registered with the NCAA. He was also scheduled to participate in weekend tournament assignments with other redshirts to videotape games and setting up the pool for games throughout the season. The videotaping assignments always included two redshirts to each camera so that the entire meet is recorded and nothing is missed, even if one student needed to take a break. It defies common sense and logic for assistant coach Moon to suggest that Johnny wasn't there after the first day, especially since Johnny was assigned to videotape games throughout the season.

As shown below, Johnny was asked by the assistant men's and women's water polo coach for the size uniforms he needed, and he traveled with the rest of the redshirts for away team matches.

Stefan Luedecke <luedecke@usc.edu>
John Wilson <johnbwil@usc.edu>
Sent: 8/9/2014 11:30:29 AM
Subject: Re: USC Apparel Information

what is your water polo suit size please?

Stefan Luedecke

Men's & Women's Water Polo
Assistant Coach

Cell (213) 280-6604
Office (213) 740-2159
Fax (213) 740-6177
http://www.usctrojans.com

University of Southern California
Uytengsu Aquatics Center
1026 W. 34th Street
Los Angeles, CA 90089-2511

Follow USC on Facebook and Twitter
http://facebook.com/USCTrojans
http://twitter.com/USC_Athletics
http://twitter.com/uscwaterpolo

On Aug 8, 2014, at 11:57 AM, John Wilson <johnbwil@usc.edu>
wrote:

Yes I am very exited to play this year. I am not sure about the suit size so I would like to order a medium and a large.
shoe size: 12
shirt size: xl
polo shirts: xl
sweatshirts: xl
warm up top: xl
warm up bottom: xl
shorts: xl
parka: xl
6'0 192 lbs

Thank you,
Sincerely Johnny

On Thu, Aug 7, 2014 at 3:10 PM, Stefan Luedecke <luedecke@usc.edu> wrote:
John,

USAO-VB-01605508

I hope all is well. Season is around the corner and I need your sizes for our Nike outfits. Please send me the following information as soon as possible

Water Polo Suit (S=30, M=32, L=34, XL=36, XXL=38)
Shoe size
T-Shirt (S,M,L,XL,XXL)
Polo Shirt (S,M,L,XL,XXL)
Sweatshirt (S,M,L,XL,XXL)
Warm up top (S,M,L,XL,XXL)
Warm up bottom (S,M,L,LT (Long and Tall) XL,XXL)
Shorts (S,M,L,XL)
Parka (L,XL,XXL)

Also, please send me your hight and weight. Thank you.

Fight ON!

Stefan Luedecke

Men's & Women's Water Polo
Assistant Coach

Cell (213) 280-6604
Office (213) 740-2159
Fax (213) 740-6177
http://www.usctrojans.com

University of Southern California
Uytengsu Aquatics Center
1026 W. 34th Street
Los Angeles, CA 90089-2511

Follow USC on Facebook and Twitter
http://facebook.com/USCTrojans
http://twitter.com/USC_Athletics
http://twitter.com/uscwaterpolo

Leslie and I travelled from Europe to Palo Alto, California, to meet with the other team parents and the redshirts to cheer the team on for their game against Stanford. We flew ten hours each way, multiple times and attended multiple practices and other team games as well. The photos below are from the NCAA national water polo championship tournament held in December 2014 in San Diego. You can see from the photos I took of the team, the redshirts in the stands cheering the team on, a close-up of Johnny with one of his teammates (and as shown in an earlier chapter) and one of me and Johnny together the same afternoon.

Why would we do any of this if Johnny were not on the team?

Photos from NCAA National Championship Tournament 2014 in San Diego

***

We filed a lawsuit in September 2024 against USC for defrauding us when we met with school officials back in 2013. We learned of this fraud during my trial in 2021. That's when the USC witnesses effectively said that the representations made to us by multiple senior USC officials during our in-person visit in 2013, as well as many interactions we and our son had with USC coaching and medical staff members during his time on the team, were against school policy and fraudulent.

It seemed more than strange to us that USC fought extremely aggressively throughout the trial to keep their internal admissions data, emails, and practices secret and blocked from the jury and public—even after the materials were redacted to avoid sharing any private names or information. These documents were all filed under seal. If they were truthful and had nothing to hide, why was it necessary to go to such extremes to keep this redacted information away from the jury and public scrutiny.

All the information we did see during the discovery and trial preparation, confirmed what we had been told during our in-person visits to the school in 2013—specifically, that USC had a widespread practice of giving help in admissions to donor families, or potential donor families, through both the VIP process and athletic subcommittee process.

Yet, the USC witnesses who testified in 2021 said just the opposite. Taking their testimony given under oath as the truth, all the USC representations to us and related actions from 2013 and 2014 were fraudulent. USC representatives either defrauded us in 2013 and 2014 or they lied on the stand in 2021.

This led us to believe that there were multiple embarrassing secrets about how many donor families were treated by USC in the admissions process which the school did not want to disclose.

Below are portions of two articles about the USC lawsuit from *Sportico* and the *LA Times* and the press release about the lawsuit.

THE SCANDAL WITHIN THE SCANDAL

Sportico

VARSITY BLUES FALLOUT PRODUCES FRAUD ACCUSATION AGAINST USC

BY MICHAEL MCCANN September 24, 2024 2:00pm

A lawsuit brought by a Varsity Blues parent accuses USC of fraud.
PHOTO BY MARIO TAMA/GETTY IMAGES

With one notable exception, the few dozen parents caught up in the Operation Varsity Blues scandal have seemingly moved on from that turbulent period in their lives. Most have kept quiet about a prosecution that, for some, led to prison sentences and public shaming over standardized test cheating, fake athletic credentialing and other illicit efforts to ensure their kids gained acceptance into prestigious universities.

John B. Wilson is the exception.

A father of three who was one of the few parents to take his chances in court rather than cut a plea deal, Wilson beat the feds last year when the U.S. Court of Appeals for the First Circuit **overturned** his conviction. The appellate court concluded his actions didn't amount to crime. Last month, a Massachusetts judge **advanced** Wilson's defamation case against Netflix over his portrayal in the film *Operation Varsity Blues: The College Admissions Scandal's*.

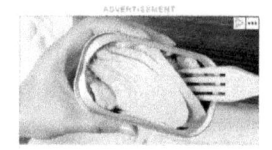

The Best Tuna In The World

The Quality of This Tuna Has Everyone Asking Why Wasn't This Quality Available Before?

Natural Catch Tuna

Open >

POPULAR STORIES

WHY NORTHWESTERN WANTS BIG-TIME FOOTBALL'S...

MICHAEL JORDAN AND NASCAR REACH DEAL AS LAWSUIT...

USC accused of fraud by 'Varsity Blues' parent whose conviction was overturned

BY HARRIET RYAN, MATT HAMILTON

SEP 20, 2024 | 20:36

A Massachusetts father implicated in the "Varsity Blues" scandal filed suit Friday against the University of Southern California, seeking the return of a $100,000 donation he made in connection with his son's admission, along with $75 million in damages for what he claims was fraud and deceit by the university.

John Wilson, a former executive at Gap and Staples, was convicted in 2021 of conspiracy, fraud and bribery in the college admission scheme. An appellate court tossed those charges last year, ruling prosecutors had not proved an "overarching conspiracy" with corrupt college counselor Rick Singer, and Wilson has since embarked on a campaign to clear his family's name.

In addition to the suit against USC in Los Angeles County Superior Court, the 65-year-old has brought a defamation case against Netflix over a film about the scandal and gone on a media blitz about what he describes as an unjust prosecution that cost him his life's savings.

> "I do think it's important for us to try to set the record straight and do whatever I can to help rebuild my family's reputation," Wilson said in an interview Friday.

> Wilson hired Singer in 2010 to tutor his son, Johnny, and later advise him on college admission. The teen was admitted to USC as a water polo recruit in 2014 after Singer advised the family to donate $100,000 to the athletic department.

THE SCANDAL WITHIN THE SCANDAL

Federal prosecutors characterized that donation as an illegal bribe to USC. In his suit, Wilson contends that he confirmed Singer's instruction to donate to the university with two employees — the head water polo coach and an athletics department administrator — who both said the gift would facilitate his son's admission and was "in accordance with accepted school policies and certainly was not illegal or illicit."

After federal prosecutors indicted Singer and 33 parents in 2019, USC said it had been a victim in the scheme and that it was a violation of university policy to accept donations to facilitate admissions.

Wilson's suit called that stance by USC "nothing short of reprehensible" in light of what he said university employees previously told him and said it fueled the criminal case against him. The suit criticized USC's decision to keep the Wilson donation as "a deeply troubling double standard and a gross misuse of donor trust."

In a statement, USC said, "This lawsuit, which dredges up events that occurred as many as 10 years ago, has no legal merit."

The statement added that, in the wake of Varsity Blues, "USC made a number of significant changes to prevent abuse of the athletics admission process" including multiple layers of oversight.

Singer, the mastermind, was sentenced last year to 3½ years in prison. Some of his high-profile clients, including actors Felicity Huffman and Lori Loughlin and Loughlin's husband, fashion designer Mossimo Giannulli, served terms of five months or less.

> Felicity Huffman says college admissions scandal was 'only option' to help her daughter
>
> Dec 1, 2023 | 12:36
>
> A jury convicted Wilson of filing a false tax return, bribery and several fraud-related charges, but his defense team appealed, arguing that admissions slots were not considered property for the purposes of mail and wire fraud. An appellate court agreed, throwing out all but the tax charge. After prosecutors declined to retry

The lawsuit is pending in Los Angeles. Below is the release from that lawsuit.

THE SCANDAL WITHIN THE SCANDAL

Exonerated 'Varsity Blues' Parents File $75 Million Lawsuit Against USC for Fraud

NEWS PROVIDED BY
Law Offices of William Charles Tanenbaum, Esq →
Sep 23, 2024, 15:46 ET

John Wilson, Cleared of Charges in College Admissions Scandal, Seeks Justice

LOS ANGELES, Sept. 23, 2024 /PRNewswire/ -- John Wilson, a Massachusetts businessman and former defendant in the high-profile "Varsity Blues" college admissions scandal, and his wife, Leslie Q. Wilson, have filed a lawsuit against the University of Southern California (USC) for fraud. The suit, filed in Los Angeles County Superior Court on Sept. 20, 2024, by the Law Offices of William Charles Tanenbaum, Esq., seeks $75 million in damages from USC for its role in Mr. Wilson's wrongful conviction in the sensational and star-studded 2021 federal case which drew national media attention. After a protracted legal battle, all of Mr. Wilson's core convictions in that case were ultimately overturned by the U.S. Court of Appeals for the First Circuit in May 2023.

"As it relates to the Wilson family, USC was not a victim, but rather, they were the architects of an athletic-related donations process that put a legal target on Mr. Wilson," said William Charles Tanenbaum, the Wilsons' attorney who filed the suit. "USC not only misled the Wilsons into making their donation under false pretenses but also had the audacity to keep the money even after labeling it, many years later, as an illegal bribe. This is a disturbing betrayal of donor trust and a disappointing example of institutional hypocrisy."

In part because of USC's actions, the suit alleges, John Wilson was charged on several counts in the Varsity Blues case including making a $100,000 donation to USC's Trojan Athletic Fund which the university assured him was legal and conformed to the institution's donation policies. The Wilsons relied on the representations of USC's Head Water Polo Coach Jovan Vavic and Assistant Athletic Director Alex Garfio that the donation was proper and an accepted part of USC athlete recruitment for non-scholarship players. John and Leslie both met with officials on USC's campus as part of their due diligence before donating.

Johnny Wilson, back left corner, stands with the rest of the University of Southern California water polo team in 2014 for a team picture.

Taking on the Trojans

The lawsuit further claims that USC engaged in "reprehensible" and exploitative behavior by misrepresenting its donation policies directly to the Wilsons then, according to Tanenbaum, "later ratified their in-person representations in a written 'thank you' letter sent to the Wilsons, which was printed on USC Athletics Department letterhead and signed by Associate Athletic Director Ron Orr, copying the USC water polo coach. USC further confirmed to the Wilsons the propriety of their donation by corresponding with the Wilsons during their son Johnny's freshman year as a full-time "redshirt" player on the USC water polo team, and as verified on the team's website and NCAA records.

Though dozens of other parents, including several Hollywood celebrities, pled guilty and were convicted of a variety of illegal activities in the Varsity Blues case, the Wilson's never misrepresented their son's credentials, nor falsely portrayed his academic and athletic record which made him a strong candidate for admittance to USC under any circumstances. Unlike many, if not all of the other defendants in the Varsity Blues case, the Wilsons' son was well-qualified to attend USC with a 3.8/4.0 GPA and a 93-percentile score on the ACT college entrance exam. He was an elite high school water polo player, who was twice invited to join the U.S. Olympic team development program and who was being recruited by other Division I colleges. He participated in the 2014 USC water polo team where his certified swim times proved he was one of the fastest swimmers on USC's 2014 team.

The suit claims John Wilson and his family endured a harrowing experience from false charges brought by Boston federal prosecutors seeking venue in the Wilson's home state of Massachusetts for this high-profile case, in part due to USC's actions regarding the Wilsons. The prosecution caused Mr. Wilson to spend nearly all his life savings on legal fees, fighting false allegations for over five years until all the core charges against him were overturned.

"Fighting these false charges has been a five-year emotional, physical and financial nightmare for my entire family," John Wilson said. "Worst of all, the reputations of our teenage daughters, who earned perfect and near perfect ACT test scores, were also falsely maligned in the media, all for crimes we did not commit."

"We did our due diligence and met with multiple senior people at USC to confirm our donations and the athletic admissions process and we did everything the school requested," said Leslie Wilson. "We were dedicated parents who supported our children throughout their academic and athletic careers. We would travel to team practices and games to support our son and the entire USC team, and we continue to have fond memories of the education our son received at USC. But, we need to set the record straight regarding the admissions process that USC created and guided us through."

The case is expected to be closely watched by legal experts, education professionals, and the public as it progresses through the court system, potentially setting precedents for how universities handle donations and admissions in the future.

The full lawsuit is available at **www.scandalwithinthescandal.com**.

Contact:
Mark Hazlin
Email: **Mhazlin@xenophonstrategies.com**
Ph: (202) 289-4001

SOURCE Law Offices of William Charles Tanenbaum, Esq

On February 24, 2025 we filed an opposition to USC's motion to dismiss our fraud case against them (a motion to dismiss is called a Demurrer in the California legal system.) USC's primary grounds for Demurrer are based on statute of limitations. The first few pages of our case address this issue and are shown below.

William Charles Tanenbaum, Esq. - SBN 305030
LAW OFFICES OF WILLIAM CHARLES TANENBAUM, ESQ.
9701 Wilshire Blvd., Suite 1000
Beverly Hills, CA 90212
Telephone: (310) 628-0989
Facsimile: (310) 859-1960
Email: tanenbaum@tanenbaumlegal.com

Steven A. Engel, Esq (*Pro Hac Vice* forthcoming)
DECHERT LLP
1900 K Street NW
Washington, D.C. 20006
Telephone: (202) 261-3300
Facsimile: (202) 261-3333
Email: steven.engel@dechert.com

Attorneys for Plaintiffs
John B. Wilson and Leslie Q. Wilson

SUPERIOR COURT OF THE STATE OF CALIFORNIA

COUNTY OF LOS ANGELES – CENTRAL DISTRICT

JOHN B. WILSON, an individual, and LESLIE Q. WILSON, an individual, Plaintiffs, v. UNIVERSITY OF SOUTHERN CALIFORNIA, a California nonprofit corporation, and DOES 1-30, Defendants.	Case No. 24STCV24447 (Assigned to the Hon. Holly J. Fujie, Dept. 56) **OPPOSITION TO DEFENDANT UNIVERSITY OF SOUTHERN CALIFORNIA'S DEMURRER AND REQUESTS FOR JUDICIAL NOTICE; MEMORANDUM OF POINTS AND AUTHORITIES** DATE: February 24, 2025 TIME: 8:30 a.m. DEPT: 56 Complaint Filed: September 20, 2024 Trial Date: Not Set

MEMORANDUM OF POINTS AND AUTHORITIES

I. INTRODUCTION

Senior University of Southern California ("USC") officials lied to John and Leslie Wilson about their admission policies, and those misrepresentations nearly destroyed their lives. In 2013, USC officials brazenly defrauded the Wilsons to solicit a large donation from the Wilson family. Multiple, independent, USC Athletic and Development Department staff repeatedly and falsely represented that the Wilsons' donation in support of their son would be common, lawful, and entirely consistent with USC's admissions policies. Those misrepresentations directly led to the criminal prosecution of John Wilson and to a financial and reputational nightmare that ended only when the U.S. Court of Appeals for the First Circuit held that the government should not have prosecuted him for making the purportedly unlawful donation in the first place. But the Wilsons' nightmare all began with the lies told by numerous representatives of USC starting in 2013.

USC's bad behavior continues to this day and cannot deprive the Wilsons of their day in court. Few rules are more familiar in California than the demurrer standard. A trial court considering a demurrer must "deem to be true all material facts properly pled" in the Complaint, *Montclair Parkowners Ass'n v. City of Montclair*, 76 Cal.App.4th 784, 790 (1999), and then decide whether "the plaintiff has described a cause of action under any possible legal theory," *Aubry v. Tri-City Hospital Dist.*, 2 Cal.4th 962, 966-967 (1992). In their rush to avoid accountability, and a public trial focused upon their deceit, USC blows through this black-letter standard and asks the Court to sustain the demurrer based solely upon Defendants' untested version of events and multiple documents falling outside the Complaint.

In April 2013, the Wilsons visited USC and spoke about their son's potential application to the school. USC officials confirmed that a donation from the Wilsons would be a "win-win" for all concerned, and the university reinforced those misrepresentations by taking concrete steps to ratify the legitimacy of the donations. USC's agents memorialized the approval of the donations that the Wilsons made through Richard Singer's organization, with USC's Associate Athletic Director, Ron Orr, sending a letter to the Wilsons thanking them for contributing to USC

1
OPPOSITION TO DEMURRER

Athletics. USC then further justified the Wilsons' reliance by enrolling their son at the school and allowing him to walk-on to its powerhouse water polo team in his freshman year.

As the Complaint reveals, the Wilsons reasonably relied on USC's multiple misrepresentations, which were made directly the Wilsons. The Athletic Department's "Thank You" letter ratified those statements. Moreover, the Wilsons also learned of many other families who made similar donations to bolster their children's chances of admission and placement on athletic teams, all with USC's apparent blessing. And the Wilsons had no reason whatsoever to question why their son, Johnny, made the team. Johnny had spent high school starting for multiple top club teams. Johnny's nationally recognized high school coach had called USC to recommend Johnny for the team. And Johnny participated as a full member of that 2014 team, dedicating over 40 hours a week to it, only resigning after suffering a career-ending concussion.

USC's fraud set the Wilsons up for years of criminal litigation, financial devastation, and reputational ruin. Because the Wilsons had relied upon an unscrupulous adviser, Richard Singer, in connection with their application, John Wilson was charged as one of many Singer clients in the infamous "Varsity Blues" conspiracy case. The federal indictment cost John his career. The public outcry cost the Wilsons their friends and their reputation. And the attorneys' fees cost the Wilsons their life's savings. Yet through it all, the Wilsons knew that John would eventually be exonerated. That confidence arose in no small part because they believed they had followed USC policies as explained to them by multiple USC officials and that USC officials, when called to testify at trial under oath, would admit that USC had advised the Wilsons that they considered the donations entirely lawful and consistent with USC practice.

USC's chosen representative at trial buried those hopes at trial on September 21, 2021. That day, a USC admissions officer, whom the Wilsons had never met, testified that financial contributions were not a legitimate part of the admissions process for non-scholarship athletes seeking to join a USC team. In other words, USC's testifying witness *admitted* that USC's coaches and athletic personnel had *repeatedly lied* to the Wilson family, leading the family to make the donations that led to the catastrophic federal indictment. It was on that day that the Wilsons discovered that they had been defrauded.

> John Wilson has since beaten the federal charges levied against him because of his USC donation. But the harm inflicted by USC's fraud remains. The Wilsons would not have suffered that harm had *just one* USC official told them the truth—that the school considered the donation improper and contrary to their admissions policies. The Wilsons now have brought this action in an effort to hold USC to account and to make the family whole. The Complaint adequately alleges facts in detail that, taken as true, are more than sufficient to demonstrate liability for fraud and negligent misrepresentation.
>
> The Demurrer offers no reason to hold otherwise. Rather, the Demurrer reads like a summary judgment brief that offers untested and defamatory assertions that directly contradict the well-pleaded factual allegations. This Court will have ample opportunity to evaluate the merits of this case, and the Wilsons will be entitled to full discovery into USC's admissions policies; its consideration of donor's contributions in connection with admission; and what USC has represented to other parents on those subjects. But the Court should not countenance USC's effort to try to pretermit discovery through a demurrer that relies entirely upon purported facts and argument falling outside the Complaint.

We did not learn that USC defrauded us in 2014 until USC witnesses testified at my trial in September 2021. This legal filing also discusses assistant coach Moon's testimony stating,[39] "Moon's false testimony conflicted with USC's own records demonstrating that Johnny regularly attended team practices and performed weekly work assignments with other redshirt players, USC medical records about Johnny's concussion, the official team photo, and official team records submitted by Moon to the NCAA."

As stated previously, it was devastating when the prosecutor and trial judge wouldn't allow overwhelming amounts of impeachment evidence (evidence which discredits a witness' testimony in a trial) to be shared with the jury during my trial. This blocked evidence could have helped to prove the falsity of many of Moon's statements on the stand.

---

39 *Newswire by William Tanenbaum, Exonerated 'Varsity Blues" Parent Challenges USC's Wrongdoing & False Testimony, February 11, 2025*

OPPOSITION TO DEMURRER

placed him on the team roster, and otherwise treated him as a full member. (Compl. ¶¶ 56-59).[1] Johnny finished out the 2014, and only resigned from the team in January 2015 after suffering a concussion.

C. The Wilsons Did Not Learn Of USC's Fraud Until USC's Witness Testified At John Wilson's Criminal Trial.

In 2019, the Department of Justice indicted John Wilson for allegedly conspiring with Singer in the so-called "Varsity Blues" conspiracy. (Compl. ¶ 3). According to the indictment, John joined other parents in using Singer's services to defraud USC and other universities by bribing officials and coaches to accept their children to fill athletic positions. (Compl. ¶ 3). As the sole Singer client who lived in Massachusetts, the Boston-based federal prosecutors used John as a "venue hook," allowing them to charge and potentially try Hollywood celebrities and dozens of other alleged West Coast conspirators for this high-level case in Massachusetts federal court. (Compl. ¶ 4). Although most defendants pled guilty, John Wilson fought the charges because he knew that he was innocent, not least because USC—the purported victim of the alleged bribe—had *repeatedly represented to him* that his donation was above-board and consistent with USC policies. (Compl. ¶¶ 3-14).

The Wilsons had no reason to think that a USC witness, when placed under oath, would say anything different. As the Complaint explains,

> After 2014, the Wilsons learned about other parents who made donations to other various sports programs at USC with the understanding that such donations were helpful in the admissions process of their children which served to confirm the propriety in the minds of the Wilsons of what was represented to them by Coach Vavic and Mr. Garfio. The Wilsons learned of many specific examples of donor families getting admissions help for non-athlete children on multiple USC sports teams over several years, many of whom made donations to USC unrelated to Singer's organization.

---

[1] The government never filed charges against, and USC's Athletic Department never fired, Moon, who is currently the women's water polo coach, despite his testimony at the criminal trial that USC purportedly did not consider Johnny a member of the team and that he had worked with Javic in building Johnny's athletic profile. (E.g., Compl. ¶¶ 61, 64, 72). Moon's false testimony conflicted with USC's own records demonstrating that Johnny regularly attended team practices and performed weekly work assignments with other redshirt players, USC medical records about Johnny's concussion, the official team photo, and official team records submitted by Moon to the NCAA. (E.g., Compl. ¶¶ 56-61).

It is unfortunate that certain individuals within an institution dedicated to educating young people have not upheld the integrity and values they are meant to instill. Their actions in concealing the truth and falsely smearing the reputation of one of their *own* students to protect themselves from legal actions and safeguard their own dark secrets are deeply concerning.

As a private institution, we believe that USC should have the autonomy to structure its admissions process as it deems appropriate. However, if preferential treatment is extended to certain groups, we feel that it should be applied consistently and be done with public transparency. The recent change in California law prohibiting legacy and donor families from getting help in admissions may end a couple of those practices.

However, there still may be other preferred categories and opaque admissions practices. A long-term solution will likely remain out of reach unless USC addresses their past admissions issues truthfully and provides transparency in all aspects of their admissions process.

On March 28, 2025, we submitted an amended complaint against USC and a hearing on USC's expected motion to dismiss is likely sometime in the summer or fall of 2025.

USC has an opportunity to set the record straight and tell the truth about our son, clarify what truly happened with our family, and bring transparency to their admissions process.

EPILOGUE

Our Fight to Restore Our Family's Honor Continues

When it comes to defending our family's reputation, we want to leave our children with a legacy of standing up for what is right. We believe an inheritance of honor holds more value than wealth. Although the journey ahead will be long and challenging, fighting for our principles is the only path where we can maintain our dignity and all hold our heads high.

***

> Setting expectations in any long-term endeavor is critical to success. Sustaining your energy, resources, and focus over prolonged periods requires perspective. Winston Churchill, as part of a 1942 speech after the Allied victory over Rommel's Nazi forces in North Africa, made this point well when he said, "Now is not the end. It is not even the beginning of the end. But it is, perhaps, the end of the beginning."
>
> **Winston Churchill**
> "Now this is not the end,
> It is not even the beginning of the end.
> But it is, perhaps, the end of the beginning."

THE SCANDAL WITHIN THE SCANDAL

> Churchill was trying to pace an entire nation and the Allied forces in an existential struggle against Nazi Germany. While his words may have been disheartening to some, they added perspective, resolve, and determination to others. His timing was also impeccable. He shared this harsh reality after a massive victory. As painful as the war had already been, the nation was ready for a renewed long-term war commitment.

***

We know all too well that our struggle against three Goliaths demands extraordinary courage, resilience, and grit. It isn't just me in this fight; Leslie is always there by my side, a pillar of strength, especially when I need her most. Our children, facing their own heartbreaks and struggles, continue to impress us with their resilience. We lean on each other to ensure truth will ultimately prevail.

This was not a fight *we* chose, but it was one we had to face. To cower would mean allowing lies and half-truths about our integrity and our character to define us forever. For us, this is much more than simply winning—it's about standing tall against the tidal wave of injustice threatening to consume us. While the pain and the toll are undeniable, so is our resolve.

This fight has revealed shocking truths, truths that extend far beyond our personal case. It has exposed multiple scandals within the scandal: a justice system that was weaponized and corrupted for prosecutor career gains, a media machine that profited from sensationalized false narratives, and universities who did everything possible to hide their own dark secrets. Each of these institutions knowingly distorted the truth, brutally and falsely attacked our innocent children, and did all they could through wars of attrition to punish those who dared to stand up against them.

***

Epilogue

At the center of the Varsity Blues case, was a headline-grabbing saga that featured Hollywood celebrities and dozens of wealthy parents who confessed to cheating, bribery and fraud to get their unqualified children into top universities. These parents' outrageous acts deserved to be punished.

The Boston federal prosecutors went beyond this group of bad actors and wrongly grouped us with these other parents to bring all the trials (and the career-boosting media spotlights) in this case to Boston. It's revolting how they trampled over our innocent children as collateral damage in their destructive path to win any turf battles to keep this case in Boston.

These prosecutors were able to leverage public outrage into career advancement, turning this case into a personal stepping stone. They manipulated the media and wielded their power with extreme vindictiveness, filing excessive charges designed to intimidate and force me to plead guilty. This abuse of prosecutorial discretion was not only appalling but also demonstrates how our system of justice can be weaponized by media-hungry prosecutors to serve their own ends.

The universities, particularly USC, were also complicit. They sought to protect their status quo by hiding and denying the truth, crafting a web of opaque admissions practices designed to favor those who could help the university financially, politically or otherwise. Instead of owning up to the cold realities of the favoritism the university purposely architected into their admissions processes, they chose to deceive, deflect blame and tarnish families like ours.

USC's refusal to release internal emails and admissions data during the trial, hiding behind a veil of secrecy to protect their unfair practices and reputation at the expense of the truth and one of their own students' well-being, continues to this day.

Netflix added another layer of harm, turning our family's ordeal into a false sensationalized drama played out on a global scale. They described their movie as a documentary to induce their audience into believing that what was depicted was truthful when they, in fact, manipulated the script to take statements out of context, even splicing words from different conversations together to feed their false depictions. They falsely made me the ultimate villain parent, with the actor portraying me getting second billing—only second to the actor playing Singer. The result? An unimaginable tsunami of public shaming, character assassination, and permanent ruin to our family's reputation.

To make matters worse, the film was aired before my trial, tainting the jury pool with its vicious narrative. And the damage continues as their film is still shown to this day.

**

We are committed to fighting and doing everything we can to clear our family's name and champion at least these ten truths that were all documented and known by the prosecutors, Netflix, and USC:

1. **Our children were all qualified** for admissions to each of the colleges they applied to based on their own hard-earned merits.
2. **No one in our family cheated** on college tests or gave any false information to Singer or to any college.
3. **Our son was a Division I water polo athlete**, and his nationally recognized high school water polo coach personally called the USC staff to recommend Johnny as a walk-on recruit for the USC team.
4. Coach Bowen stated that **"without a doubt, Johnny was legitimately in the group of Division 1 recruitable college athletes,"** and could be a starter by his junior or senior year at USC.
5. **Our son was one of the fastest documented players** on USC's 2014 water polo team, and he participated as a redshirt player for the entire season and postseason.
6. **We discussed our twin daughters for team manager roles** and never submitted any false information to Stanford or Harvard.

7. Three separate senior **USC officials** confirmed that our donations through Singer's organization were **proper** and would be helpful to the admissions process.
8. Our donations through Singer's organization went to **college foundations and his IRS-certified charity**, not individuals. Singer ultimately stole half of our donations.
9. **USC gave us a receipt for our donations and has kept our money to this day**.
10. Using the invoice from Singer's company instead of the donation receipt we had received from USC on our tax return was a simple, **honest mistake,** verified through rigorous polygraph tests.

***

Reflecting on the Varsity Blues case since it began in 2019 has provided us with several unique perspectives.

It has been horrific beyond words being the targets of extreme government overreach and deliberate abuse. What sickens us the most is the conscious disregard for the harm inflicted on our innocent children by these government, media, and university employees. The excessiveness of the charges and government resources used in this case also reveal a troubling reality about our legal system: those entrusted to run it can sometimes put personal ambition over justice and the search for truth.

Was the 8% change in a swim time that Singer made on our son's profile (without our knowledge) really a federal felony? Was using Singer's invoice instead of the receipt we got from USC in my tax returns really a federal crime? Even if these allegations were true (and they weren't), did they justify nine federal felony charges, 180 years of potential prison time?

The government's disproportionate approach to my case, especially since they had overwhelming evidence which proved my innocence from the start (including evidence from that FaceTime call which somehow "disappeared"), has been outrageous at every level.

With all the challenges in our world, how did any of this make sense?

When something like this doesn't make sense, I look at who benefitted the most and who was harmed to understand what really happened and why. I often find it helpful to peel back the layers of the onion to identify which individuals or institutions may have exploited the situation to serve their own agendas. In other words, who had the most to gain from pursuing the Varsity Blues case?

The biggest personal beneficiaries of this case were the Boston federal prosecutors who weaponized our system of criminal justice and leveraged the public outrage and media attention for personal career gains. Several went from $100,000 to $160,000-per-year government jobs to partner roles in prestigious law firms with million-dollar-per-year upsides. One former office leader was featured in his own hour-long podcast bragging about the media coverage he was able to garner for this case.

Another former prosecutor bragged in an interview about the collateral consequences they intentionally inflicted upon all the families charged in this case stating, "They were ridiculed, humiliated, stained and had major disruptions to their careers."[40] His quote almost seemed gleeful at the severe harm they inflicted on the parents and children.

Is this level of weaponization and vindictiveness what we want from our prosecutors?

***

Perhaps the biggest individual beneficiary in this case was USC assistant coach Moon. As stated in a public filing, "The government never filed charges against, and USC's athletic department never fired Moon…despite

---

40 *Sportico, Varsity Blues Affair Winds Down as Ex-USC Official Now Free*, by Daniel Libit, July 12, 2023

Epilogue

his testimony at the criminal trial that USC purportedly did not consider Johnny a member of the team and that he had worked with Vavic in building Johnny's athletic profile."[41]

As William Tanenbaum stated publicly[42] in the USC case, "Moon falsely testified that Johnny Wilson was a no-show member of the team after day one." Instead of being fired by USC, Moon was rewarded and promoted by USC. Moon was also the only person (that we are aware of) who admitted he submitted false information into a student's profile who was not charged by prosecutors with a crime. It's reprehensible to think that Moon may have been willing to make false statements about our son participating on the USC team to help the prosecutors' fabricated criminal case against me. The inducement to stay out of prison and keep their job can be a powerful motivator for someone to lie under oath.

The biggest institutional beneficiaries were USC and the other universities who got to protect their dark secrets about how their admissions practices truly work. They were able to keep multiple categories of "unfair" admissions (purposely designed to help with fundraising and other goals) opaque to avoid public criticism. Giving admissions preferences for legacies, donors, political VIPs, faculty children, dean's recommendation lists, board of trustee referrals, athletes, full-tuition-paying families, and so forth continues at many schools to this day.

As noted in Mr. Tanenbaum's public filing, "USC's misrepresentations of their admissions policies to the Wilsons and the subsequent contradictory false testimony about… Johnny's membership on the USC water polo team" had a devastating impact on the Wilson family. To be clear, we believe that private institutions should be able to use whatever criteria they choose when accepting students. However, we believe that they should be transparent about their practices.

---

41 Opposition to defendant USC's demurrer in the Superior Court of California, filed February 10, 2025

42 Tanenbaum Law Offices release, Exonerated 'Varsity Blues" Parent Challenges USC's Wrongdoing & False Testimony, February 11, 2025

USC was able to hide all this damning evidence under seal and then the prosecutors and trial judge blocked all of this evidence from being shared at my trial or with the public. Blocking all this embarrassing evidence was clearly improper as the appeals court unanimously noted.

The biggest profit beneficiaries were the media, in all forms, who accepted the false narrative being fed to them about our family and helped sensationalize the story (smearing us with the bad acts of other parents) to maximize viewers. Netflix, with its big-budget purported documentary, fueled the public's anger with tens of millions of global viewers.

The final group of beneficiaries were the dozens of law firms representing the fifty-plus defendants as well as the universities and Netflix. It was a multimillion dollar payday, in aggregate, for all the law firms involved.

***

Who were the people or groups who were negatively impacted by the Varsity Blues case?

In the end, students and society overall, were the most adversely impacted groups—because the systemic unfairness colleges have designed into their admissions processes continues. We feel particularly badly for those less fortunate children who were highly qualified and bumped by less qualified or unqualified children whose parent made donations or were otherwise connected.

As parents we would never want unqualified children to bump more qualified students. We made sure that our children's test scores showed that they were more than qualified compared to the majority of students attending each school they applied to. We did this to make sure that there was never any need to bump more qualified, less fortunate students and to make sure that our children could succeed academically at each school they applied to.

Epilogue

Many college admissions policies remain largely unchanged and their administrators have avoided public scrutiny of their underlying processes. In fact, many universities continue to keep their admissions practices deliberately opaque, labeling them "holistic" and so forth to avoid public criticism and ill will.

Because the prosecutors chose not to pursue the powerful universities, they missed significant opportunities for systemic changes which could have truly helped society.

The second group of people who were harmed in this case were the taxpayers. In a country facing enormous challenges, was it the highest and best use of tens of millions of dollars and nearly eight years of federal prosecutors and FBI resources (recall the investigation began nearly a year before the charges were publicly announced and continue to this day) to prosecute thirty parents (out of Singer's 3,000 parent clients) with felony charges for cheating on SAT tests?

The third group of people who were harmed were the children of the wealthy parents who knowingly lied, cheated, and bribed officials to corrupt the admissions process to have these *unqualified* children bump more qualified applicants from the admissions queue. The impact of these parents' corrupt actions not only violated the law and common decency but could also have lasting negative consequences on their children's mental health and wellbeing. While we have little sympathy for these parents, we do feel badly for their innocent children.

Of course, the people we feel most badly for in this case were *our* innocent children—who despite being *highly qualified* for admissions based on their own hard-earned merits and doing absolutely nothing wrong—have been mercilessly attacked and profoundly impacted by the prosecutors and the media. As parents, words still can't describe the gut wrenching pain of being forced to see our innocent children suffer at the hands of the federal government.

THE SCANDAL WITHIN THE SCANDAL

For federal prosecutors (who are supposed to defend innocent children) to deliberately feed false smears about our children's qualifications to the media (behind the scenes to avoid liability), in order to help their case against me and to bring all the trials in this career building case to Boston, is ethically and morally bankrupt. It's still hard for us to understand how these prosecutors could treat our children as mere collateral damage in their pursuit of fame and power. For these same prosecutors to go to the extremes they went to in my case and against our children to hide their misdeeds and then award themselves citations for heroism is beyond words.

***

We are fighting back…and starting to win.

In fact, the multiple wins we have achieved so far, each against nearly impossible odds, have added extraordinary emotional fuel to motivate us to continue our fight for the truth and our family's honor.

Our first big win was at the appeals court. We were told by multiple experts that getting all your core convictions overturned by an appeals court was a one-thousand-to-one long shot.

Our case was so unique, our facts and truth so powerful, and our will to fight so strong that we beat those odds (with the help of our great defense and appellate lawyers and unbiased appellate judges). That moment was not just a legal triumph; it was a beacon of hope, a reminder that perseverance, the truth, and integrity can prevail.

The road to that victory was anything but ordinary. More than six years of intense effort and careful documentation finally revealed the deeply flawed nature of the case against me.

The charges and trial were so egregiously flawed that eleven former US attorneys took the extraordinary step of publicly criticizing their former colleagues, declaring, "John Wilson did not receive a fair trial." It's impossible

Epilogue

to overstate the power of these unpaid and unrelated former prosecutors coming to our aid. Their voices brought validation to what we had been saying all along—that, at least in this instance, the legal system had failed us in a profound way.

***

The appellate victory was a massive, almost unprecedented win. It helped breathe fresh life back into our souls, and the unanimous decision started to turn the media tide and public opinion, ever so slightly, in our favor. For the first time in years, we felt seen, heard, and believed in the media. That feeling—however fleeting—was priceless.

The next big win for us was when the prosecutors dropped *all* the overturned charges. This was a monumental moment, one that many lawyers described as our true exoneration in this case. The vindictive prosecutors chose to drop all the overturned charges rather than retry the case with a new, randomly selected judge. It was as though, finally, someone was willing to admit that justice, in my case, had been mishandled. It was not the end of our fight, but it was a moment of immense relief—a glimmer of fairness in an otherwise merciless process.

The prosecutors didn't drop the charges against me to simply move on. Believe it or not, after seven-plus years, the government (which started this case nearly a year before they publicly launched their charges) has not yet moved on. They are still actively pursuing appeals cases against the USC head coach and other parents who are trying to rescind their plea agreements (after the key decisions by the appeals court in my case).

Another big win was the sentencing decision of probation for the $1,425 tax conviction—despite *four* prosecutors coming to my sentencing hearing to argue vehemently for a sentence of fifteen months in federal prison! The judge gave me a small fine, some community service, and probation.

THE SCANDAL WITHIN THE SCANDAL

This decision, while small in the grand scheme, felt like another measure of common sense finally breaking through in the Boston district court.

The next small win was when my probation officer decided to forego an ankle bracelet during my six months of home confinement. They said tracking my cell phone was sufficient. It was the first time someone in the government seemed to have a reasonable perspective on my case. For the first time in months, I could breathe a little easier in my own home.

***

The first big public win was my speech at Harvard Business School, where more than three hundred alumni gave me a standing ovation. Multiple people came up to me after, thanking and congratulating me for fighting so fervently for justice. Their support brought tears of joy and appreciation. To stand in front of such an audience and share my truth was both cathartic and reaffirming. It reminded me why we fight—not just for our family, but for anyone who has ever been wrongfully accused.

The next public win was getting my op-ed published in the *Boston Globe*.[43] It took months and lots of fact-checking by the *Globe*, but the power of our story prevailed. This was especially satisfying since it hit our hometown audiences.

Another media win was the *Wall Street Journal* op-ed written by Harvey Silverglate.[44] It was an amazing piece written by a man unrelated to me and unpaid by me. It helped open some minds and doors to what really happened. The title still resonates: "How 'Varsity Blues' Swept up an Innocent Father." I went to his office in Cambridge, Massachusetts, to meet and thank him after his article came out.

---

[43] "I was unjustly targeted in the college admissions scandal. This is my story," Boston Globe, December 25, 2023.

[44] "How 'Varsity Blues' Swept Up an Innocent Father," Wall Street Journal, July 29, 2024.

Epilogue

Soon after that, another one-thousand-to-one legal victory happened when a federal judge ordered the prosecutors to return the money they had confiscated from us during their setup calls from 2018. This rarely happens, and the prosecutors vehemently fought against it. The ruling was not just a win for us but a powerful message against government overreach.

Then in August 2024, we won a major legal battle in our civil defamation suit against Netflix. A Massachusetts superior court judge denied Netflix's motion to dismiss our case. The decision is also a powerful warning shot for the media to take greater precautions when blurring the lines between fact and fiction in a documentary for profit. The fight is far from over, but this victory gives us hope that the truth will eventually prevail here too.

Additionally, in September 2024, we filed a lawsuit against USC for defrauding us.

In October of 2024, a ten-minute feature story was broadcast on Sheryl Attkisson's *Full Measure* series to tens of millions of households. Seeing our story shared with such clarity and fairness was also strong validation of the truth in the sea of misrepresentation we had endured.

While each legal victory reenergizes us and builds momentum, our battle is far from over. As Winston Churchill noted, proper perspective is critical to long-term success. The legal disputes with Netflix and USC will likely drag on for several more years. Indeed, the struggle to restore our family's reputation and honor may well last for the rest of our lives.

***

In addition to standing up for our family's honor, I am also passionate about reigniting my professional career. I am fortunate that I still have the skills and energy to help make a difference again in the business world. My focus is on continuing to be the principled leader I have always been, committed to helping organizations achieve their full potential.

Reflecting on my life, it's hard to believe that the wide-eyed boy, sitting around those campfires decades ago in Hartford, Connecticut, with veteran Big Sam, managed to break out from my family's cycle of poverty and abuse. I even got to see the world—including the palace of Versailles—or as Big Sam would have preferred it, "Ver-sighhhhh"!

It's perhaps the ultimate irony that the scholarships I received in my youth were my ticket to escape poverty while my later donations to fund similar programs for others nearly became my ticket to prison.

Regardless of what the future holds for us and our children, we take pride in fighting for the truth, our honor, and our children's futures.

Our wins, however, have not erased the harm done. Each small victory—whether a court win, a vindicating media narrative, or a standing ovation from a supportive audience—helps us rebuild. However, it doesn't undo the damage. The fight for our family's honor is far from over, and we will not stop until the truth is fully revealed and we hold the major wrongdoers accountable.

We realize that the far easier path would have been to give in to these giants. We could have preserved our life savings. However, standing up for what's right and fighting for the truth is the only path where we can all hold our heads high. We also hope that our fight will inspire others to take on the injustices they face.

***

Varsity Blues: The Scandal Within the Scandal exposes just a fraction of the extreme measures three institutional Goliaths took to advance their own self interest versus the truth. It's beyond despicable when we reflect back on how they each nearly destroyed our innocent family and treated us as mere collateral damage in the process.

Epilogue

Some sharp daggers continue to cut into our family to this day. For example, Netflix's defamatory and sensationalized "documentary" about our family (which they haven't updated or changed to this day) still streams to more than 280 million worldwide subscribers and through their contracts with other streaming platforms to maximize their profits.

As we write this final chapter, there are three profound examples (of the many outrageous behaviors) which still shock us to our core.

First, is that the prosecutors deliberately threw me into a federal prison for two days, putting my life at risk to intimidate and coerce me into taking a plea deal. For what? Making donations to college foundations to help our highly qualified children's chances of admissions. Throughout this process, the prosecutors' actions have been so disproportionate to any alleged crime that it's still hard for us to believe.

Second, and perhaps most painful, was how the federal government, USC, and Netflix, knowingly and falsely smeared our innocent son's hard-earned athletic credentials. They did this by misleading the media through off-the-record statements, by misleading the jury during my trial, and by misleading viewers with defamatory filmmaking innuendo, respectively. These three, once highly trusted, institutions deliberately disregarded the truth and the facts that they each had in hand to destroy our son's reputation, boost their careers, hide their dark secrets, and maximize profits.

Third was how vindictive the prosecutors have been throughout the past six plus years—even after they lost on all the core charges at the appeals court level and were ordered by the district court to return the donations they confiscated from me as part of their setup calls in 2018. The prosecutors brought four attorneys to the sentencing hearing and continued to viciously attack me and smear our highly qualified children.

The prosecutors argued for forty-five minutes that I should serve fifteen months in prison for mistakenly using the Singer invoice instead of the receipt from USC for my donation on my 2014 tax return (a $1,425 error in a year which the government acknowledged I overpaid my taxes by more than $100,000.) This prosecutor overreach seemed to be vindictiveness on steroids.

As parents, it is impossible to fully describe the pain of being helpless while our innocent children have suffered from years of vicious, false and brutal attacks. The originators and perpetrators of these odious acts were not uniformed internet trolls or schoolyard bullies. The prosecutors were aware of the overwhelming amounts of evidence which proved my innocence and our children's qualifications. We know they were aware of this evidence because they blocked it all (hundreds of times, piece by piece) during my trial.

We heard from many legal experts that the prosecutors' actions were beyond morally bankrupt. We also realize that calling this bad behavior puts us at risk of retaliation. For example, the prosecutors could try to find some other minor pre-text (like charging us for deducting an expense on the wrong line on our tax returns) to come after us.

Similarly, what Netflix and USC did to our family, especially to our innocent children is beyond reprehensible. Despite the costs and risks of fighting these three Goliaths, we feel compelled to address their outrageous misdeeds and to hold those who purposefully engaged in them accountable.

Our system of criminal justice, Netflix and USC can and must be better than this.

***

What happened to us should never happen to anyone in America. It is especially disturbing how federal prosecutors can weaponize our criminal justice system to serve their own agendas. The scariest part of this story is that if prosecutors can do this to our family, it can happen to others.

Epilogue

We will continue fighting to defend our family's honor, to call out government overreach and to compel Netflix and USC to put the truth ahead of profits and hiding dark secrets, in order to help prevent this from happening to anyone else.

Our fight is far from over ...

ACKNOWLEDGMENTS

We could not have survived this ordeal or authored this book without the support of so many people. Our hearts swell with pride and gratitude as we reflect upon all the people who have helped us in so many ways; it gives true meaning to the adage that "a friend in need is a friend indeed."

To Leslie, my wife of nearly thirty-five years: you are the best thing that ever happened to me and have been there for me every step of the way, holding my hand and hugging me when I needed it and kicking me in the butt when I needed it too. To our son Johnny, whose amazing accomplishments and kind spirit always inspires us to "Fight on!" To our brilliant and lovely daughters Mamie and Courtney, who light up our lives whenever they walk into a room.

To my brother Cliff, who was there for us countless times helping from day one in Houston and every step of the way since: your daily calls and in-person visits helped us make sound decisions and keep our sanity in the courtroom and on the phone. We can never thank you enough.

To Sam and Alison Gersten, who were always there for us—even at 2:00 a.m. We will never forget how you stayed with us in the courtroom each day, helped us fend off the media throngs, and just listened when we needed that.

To our extended "family"—Ken and Laurie Quartermain, Anna Laughlin, Jim Erbs, Shan Atkins, Carol Rickless, Christian and Chris Sagherian, Jackie Bastien, Pat Sheehan, Brian and Sandi Curley, and Polly Bryson, Debbie Snow, the Raftery family, the Elliott family, and Ellen Slawsby for supporting us and always encouraging us to hold our heads high.

THE SCANDAL WITHIN THE SCANDAL

To Fred Lukens, my dearest friend for fifty-plus years: every moment across those five decades together has been amazing. I will never forget all your advice and help with my life, family, career, and business and with authoring this book.

To my business school friends for over forty years—especially David and Dawn Merrill, Lorne and Victoria Adrain, Deborah Gelin, Joe Loughran, Craig Coy, Phil Blumberg, John Macomber, Andy Studley, Doug Hansen, Randy Christofferson, Doug Thomas, Janie DeCelles, Diane Cutler, John Pittenger, Michael Rabin, Jennifer Devitt, Michael Zaoui, and Fran Kelly—I will never forget your support and willingness to spend time on countless phone calls and in-person visits to support me every time I needed it.

To Mark and Kelly Mandel and the thirty years you have helped me and our family: from playing sports with our children to our wonderful philosophical discussions contemplating the meaning of life, you have always been a great sounding board and friend.

To John Lukens, Chuck and Colleen Saftler, Rick and Debbi Bocci, Bill and Ginger Hedden, Joe Beaulaurier, Al and KC Vincelette, John and Lynda Marren, Debbie and Stuart Rosenberg, Stephen Martin, and Bob Smith for your long-distance support.

To our Boston-area friends, especially Charlie and Jill Nilsen, Don and Marie DeAmicis, Bill and Christy Cadigan, Tom Fitzgerald, Margaret Boles Fitzgerald, Ian and Wendy Carver, TJ and Kristin Hughes, Phil and Pat Dubuque, Bill and MJ McPhee, Scott and Carol Williams, Chris Wilson, Martin and Cathy Deale, Steven Campbell, and Lisa Simmons: your unwavering support and warm shoulders to lean on will never be forgotten.

To our Cape Cod friends who remained steadfast supporters throughout this challenging period: thank you for being kind to our children and making them feel welcomed and supported in our small village throughout this ordeal, especially Dick and Martha O'Keefe, Chris and Julie Barker, Lance and Tracy Isham, Nick and Pam Lazarus, David and Joan Hill, John

Acknowledgments

and Heather Schneeberger, Jim and Lorine Hutchins, Eric and Sally Bacon, Garry and Ruth Schaefer, Jon and Cathy Duane, Ted and Margot Mehm, Fred and Marcia Floyd, Linda Woodwell, Jim and Monica Shay, Drew and Shannon Hayden, Artie and Maureen Demoulas, Richard Clark, Frank and Penny Floyd, Bob and Nancy Solomon, Brian and Miriam O'Neil, Gary and Julie Holloway, Ron and Carol Gwozdz, Peter McLoughlin, Jim and Susie Whelan, Jim and Denise Plunkett, Kevin and Ali Joyce, John and Lynn Harrison, Elise and Jim Gustafson, Richard and Beth Strachan Hank, Margaret Erbe, Michael O'Sullivan, Pat Donahoe, John Gregg, Paul Crosby, Stephen and Bobbi Leek, Steve and Lisa Andrews, Jake and Gretchen Filoon, Peter and Catherine Dryoff, John and Pam Saidnawey, Joe Driscoll, John Driscoll, Peter Barbey, the Hughes family, Tim and Sue B. O'Keefe, Peter and Brenda O'Keefe, Michael and Margaret Kerr, Harry and Katie Alverson, Jack and Betsy Campo, Bruce and Lissa Stepanek, Frank and Penny Floyd, Chris and Carol Page, John Muir, Mike and Florence Doud, Scott and Lisa Hilinski, Joe and Pam Scattaragius, Trey and Marina Reik, John and Leslie Strachan, Bill and Rena Patterson, Sam and Julia Wilson, Sam and Jane Barber, Dana Delorey, Chris and Sheila Kennedy, Ted and Kiki Kennedy, Bobby Kennedy, Max and Vicki Kennedy, Kerry Kennedy, Anthony Shriver, Tim Shriver, and Mark and Jeanne Shriver, Sam Yogis, Ben Yogis, Nate Yogis, Matt Gazoorian, Frank Donovan, Fred Stefanis, and Brian Merrick.

To our YPO colleagues, especially Bill and Tammy Crown, Nanci and Gary Fredkin, Susan Butenhoff and Chris Mani, Michael and Santi Dunn, Greg and Tracy Johnson, Jason Phillips and Sheila Schroeder, Kimi Glen, Jan Harris, Mikey Hoag, Susan Charlotte and Todd Yates, Alison Davis and Matthew LeMerle, Beth and Peter Vanderslice, Laura Scher, Melissa Ma, Anthony and Lisa Vidergauz, Bill and Jessica Jesse, Laura and Steve Yecies, Karen Kalinske, Wendy Petersmeyer, LouAnn Winchell, and Anthony Bourke: your advice and camaraderie over the years have been invaluable.

THE SCANDAL WITHIN THE SCANDAL

You each helped me in many ways to maintain my balance and long-term perspective throughout this difficult period.

To my autism board colleagues Jon Shestack, Mark Roithmayr, Portia Iverson, Sallie Bernard, Ricki Robinson, Marcia Goldman, and Bob Wright: I'm proud of what we accomplished together and thankful you stood by me.

To my professional colleagues and our friends, especially Ron Sargent, Gary Crittenden, Vern Altman, Dave Siegel, Karl Blanchard, Ken Pilot, Claudio Brasca, Shahzad Malik, Patrick Legro, Henrik Zadig, Gogi Grewal, Coen Bouve, Mathew LeMerle, Monica Roose, Monique Duvalois, Viola de Bellis, Todd Krasnow, Kevin Milliken, Bob and Joan Mayerson, Mats Karlsson, Patrick Olson, Pat Hickey, Faisal Masud, John Barton, Tom Conophy, Peter Schwarzenbach, Bob Spellman, Dymfke Kuijpers, Ivo Bozon, John Burke, Gordon Glover, Mike Patriarca, Rikke Wivel, Kyle Pounds, Louise Good, Karen David-Green, Joe Isaac, Ellen Chin, Ede Holliday, Jenny Johnson, Mary Choksi, Larry Thompson, Gary Wilson, and Mark Mills: you all reached out to show your support when I needed it most. Thank you.

To Teddy Bogosian, David Fuscus, Mark Hazlin, Ann Baldwin, Mitchell Schwenz, Victoria Wilson, Maria Blauner, and Mike Bell for your help in crafting my communications and giving my messages the clarity and brevity that I so desperately needed.

To Kendall Shull and Don Kraphol: thank you for helping to prove to the world that I have been telling the truth about this case from day one. Your ability and credentials are unparalleled.

To Noel Francisco, Yaakov Roth, Mike Kendall, Andy Tomback, Hal Hardin, Hank Asbill, Bill Tanenbaum, Howard Cooper, and Christian Kiely, for your legal expertise, genuine caring and belief in us.

To the eleven former US attorneys, law school professors, and National Association of Criminal Defense lawyers whom I have never met who cared

Acknowledgments

enough about justice to write amicus briefs (without any compensation) in support of my case.

To Coach Jack Bowen: thank you for the six wonderful years you coached our son and ingrained in him the values of hard work, integrity, and being the best version of himself possible—it has helped make him a better young man. I also wanted to thank you for your time and effort to fly out and testify at the trial.

Saving the best for last, to Marigale Walsh and Tom Zenner, without whom this book would not have been possible: your positive energy and tireless efforts helped us share our story. We make a wonderful team and are proud to call you both our friends.

ABOUT THE AUTHOR

John and his three half-siblings were raised on welfare by their single mother in the Bowles Park housing projects of Hartford, Connecticut. He hand-picked tobacco from age 12 to 16 to help his family make ends meet. After he was adopted by Tom Wilson, a career Air Force sergeant, formal education began to transform John's life. He earned a BS in chemical engineering from Rensselaer Polytechnic Institute and graduated with an MBA from Harvard Business School at the age of 23, the youngest in his class..

He built a successful business career rising from entry level positions to leadership roles in multiple Fortune 500 companies. A global executive who has traveled to more than 95 countries, John is an effective change agent with a proven track record leading organizations to their full potential. At 29, he became the youngest partner in Bain & Company's history. As CFO, he helped Staples become the fastest company to reach the Fortune 500. As COO of Gap inc., he led 80,000 associates to become the first specialty retailer to achieve $50 billion market value. John also was the president of Staples Int'l and senior operating partner at McKinsey.

John has lived on Cape Cod, Massachusetts with his family for twenty-five years.

www.ingramcontent.com/pod-product-compliance
Lightning Source LLC
Jackson TN
JSHW072029180425
82917JS00017B/89